THERE AND BLACK AGAIN

DON LETTS

WITH **MAL PEACHEY**

OMNIBUS PRESS

London / New York / Paris / Sydney / Copenhagen / Berlin / Madrid / Tokyo

Copyright © 2021 Don Letts and Mal Peachey
Published by Omnibus Press
(A division of the Wise Music Group
14–15 Berners Street, London, W1T 3LJ)

Cover designed by Amazing15
Picture research by the authors

ISBN 978-1-913172-09-1

Typeset by Evolution Design & Digital (Kent) Ltd
Printed in the EU

A catalogue record for this book is available from the British Library.

www.omnibuspress.com

'When they approach me they see only my surroundings, themselves, or figments of their imagination.'

Ralph Ellison, *Invisible Man* (1952)

'If you have no reason for living/don't determine my life'

Dr Alimantado, 'Born For A Purpose' (1977)

Contents

Scene

Interior. Day. A domestic kitchen in West London. Through large glass doors and windows, a long London garden with a tree to the left, a small patio and a snaking path leads to a 'home office' structure of wood and glass. The sky is an indeterminate colour somewhere between teal and grey. Inside the kitchen two men sit opposite one another. One at a table pushed against the right-hand wall, the other on a deep couch that takes up the left side of the extension. Pan around to show a family kitchen; we see smart grey cupboards, worktops, hob, sink, and door into the rest of the house. Pass over a fridge with various photos and kids' drawings fixed to it, linger for a couple of seconds on a pillar so we can make out lines marking the heights of two children showing their progress from toddlers through to late teenage.

The men are talking.

M: So how are we going to start this book, Don?

D: Don't these things usually begin at the beginning, Mal? Or with some major event in the life of the author?

M: You mean like in a great film noir?

D: Yeah – I walk into your office and say, 'I want to report a murder,' and you ask whose. To which I reply, 'Mine!'

M: Or we open on a body in the foreground of the shot, a knife sticking out of her back – it's always a female victim – and you waking up beside her, with blood on your hands, looking horrified as you realise the spot you're in.

D: Except I haven't killed anyone or been accused of it. I've been accused of a lot of things, but murder ain't one of them.

M: So, what dramatic event from your life should we tease the reader with?

D: It should probably involve someone famous, shouldn't it? How about sitting with Joe Strummer feet away from Alexandra Palace as it burned down in 1979, passing a joint and wondering what had happened?

M: Do you want to begin with The Clash, though? Seems to me that too many people associate you with them, when you've done a lot more work that doesn't involve Joe, Paul or even Mick.

D: How about the story of the photo that Rocco took, and Paul Simonon put on the cover of *Black Market Clash*, me against hundreds of coppers at the 1976 Notting Hill Carnival riot? That's the image of me that everyone knows.

M: Yes, and you've told that story too many times. Everyone knows that the angle the photo is taken from is telling an untrue story, that you're actually heading away from them and the fight, toward safety in a friend's place up the road.

Portobello Road, 1976, at the Carnival.   ROCCO MACAULEY

D: But that's it, though. My story as we're putting it down isn't anyone's truth but mine, it's what I made of a life, remembered as hazily as I can. Other people see me, a Black man, in situations and places where their prejudices and preconceived ideas can't quite make sense of it.

M: Like the way Bob Marley couldn't help but have a go at you for wearing bondage strides in 1977, or that MTV executive who embarrassed himself having to tell you that they didn't know you were Black.

D: Yep, and the Jamaican customs officer who had to be relieved of his post because he couldn't get how I was the boss of a white documentary crew – and that wasn't too long ago. I've had to deal with other people's idea of who I am while trying to be me, as the real me watches on. How many points of view is that?

M: Edith Sitwell wrote in one of her biographies 'there is no truth, only points of view', and the thing is that you, Don Letts, have been the focal point of a lot of different people's points of view, written into their autobiographies as who they thought you were. Chrissie Hynde, John Lydon and even your brother Desmond have written about a Don Letts who, I have to say, I don't fully recognise. Do you?

D: I recognise the times, the places and events, but not in exactly the same way as they do. I'm sure what they've written is how they remember it, and it's their point of view. I've learned to do that out of necessity. Even today, if I'm talking to someone about work, especially if it's a younger white guy, I have to be careful about what I say, to make sure that I word things so that they can repeat it back to me in a couple of minutes as if it's their idea.

M: Do we start there, then? How the fuck do you manage it?

D: Herb. It's part of my survival kit; it helps defend against people who're insensitive, racist or downright insulting. It can annoy white people that I know more about their culture than they do, and way more about my own, of course. I have to self-censor so as not to appear to be too smart. Which is boring.

M: But all those documentaries that you've made about white youth culture – skinheads, punks, mods – are all proof that you have a deep and wide-ranging knowledge of their culture. Surely people understand that?

D: Yeah, but remember that after more than forty years of making films about youth culture I'm the man they thought of as 'Britain's only Black video director'. Not that I ever planned it to be that way, and this book should show that nothing I ever did was premeditated. I was never content to do what I was 'supposed' to. Society made me the way I am because it was always telling me I couldn't do something, and I took that as a challenge, I had to prove them wrong. I became the Don Letts that people see in public because of the cultural climate I existed in. I always had to watch myself being *that* Don Letts the video director, or *that* Don Letts the pop star, the DJ. You could say that I've directed my own biopic without a script, criticising things I've done after the fact and dealing with it in my own head as best I can. I've compiled my own soundtrack from stuff that I've heard and loved throughout the past sixty-four years regardless of where it came from and whether I 'should' be into it or not.

M: A biopic. There's an idea – how about we set this out as if it's the basis for a biopic? Start each 'chapter' with a scene in which we reimagine the place, people and conversations that went on at different times in your life? We can move the narrative on in a filmic way.

D: There's no way I can remember conversations I've had with people over the years.

M: Of course you can't – who can? But that doesn't matter, because this is your story, your point of view of the truth, right?

D: Y'know what? Fuck the truth, I'm an artist.

M: So, let's start this story at the beginning, setting the scene for Don Letts the director to show us Don Letts the child . . .

London
(Is the Place for Me)

Interior. Night. A cramped kitchen in a terraced house in Brixton, London, 1960. A well-scrubbed wooden table for four is pushed against a wall adjacent to the door, which is not quite closed. A Blue Spot gramophone has pride of place against one wall. Two men in white shirts, no ties, woollen trousers and dark brogue shoes, and two women in shift dresses of bright colours, their hair teased into beehives, their feet in sharply pointed stiletto-heeled shoes, stand laughing in the cramped space between the sink, a mangle and the table. They're aged somewhere in the early to mid-thirties. Just outside the door, peering through the crack between jamb and door, is a small boy in his pyjamas.

My father and another big man, their shirt tails hanging out, arms on one another's shoulders, are swaying and shuffling in our kitchen as a high-pitched voice with a scratching rhythm and sparse guitar makes a happy noise. They're singing along with it. My mother is in the room too. She's relaxed – which is a rare thing in these grey, wet days when the washing won't dry, and the windows steam up inside whenever the kettle boils. 'Cha!' she laughs, scornfully waving away her husband. 'What you singin' 'bout that for, we don't see no Yankee dolla roun' 'ere!'

The woman perched next to her on the edge of the table laughs too, then she gets up and gently pushes the men to one side and reaches

1

inside the radiogram. A swooshing scratch sounds as she takes the arm off Lord Invader's 'Rum And Coca Cola'. My dad stumbles back to lean against the door frame, where he bends over panting. The other man moves toward the Blue Spot as if to stop his wife, but she shoulders him aside and sets a new disc on the turntable.

Click, whirr, click, whirr, click. Treble piano notes sound out the ding-dong, ding-dong, dong-ding, dong-ding of Big Ben sounding the hour, before a similar voice but not that of Lord Invader sings about London being the place for him.

It's the turn of both men to laugh now, but not like they heard a joke. My dad takes two steps to the record player just as the singer mentions America. 'Lord Kitchener, pah,' my mother says dismissively, 'what he know?' Dad swipes the fat grey arm from the big record and lifts it off the metal spindle.

'Bwoy Fats is my man!' he half-shouts as he takes a smaller disc from the stack on the top of the Blue Spot and puts it on the deck. He places the arm heavily, so that it skips, missing the run-in. A piano with someone whistling over it sets up a rolling rhythm. Both men start to shuffle around the kitchen, their arms stretched out to the women, trying to get them to dance as Fats Domino cries that he's going to New Orleans. From my spot behind the door, I can see and hear everything. The kitchen is bright and warm, the mood unusually matching the surroundings. My parents haven't often had people to the house in the years before I started school, but when they do, the music always draws me from wherever I am, whatever the time, filled with a need to be as close to its source as possible.

By my reckoning, I'm as old as rock 'n' roll, having been born in 1956 (the year of Elvis's 'Heartbreak Hotel' and 'Hound Dog', Little Richard's 'Tutti Frutti' and 'Rip It Up', Chuck Berry's 'Roll Over Beethoven' and Fats Domino's 'Blueberry Hill', among others). As much as Babylon would have liked to send me down another road, my virtual twin, rock 'n' roll music, has taken me on a different path. I don't recall how old I was when I realised that music was how my father connected with not just us, but neighbours and strangers, too. It probably came to me when watching him DJ at the church halls and gardens where he'd set up his sound system, Duke Letts Superstonic Sound, after Sunday service. His 'sound system' was relatively small and nothing like the gargantuan set-ups of today, his role in the tradition of the original DJ whose main talent was as 'selector', choosing records for the people at his events who'd arrive carrying Bibles and not bags of weed. He never set up in the sh'beens in neighbourhood basements lit by a single red bulb, where curry goat and rice was served along with Red Stripe.

My father, St Leger 'Duke' Letts, worked as a London bus driver when I was very young, later becoming a limousine chauffeur, and he was hugely admired among our respectable neighbours for his collection of 78 rpm shellac 10-inch and 45 rpm 7-inch vinyl records, and his ability to start a party and keep it going long into the night. His record collection was large, varied, including some that he'd brought with him from Jamaica four years before my birth, along with many more that he'd bought in London during his first decade here. Some of my earliest memories are of occasional Sundays and holidays when he'd play singles by the likes

The original angelic upstart, 1960-ish.

of Lord Flea, Fats Domino, Prince Buster and Jim Reeves, as people from the neighbourhood and church talked, smoked, ate, drank and swayed around the church hall with plates of plantain, rice and peas or chicken in hand. When I was 4 or 5 years old I had the time of my life running around people's legs, trying to evade women who'd want to pick me up and smother me with kisses, or swipe at me to get away in case I ladder their stockings. Those occasions gave me a small idea of what it was that my parents had given up in coming to England, especially when a soca, mento or calypso record played, and the patois sounded above the dance tunes. As the beat built and the music turned up louder, I'd hear people talking about Kingston while husbands and wives (or in-laws, which always created a chorus of 'tchs' and whoops from onlookers) started close dancing. I was lucky because music often seemed to be playing somewhere in the house, whether it was on the transistor radio, Blue Spot, or my older brothers' Dansette record player in our bedroom. The great thing was that there'd never be the same sounds played for too long; there was always new music to hear.

I was the third son of four in the Letts house, but the first to be born in London and to both my parents. As was surprisingly common in Jamaican families of the time, my parents had left behind a complicated life. My eldest half-brother Derrick was my father's son, born to a different woman in Jamaica, and Desmond was my mother's son, born in Kingston, his father a white sugar cane plantation overseer. Derrick is ten years older than me, and Desmond five. Both half-brothers had been left behind until my parents settled in London, where they had me and then Norman. Derrick came to London first, around the time I was born, and I have very few memories of his living with us because he was so much older. He was already well into his teens when Desmond arrived at our council house aged 10, in 1961. Desmond had lived with his father for most of his life, where he was treated with deference due to being the boss's son. He rode his father's horse with him, ate good food, had a governess and servants, but no memory of his mother. He did know his maternal grandmother and aunts because he'd spent holidays and some of the summer with them in the cooler mountain area where they lived, and he loved them.

When Desmond arrived in London, he must have had a hell of a shock. Not just from the change in the weather, but more because of the change in his position. We had no servants, and us kids had to do chores that, if not done to her satisfaction, would result in a beating from Mum. She ran the house, and what she commanded, everyone did, because if we didn't then she'd use whatever came to hand to remind us of who was boss. We couldn't speak disrespectfully to her; saying 'no' in the wrong tone, giving her bad 'looks' or 'kissing' your teeth would be dealt with swiftly and firmly. I still bear a scar on my hand from a bread knife she happened to be holding one day when I cheeked her. My mother's power lay in a swift and deadly execution of punishment – how just it might have been was another matter.

By the mid-1960s Derrick was giving my parents trouble. He'd discovered sex, music and the Ram Jam Club on Brixton Road, so was coming home late or not at all – he'd be locked out if not home by 11, anyway. Although we didn't talk or exactly bond (I was barely 10), I couldn't help but love the way he dressed. Later I'd recognise that he'd been a rude boy with his mohair suit, roll-neck sweater, dark glasses and Otis Redding on the Dansette. After a few late-night shouting matches between Derrick and my father about clubbing and the 'type' of girls he was hanging with, their final confrontation ended with Dad saying, 'If you think you're a man now you can find somewhere else to live.' Which Derrick did, and I'm sorry to say that we've had very little contact for the rest of our lives.

With Derrick gone, his chores were handed to Desmond, which made him even more annoyed than he already was. One of those chores was to empty the chamber pots – we had no indoor toilet or bath, so at night all four of us pissed in a pot which was kept under the bed – and one morning Desmond unfortunately tripped down the stairs while carrying a full pot. He was drenched and I stupidly laughed, and then even more stupidly later that day told a friend of mine about the accident. When kids started taking the mickey out of Desmond about it, he first punished them, and then found me and did the same.

Our house had only two bedrooms, and our parents' was also the TV room because we'd let the back parlour downstairs to a woman for the rent money. The front room was never used, it was only for show and the sofa and chairs in there were kept in their plastic wrapping, permanently watched over by a portrait of Queen Elizabeth. Our mother was a proud woman who did things the 'proper' English way, which included standing for the national anthem at the cinema and respecting authority. She hated being shown up and would direct her fury at us when we did anything to embarrass her. Even with Derrick gone it can't have been easy trying to keep three boys aged from 6 to 13 in line. Especially when we got into all kinds of trouble, despite the threat of corporal punishment. One time I accidentally punished myself in an act of daring stupidity when Desmond, Norman and I decided to play Batman. If there was ever a really stupid thing to do, Norman was usually first in line to try it since he was the youngest, but on this occasion I decided to jump out of our second-storey bedroom window because, of course, I was Batman. Except I was more of a Fatman, being overweight until I got to my teens, and so I couldn't hold onto the rope, which was too thin in the first place. I must have hit the ground at 60 mph and with severe rope burns to both hands. Desmond got the beating from our mum that time, because he was supposed to be looking after us and I was too hurt from the fall to take any more punishment. ('Serves y'right,' I think was the first thing she said when she found me screaming and crying in the garden.)

Desmond almost mercilessly bullied me and Norman; he'd lock us in a cupboard if left 'in charge' when our parents were out of the house, punch and kick me when I wasn't expecting it, ridicule me in front of my mates – the usual big brother crap. But he also showed me how to tie string to bees so they could be 'flown' like a kite (when bored we let go of the strings and watched them fly into power lines overhead, get caught and die in a frenzy of buzzing). He showed me how to tune the transistor radio and how to blame Norman for everything that I – we – did to deserve punishment, such as using our shared bed as a trampoline until it broke, for which Norman was beaten with a hairbrush by my mum even though Desmond was bigger and I was fatter.

When not at school and allowed to play out on the streets, I ran around with a gang of (mostly white) boys playing war or cowboys and Indians, 'shooting' Irish, English, Greek and West Indian kids. Sometimes the fun turned into real violence, but never for long and never dangerously. When not being cowboys and Indians, we were soldiers fighting the Nazis. This was only twenty years after the War and it was hard to forget, especially when the television and movies always seemed to be full of it.

There were also a lot of black-and-white gangster movies of the 1930s and 40s on the TV, starring tough guys like Edward G. Robinson, Humphrey Bogart, James Cagney and the original *Scarface*, Paul Muni. We'd yell memorable lines from some of them at each other: 'Look Ma, top of the world!', 'Why I oughtta...', 'Come and get me copper!' Then there were the more recent younger guys with cool haircuts, like Tony Curtis (*Spartacus*, 1960) and Steve McQueen (we all wanted to ride motorbikes after *The Great Escape*, 1963).

I loved the cowboy pictures best, though. We'd sing-shout the theme tunes to Western TV series as we ran around – *Rawhide* ('Yee-haw!'), *Davy Crockett* ('king of the wild frontier'), *Maverick* ('Maverick is the name'), *Champion the Wonder Horse*, even the *Lone Ranger*, or Rossini's *William Tell* overture ('taa-rum taa-rum taa-rum-dum-dum'). Cowboy movies were as popular in Jamaica in the 1950s and 60s as they were everywhere, and while country and western music never did anything for me, there were records that my father liked a lot, such as Marty Robbins' *Gunfighter Ballads* (released in 1959, it included 'Big Iron' and 'El Paso'), Johnny Cash's 'Ring Of Fire' (1963) and Roger Miller's 'King Of The Road' (1965), to name but a few. It wasn't a huge leap for him when DJing to go from Prince Buster's 'Al Capone' (1964) to Jim Reeves' 'Distant Drums' (1966) – especially when he was working in the church hall after morning service on a Sunday. I guess he identified with the *High Noon*-style, morally correct cowboy that the likes of Jim Reeves and Marty Robbins sang about, and he loved Alan Ladd as *Shane* (1953).

My parents were law-abiding, church-going citizens who thought it for the best that they become Anglicised as much as possible, to 'fit in' and not bring attention to themselves. But being first-generation British-born Black meant I was hearing and witnessing things at the homes of my white mates that were alien to my parents. I was seeing how the white half lived, ate their food, talked with their parents, and I'd go through their record collections whether invited to or not. For which I am grateful, because the duality of my existence meant I was getting the best of both worlds, at least musically speaking.

It wasn't generally easy to hear a lot of different music outside of your home back then because there were so few channels to hear it on.

My mother, Valerie Victorene Letts, before she left Jamaica, and my father, St Leger Letts.

We only had vinyl records that we'd bought, stolen or borrowed, and until the end of the decade there was only one radio station legally allowed to broadcast pop music in the UK, and that was part of the BBC. The Light Programme had *Saturday Club* (which began as *Skiffle Club*) on from 10am to 12pm, and *Easy Beat* on Sundays from 10.30 to 11.30am, both presented by Brian Matthew. *Pick of the Pops*, hosted by Alan 'Fluff' Freeman, played the pop chart rundown for two hours on a Sunday, while the hour-long *Pop Inn* aired on Tuesday lunchtimes, presented by Keith Fordyce, who played request records and had guest musicians in the studio to perform their latest singles, but not many of them were 'beat' groups. And that was it until 1967, when the BBC launched Radio 1, as much in response to demand as a result of the march of progress.

For those of us who had a television set (black-and-white only until 1968), there were children's television shows, like ITV London's *Tuesday Rendezvous*, where we could see a singer or band miming to a latest release (The Beatles made their first ever TV appearance in London in December 1962, miming to 'Love Me Do'). There was the BBC's *Juke Box Jury* on Saturday night presented by David Jacobs, which played new-release 45 rpm singles and a panel of celebrity judges passed verdict on whether it'd be a hit or not ('I give it five, David'). The only episode of *Jury* I remember is the one in December 1963, which drew an audience of 23 million when The Beatles made up the whole judging panel. ITV's *Thank Your Lucky Stars*, presented by Brian Matthew, featured bands performing their latest single live in the studio and The Beatles made their second ever TV appearance on January 19, 1963, performing 'Please Please Me'. But the greatest music show on TV began on ITV one clear but unseasonably chilly Friday evening in August 1963.

Even at the age of 7½, from the opening credits, which showed a couple of mods on a scooter and a couple of rockers on a motorbike revving up as traffic lights changed and The Surfaris' 'Wipeout' rattled our television's single speaker, I knew that something important was happening. 'Ready Steady Go! The weekend starts... HERE' read two cards before Keith Fordyce, a boring-looking Englishman who dressed like a teacher or bank manager in a suit and tie, welcomed us all to the studio where he was surrounded by people who looked like they'd just walked in off the street. The girls wore shift dresses, their hair bobbed, their feet in pointed stilettos; the boys wore two-piece suits with long collars and thin ties, their hair growing over the collars of their tight, two-button jackets. But the big excitement for me was seeing the one Black guy, who looked just like Derrick. I don't remember what bands were on the show that first night but whoever they were I didn't care. I made sure that every Friday night at 6 I'd be in front of the television when *Ready Steady Go!* went out live. A big attraction was added to the show when Cathy McGowan became Fordyce's co-presenter after a few episodes. She didn't look like the usual girl on TV and she giggled and got things wrong. Her hair was dark and straight, she had a low fringe and wore the kind of outfits my mates' big sisters wore.

That first year of broadcast it was the only television worth watching, and for bands like The Beatles, Rolling Stones, the Merseybeat bunch (The Searchers, Gerry & The Pacemakers, Billy J. Kramer, Cilla Black, etc.) it was the best showcase in the country. The BBC were so impressed and jealous of the programme that they came up with *Top of the Pops*, a pop chart show which went out on Wednesdays from January 1, 1964 and then Thursdays from October that year – they knew not to go up against *RSG!* on a Friday night.

As The Beatles became more and more popular it seemed as if they'd spawned a whole other world of music, culture and attitude. They helped to smuggle so much subversive material into the mainstream, bypassing parental censors with a smile and a quip and a shake of their loveable mop tops. I know it gets said a lot, and at the risk of doling out clichés, the impact that they had on not just me but all parts of culture and British society can't be overstated. It looks and sounds tame now, but John Lennon telling the Queen Mother and people in the expensive seats to 'rattle yer jewellery' from the Palladium stage on November 4, 1963 was shocking. My mother clucked her tongue, as I recall. Back then it was considered almost treasonable for a member of the working classes to even think of speaking to royalty without being spoken to first. Their stoned smiles outside Buckingham Palace for the photographers after receiving their MBEs barely two years later were subtly subversive, and only obvious to those who knew what those lopsided grins and half-closed eyes meant.

After The Beatles came along it was like someone had opened a door to let all these great bands out to tour the country, appear on the telly and get their records on jukeboxes in cafés and all the pop charts. In 1964 the charts were filled with records by not just The Beatles, but also The Searchers, The Hollies, Manfred Mann, Herman's Hermits, Brian Poole & The Tremeloes, The Kinks, Dave Clark Five, The Merseybeats, Wayne Fontana & The Mindbenders, The Swinging Blue Jeans, The Nashville Teens and The Zombies. While a few of those bands had appeared the year before, the number of successful British 'beat bands' almost doubled in the wake of The Beatles becoming so big in America in February 1964.

Then The Rolling Stones came along with their version of blues and R&B oldies, and their own hard-edged and confusing songs (why can't he be a man if he doesn't smoke the same cigarettes?). The Who's songs about being a boy and pictures of Lily added to the strangeness and, by the time I reached grammar school in 1967, my interests had turned to what was going on in the world of my older brothers and of their mates, and of the bigger world beyond Brixton and the Oval.

Music became more of a thing with me over the summer of '67, and I spent the wet and cold days, of which there were plenty that year, with a transistor radio next to my ear in the bedroom, trying to tune in to pirate stations like Radio London and Radio Caroline, or searching out Radio Luxembourg late at night to hear Emperor Rosko. The pirate stations were crucial in my musical education but, by the middle of August, Radio London had closed down and the Emperor had abandoned Luxembourg, which left only Caroline, manned by the likes of Johnnie Walker and Spangles Muldoon. Most of the pirate DJs jumped ship when the British government brought in a new licensing law on August 14 and a few of them, like Rosko, Tony Blackburn, Ed 'Stewpot' Stewart (whose *Junior Choice*, which began on Saturday mornings in 1968, was hugely important because he played pop record requests from the public), Dave Cash and Mike Raven all joined the BBC, ready for the new 'pop' station launch, and the ditching of the Light Programme.

While waiting for that during the first few weeks of school I had only Caroline and late-night, French-language Luxembourg where I could hear all of the singles that I couldn't afford to buy. That was hard, because I'd begun to sense something about music that made me feel different to my mates. Music built a kind of excitement in my head and made my pulse run faster in a way that sports didn't. It was the only source of information about an alternative Britain that existed outside my neighbourhood. Those 7-inch pieces of vinyl carried secret messages to us that our parents couldn't hear or understand. Knowing about musicians and records that no-one else around me had or could get, unless they had cool older brothers or sisters, made other kids look up to me.

Around that time, Desmond got a job in a Carnaby Street record shop on Saturdays and brought home singles (and albums) that were not likely to get into the charts or on television. Often imported from America or Jamaica, their labels had names and logos that I hadn't seen before. He introduced me to a load of new rock and pop, stuff by Cream, Traffic, Shuggie Otis, the Small Faces, Sly & The Family Stone, and that set me off on my own search for new music. I had to do my own record finding before my 12th birthday anyway, because Desmond disappeared from my life for a few years.

For some months, every Saturday Desmond would take me and Norman to the local corner shop to collect the newspaper for my father, and while there he'd slip a comic or two into my bag without paying for them. So, it wasn't exactly a surprise to me when one day a police car arrived at our house, and its occupants asked my parents if they'd accompany them to the police station to fetch Desmond. It was a deeply humiliating shock to my mother, who was enraged and mortified by the sight of the police at her door, especially with the neighbours looking on through net curtains and open windows. Like them, she'd seen the blue-and-white Morris Minor police car crawl up the street and stop outside. There were very few cars in our street, and the sight of a 'Noddy car' was never going to go unnoticed, especially in the late sunny afternoon of an August day as kids ran alongside pretending to be a police siren. I followed as my mother marched down the stairs from her bedroom, where she'd been looking out of the window. She opened the door before anyone could knock. 'Wha' you mean comin' to my house?' she barked.

'Are you Mrs Letts?' asked an officer in full uniform, taking his flat cap off.

'Why ya wan' know?'

'I'm sorry to have to tell you that your son Desmond has been apprehended while in the act of shoplifting from a clothes shop in the West End.'

The 'tsk' that came from between my mother's clenched teeth almost rattled the glass in our window, but she said nothing, so the policeman continued.

'He says he's 15 years old, is that right?'

A nod from my mother.

'Well,' continued the constable slowly, as if talking to someone who didn't understand English, 'that means he's a minor, and rather than hold him in the cells until he can be put in front of a magistrate, we thought that you'd like to take care of him and guarantee to deliver him to us first thing tomorrow morning?'

After turning her eyes from one constable to the other, she called back over her shoulder into the kitchen, 'Duke, me son in trouble with police, we got to go to the station, y'comin'?'

My father, who'd poked his head into the hallway when he heard Mum open the door, sighed deeply. 'I'll get m'coat.'

She turned back to the police officers.

'No.'

'Sorry, what do you mean?'

'I mean I won't take 'im in, I don't wan' 'im no more, I can't do anyt'ing with 'im, you can lock 'im up and throw away the key for all I care. We come to tell 'im that.'

With that, she stepped back inside the hall and reached behind the door for her hat and coat. My dad pushed past me pulling on his bus driver jacket with its badge on the breast pocket, and they left.

A couple of hours later they returned and, when I asked where Desmond was, my mother shouted, 'He ain't comin' back, he gone and so will you if y' do same stupid t'ing as 'im.'

It wasn't until some years later that I thought perhaps she hadn't wanted Desmond back with us because she'd never really wanted him at all. Before Desmond had gone, whenever Dad was annoyed with him, he'd tell his wife that 'your son' had done this or that, and a pained look would cross her face, as if she'd been stabbed gently in the heart. In retaliation sometimes she'd refer to Derrick as 'your son', but Dad wouldn't flinch in the same way. It all made a kind of sense when I learned that while Derrick was my dad's son from a failed love affair, Desmond had been conceived when my mother was 'seduced' by Desmond's father. She was a teenager, working as a maid at his house and he'd flattered her with attention, given her trinkets, and essentially groomed her. That he'd shown an interest in her was unusual because my mother, having descended from Indian Asians, was known mostly by the nickname of 'Coolie', an offensive colonial term used to refer to low-born Indian servants who'd been imported to JA after the abolition of slavery in order to do the lowest-paid work on the island. His grooming went on for weeks until one night, after showing how flattered she was by his attentions, he decided that it was a come-on and Desmond was conceived.

It turned out that there were children all over the island that had been fathered by this man and in the same way. He paid the girls' families to look after any female children, and any boys were brought up by him for the first ten years of their life before being sent to their mothers. I guess, because neither of them ever told us, that my mum found a kind of rescue in the imposing shape and form of my father. Although Duke hadn't married the mother of his son Derrick, everyone knew that he was the father of an illegitimate boy and neither of my parents could see a future in Jamaica which didn't include suffering the disapproval of their close family, church and neighbours. Which is probably why they came to England. A couple of years later my mother welcomed her husband's bastard son into her family, and my father accepted Desmond from the moment that he landed in the UK (although Desmond always called him 'Mr Letts' and never 'Dad').

I didn't know the true story of either of my older brothers' early lives at that time; I simply accepted that I was the third of four Letts boys, and while Derrick was a slightly distant, impressive almost-man who dressed sharp and spoke a language I barely understood, and who I looked up to nonetheless, Desmond was mostly annoying, bullying and slightly scary. He was taken to a foster home, but we were never told where it was. As happy as I was that I wouldn't have to suffer his abuse, thumps or insults any more, I was ecstatic that I got to keep and play his records, even if deep down I missed his rebellious antics.

In 1967 I developed what was close to becoming an obsession with The Beatles. It had begun after I told one of my closest friends at school, Froggy, that I'd bought a Beatles single for seven shillings and six pence ('Penny Lane' c/w 'Strawberry Fields'), which was a huge sum in those days. Froggy looked delighted and proceeded to teach me the real meaning of 'obsession', happy that he'd found someone to share it with. Luckily, my steadily growing ego saved me from the one-way street of absolute fandom, although not for a good few years and after acquiring the second largest collection of Beatles' memorabilia in England.

Born for a Purpose

Exterior. Day. A large schoolyard, early grey London morning.
Scores of boys wearing the same dark clothes mill around, some
pushing and shoving each other, others kicking tennis balls against
the wall of a large, dark brick building. There's an air of barely
suppressed violence mixed with resentment and nervousness
clinging to the damp air like a thin fog. Just inside the entrance,
slightly apart from everyone else, stands a chubby first year
wearing thick-framed black glasses. As he stares across the expanse
of hundreds of uniforms, he's reminded of something he'd seen on
television, in black and white: bare-headed soldiers standing in a
yard of some kind, looking threatening but lost. As he's trying to
remember what it was, from the corner of his eye, the boy sees the
approach of a small gang of larger boys.

'What'choo lookin' at, you Black bastard?'

I'm humming 'Penny Lane' when I hit him. I hadn't thought about
it, and as soon as my punch lands, I wonder why I'd just smacked
bully-boy on his fat, white, pock-marked nose. I move back smartly
so none of the blood that spurted between his pudgy fingers splashes
my pristine, gold-embossed, brand new leather briefcase.

My first thought is, 'Shit, Dad'll kill me if I get this dirty.'

'Aaaaargh!' screams the bleeding fat boy.

My second thought is, 'Fuck you, Bunter.'

I'd watched him and his gang moving through the crowd as I arrived, slashing the backs of legs of boys in short trousers with a metal-toothed comb (only first years had to wear shorts), and I knew he was coming for me. I think the comb was what made me think of 'Penny Lane' and its barber selling photographs. I acted instinctively, in self-defence and in the only way that my parents would have expected me to.

As the bloodied 14-year-old shrieks, his mates, who'd also stepped back when my fist landed, stand gawping at him from a distance of about three feet. Some are sniggering quietly, but a couple are beginning to look angry with the slow realisation dawning that a first year had just made their leader look like the soft, scared bully that he was. Not only that, but a Black first year in glasses, too.

The thought that I've just done something both brave and stupid comes to me with the sound of a ringing bell. As the bully's crew turns, I step quickly toward the bell ringer, thinking I could melt into a crowd of boys all wearing the same uniform. Except I can't exactly blend in with the throng as it masses toward the large, blank brick building on this day in September 1967, because I am the only Jamaican among them. Still, I keep my head down and shoulder my way past as many of the blazered bodies as I can, putting space and mass between me and the idiots who'd welcomed me to a whole new part of my so far brief life with those words, not that they were unusual.

I don't recall what happened the rest of my first day at secondary school, but I must have avoided the bully-boy and his mates, even on the way back from Oval to Brixton. That morning I'd been acutely aware of the stupid uniform I was wearing, because the shorts had rubbed against my ample thighs and the stiffness of my shirt collar and tie made my neck itch. Walking to the bus stop on my own felt weird because for the previous five years I'd ambled to school with mates who lived near me, usually taking our time, arguing about nothing, shouting at girls and taking detours to favourite play spots on the way. The first morning at grammar school was totally different, though, because I was the only one from my junior school (Christchurch Primary) to go to the Tenison. That morning walk was probably the loneliest I'd ever taken, as well as the oddest because neighbours stopped and stared at me as I hurried past in my uniform carrying a big, shiny briefcase. Some of the adults smiled, mostly the old women who'd lived there since long before the War, the Irish who'd moved in the past decade and Jamaican parents who, like mine, had settled in the area and struggled to become upright citizens. The kids gawped, though, and some of them, particularly the Greek girls who lived a few doors down our street, pointed, laughed and stuck their tongues out.

My father was as proud of me as he'd ever been (or would be for quite a few years to come) when he got the letter that informed us that I was going to Archbishop Tenison's Grammar School. He'd spent the best part of a week's wages from his job on the Routemaster buses buying that tan briefcase with its engraved initials, and all I could think was how embarrassing it was, even if I wasn't exactly sure why. To both my parents, the fact that one of their four sons had passed important exams and was going to a school which required uniforms and would be mixing with boys who (they imagined) would be a good influence was justification for their moving several thousand miles from a sun-filled Caribbean island to the dank, cold, grey, urban mess of London. They were proud to be British and desperate to fit in, to make a better life than those they'd left. That I was going to a grammar school was proof for them that they were getting somewhere, they were doing the 'right' thing.

Not that the rest of the world, or I, necessarily agreed with them. My life at grammar school involved a kind of uneasy truce with the other students, which took a year or so for me to work out. I developed a strategy of how to deal with the usual daily racist insults screamed, casually said, or whispered at me by subverting it.

'*Nigger.*'

'*Kit-E-Kat eater.*'

'*Brillo-bonce.*'

The names and insults tripped from the tongue of strangers, teachers, 'mates', (white) bus conductors, shopkeepers, street sweepers, workers on building sites and the police. Until I agreed with them. I realised that idiots who called me names would run out of insults and become confused if I responded positively, and not angrily. Then the call-and-response I played in the playground and classes became something that worked for and not against me.

'*Coon.*'

'That's right!'

'*Sunshine.*'

'Yes, that's me.'

'*Chief.*'

'Uh-huh, yeah.'

'*Sambo.*'

'Correct!'

My replies were always proudly put. It was my version of say it loud, I'm Black and I'm proud, as James Brown sang, just as the racist chorus in Britain became louder and more violent, following Enoch Powell's April 1968 speech at a Conservative Association in Birmingham. In it he claimed that one of his white, working-class, middle-aged constituents had said, 'In this country in fifteen or twenty years' time the Black man will have the whip hand over the white man.' Powell thought it was his place to report the conversation so that he could justify opposing an intended Race Relations Bill that the then Labour government passed in October 1968 – it would give more rights to immigrants and outlaw refusal of access to housing, jobs or public transport to a person because of their colour, race or ethnic origin. With his much-reported speech Powell became the voice and face of working-class racists in Britain when he predicted a coming race war and rivers flowing with blood if the Act was passed. Following the speech, a Labour MP said he'd report Powell to the Director for Public Prosecutions for inciting a riot, the Tory leader Ted Heath sacked Powell from the shadow cabinet (although Margaret Thatcher objected) and even *The Times* called the speech 'evil'. But that was all too late. Powell had made it OK for Brits to tell immigrant people to 'go home' and to paint the message 'Keep Britain White' in big letters on walls in areas where immigrants like my parents were settled. It made it OK for landlords to keep signs in the windows of boarding houses that read 'No Irish, No Blacks, No Dogs'. We had no option but to find ways of coping with it, and for me that meant diving into music, art and culture that wasn't racist or blindly obedient. It wasn't easy, and I wasn't helped by my parents wanting me to be a 'good son', to buckle down to studies, which I really didn't want to do.

At primary school I'd been very good at art, constantly top of the class, and for the first year at Archbishop Tenison School, it was my favourite subject and the one I was best at. Then came time to decide which subjects I would study through to final exams at 16, and what I wanted was not even considered by Mr and Mrs Letts. They believed that no Black person could possibly make a living as an artist, and, certain that they were acting in my best interests, they chose physics, chemistry and technical drawing for me to spend the rest of my schooldays studying. I know that my father always did what he thought best for me and Norman, because he was fond of forever telling us. 'Don't you realise how hard I work to put you through school?' he'd ask, not wanting an answer. 'I never had your opportunities.' My mother bust everybody's balls doing what she considered was for the best, including my father's, and she had a wholly unforgiving nature. My father knew that he had to defer to her judgement on everything or face being cut out of her life, because he'd seen her do it to friends and relations. If my mother thought that she'd been 'crossed' in some way then the transgressor would be excommunicated – she did it to her only brother, my uncle Albert, and his wife, Auntie Peggy. One day they were always around at ours, eating with us, and then... nothing. No more visits, 'and don't mention their name in this house again!' So when she chose the subjects I'd study, my father backed her up and the decision was made.

My problem, which continued to exist right up to when I left full-time education four years later, was that I really didn't want to do the 'right thing'. I'd always wanted to be the outlaw gunslinger or the

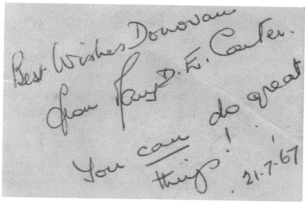

The encouraging sign-off to my final primary school report.

Cherokee warrior when a little kid, and as I grew into adolescence, I discovered a new bunch of 'outlaws' to look up to, ones who touted guitars rather than guns. The week that I started at grammar school, Engelbert Humperdinck was number one in the British pop charts with 'The Last Waltz'. Tom Jones was number two with another soppy ballad, 'I'll Never Fall In Love Again'. Everyone's mum and gran loved those records, and probably, I thought, because they sounded as if Elvis, The Beatles and The Rolling Stones had never happened. The rest of the chart that week was pretty amazing, though, and included Keith West's incredible 'Excerpt From A Teenage Opera', The Tremeloes' 'Even The Bad Times Are Good', the Stones' 'We Love You', 'Itchycoo Park' by the Small Faces, and 'San Francisco (Be Sure To Wear Some Flowers In Your Hair)' by Scott McKenzie – and that was just the Top 10. In the Top 20 were The Beach Boys' 'Heroes And Villains', Dave Davies' 'Death Of A Clown', 'Burning Of The Midnight Lamp' by Jimi Hendrix and, of course, The Beatles with the single that had dominated that summer, 'All You Need Is Love'. There weren't many reggae releases that I could put on the stack of the Dansette spindle back then – Desmond Dekker's '007' being an exception – but like plenty of others I was becoming aware of the 'new' music coming out of my parents' old country.

The Clash bass player Paul Simonon, who grew up in the same area as me and at roughly the same time, once told me that one summer when he was about 11 or 12, he walked around the streets listening to the sound of ska and reggae coming from pretty much every window he passed. That must have been the summer of 1968, because a new British record label called Trojan was putting out original Jamaican ska and reggae records and their releases were booming out of basements, cafés and the bedrooms of my brothers' mates almost constantly. Trojan Records releases became the only discs to be played at legal (and illegal) clubs where Black and white kids mixed, and every rude boy and skinhead who wanted to be a rude boy skanked and moonstomped in time to Byron Lee & The Dragonaires, Glen Adams, The Uniques, Dandy Livingstone, Denzil Dennis, The Upsetters, Wailers and others. Trojan provided the antidote to the racist poison we were constantly fed. Their releases captured the imagination of the British youth, sowing the seeds for the later flowering of Jamaican music across the UK.

The number of new reggae records in our house increased and my dad played the *Fire Corner* album by King Stitt almost endlessly, with Desmond Dekker's 'Israelites', The Paragons' 'Tide Is High', Alton Ellis's 'I Can't Stand It' and The Kingstonians' 'Mix It Up' joining his collection of old-time calypso, soca and country records on the Superstonic sound system turntable.

Trojan became my soundtrack and a musical map of my roots; it became a badge of belonging for the lost tribe growing up in England with a confused duality, and its impact was crucial. As the Jamaican recording scene established itself in the 1960s, its vibe reflected the post-colonial optimism of Jamaica, and ska evolved naturally from the various small, independent studios that sprang up in Kingston. While no-one will agree who invented ska in '59, '60 or '61, the most likely candidate was an employee of studio owner and producer Clement Dodd called Cecil Campbell, who's better known as Prince Buster. It was the Prince who told his guitarist to accentuate the offbeat to create the unique 'chug' that drove the sound of ska. Perhaps the music wasn't actually invented by any one person, though, since it spread naturally and organically across the island in the wake of independence in 1962, it was made by the people, for the people who wanted to have a good time (at last), and they did so with the island's countless sound systems. By the time each popular ska acetate wore out after being swapped among toasters and DJs, it had already been replaced with something new. Demand was partly driven by fierce rivalry between recording artists and the producers wanting to be the kings of the sound systems, and partly by economic need: no royalties were paid to musicians, just a flat fee of maybe $10 to $20 to record a track. They had to play to eat, and so quantity rather than quality became the order of the day in harsh Kingston ghettos.

Once travellers and immigrants from JA took ska to Britain, its popularity grew quickly. By 1963 it had leaked out of the Ladbroke Grove sh'beens to become one of the country's most popular underground sounds. Meanwhile, back in Jamaica, by the mid-sixties the people and musicians were hearing something new – rocksteady. It's been said that ska evolved into the slower tempo of rocksteady because of the changing social climate, but it's also reckoned that a particularly hot summer was responsible for slowing down the groove.

It's also worth considering that at the start of the sixties there was a measurable increase in tension and violence in Kingston's dancehalls, which coincided with the appearance of 'rude boys' – Jamaican youths who'd come to Kingston after independence hoping to better themselves, but found no jobs, a higher cost of living and a wariness of them among the locals. Outsiders in the city, they turned to crime to survive, forming street gangs and marking out territory that they'd 'own', enforcing arbitrary rules and excluding strangers with the use of violence – in a style not too dissimilar to the way Hollywood (and Spaghetti) Westerns showed the old Wild West being formed. The rude boys' part in the evolution of rocksteady's characteristic slower rhythm was perhaps key, though. Because it slowed down dance moves, rooting people to the spot, it allowed dancers to be more aware of what was going on around them and not get shot or stabbed in the back.

The mighty Trojan Records took its name from the trucks that owner Duke Reid used for carrying his sound system. The label went bust after only a few releases, but, in 1968, Lee Gopthal's company, Beat & Commercial, merged with Island Records in the UK and resurrected it. This time they released tracks by British artists as well as Jamaican, and featured British producers like Dandy and Joe Mansano, as well as their Jamaican counterparts Duke Reid, Lee Perry, Bunny Lee and Clancy Eccles. They were so successful that subsidiary labels like Amalgamated, High Note and Lee Perry's Upsetter were formed to take advantage of the demand for the sound of Jamaica while it lasted.

Initially only 7-inch singles were released, purely for economic reasons, but as the culture of compilation albums developed and labels like Motown built a best-selling catalogue of Greatest Hits releases featuring multiple artists as well as by individual groups (The Supremes, Temptations and Four Tops, etc.), ghetto-wise Trojan released a series of compilations called *Tighten Up* which attracted the attention of scores of teenage boys, as much for their sleeves with their photos of semi-naked Black women (except Vol. 2) as for the music.

The long-playing *Tighten Up* compilations made it easier for amateur DJs at places like my local, the Lansdowne Youth Club in Stockwell, to keep the vibe going, since they didn't have to switch records on the single deck. It was at the Lansdowne, around the time that *Tighten*

Up Volume 2 was released, that 14-year-old me first experienced the thunderbolt of sexual longing and desire when Gina Pascal walked – or rather shimmied – into the club. Watching her dance to the sounds of *Tighten Up* did things to me that I hadn't imagined until then. She'll never know what an inspiration she was to an overweight four-eyed Black kid, but that Mauritian girl was my muse before I knew what one was. Trojan Records releases were an essential, integral part of life for me and everyone I knew: the tunes dealt with themes that the youth on the street – Black and white – could identify with. Well, the youth on my street, anyway. With unbelievably infectious radio-friendly melodies, it was not surprising that Trojan scored a fair few Top 30 hits in those days.

At the same time an emerging white youth cult called skinheads, made up of essentially working-class kids who were anti-hippy in every way, from dress to musical taste and attitude to peace and war, adopted reggae music as 'theirs' along with the rude boy style of tonic suits, pork pie hats, button-down collared shirts, heavy brogue shoes and sharply creased tight trousers. While there was undoubtedly an aspect of contrariness in the choice, there was no question of cultural appropriation. Skinheads into reggae didn't want an Elvis to appear and whiten up the scene; they wanted the threat and menace that Jamaican rude boys carried to middle England (at least as far as the sensational Sunday papers were concerned). The release in 1969 of 'Skinhead Moonstomp' by Symarip (led by Roy Ellis) proved that reggae acts were as into the scene as the skins. The skinheads' appreciation of Jamaican music didn't exclude some of the more stupid ones from holding racist views, of course, like any large group, as I discovered when I was chased home from school one day by a gang of four skins who were shouting the usual insults at me (nigger, Black bastard, etc.). I made it to our front door, which flew open just as the kids – probably only a couple of years older, and none of them known to me – got to our gate. Standing in the doorway was my mum, holding the biggest kitchen knife we owned in her right hand, and her left curled into a fist.

'Wha' you want?' she stared, stony-eyed at them.

They stopped in their tracks, not sure what to do. One of them muttered 'Black cunt' and my mum took two steps toward them. They backed off.

She sucked her teeth, waved the knife at them and said, 'Go on 'ome an' look at the colour 'tween your mother's legs.'

Along with skinheads, I found something other than just great music in reggae, though – a sense of belonging. The rhythm, sound and language of reggae appealed to me in the same way that James Brown did. The Godfather of Soul was a staple of the Lansdowne Youth Club, where the sounds of Motown, Detroit, Philadelphia and Northern soul mixed with that of Kingston, creating a potent groove which had boys and girls (Black and white) dancing together. Many of the soul tracks which were being played had a political angle at the time, from The Supremes' 'Love Child' to brother James's 'Say It Loud (I'm Black And I'm Proud)' – which, simplistic as it is, was almost a mind-blowing concept because back then it was more 'don't say I'm Black' as if it made you a second-rate citizen – and The Temptations' 'Ball Of Confusion' to Marvin Gaye's 'Abraham, Martin And John', or Grady Tate's 'Be Black Baby' (among many others). That was when I started raising my consciousness by looking to America. As the seventies began, I read Bobby Seale's *Seize the Time* (1970) and Eldridge Cleaver's *Soul on Ice* (1968) and wanted to know more. My political awareness increased as I read – George Jackson's prison diaries *Soledad Brother* (1970) and *Blood in My Eye* (1971), completed only days before he was killed in San Quentin prison in August 1971, supposedly attempting to escape, were powerful books.

At the same time, when my white mates got into the likes of Captain Beefheart, Led Zeppelin and Cream I was interested and always up for a visit to their houses to hear a new album that they were all raving about, although, as I told them, listening to seven-minute guitar solos on a portable record player in a small, untidy bedroom wasn't the same as getting sweaty on a dancefloor in a club, showing off to girls. The only girls in my schoolmates' world were their sisters.

But then, the year before I was set to take my final school exams, I discovered what it was about rock music that so appealed to my white mates: it had to be experienced live and loud. On April 26, 1971 a rumour went around school that some band were going to play a free show at the Young Vic theatre in Waterloo, South London. It wasn't that far along the Thames, so a bunch of us decided to check it out. As we walked up to the big glass windows at the front of the theatre (which didn't look much like the theatre across the road from it) we heard what sounded like a dozen metal dustbins being kicked about. Pushing through the grimy, half-painted foyer unchallenged, we walked into the dark hall, unaware of how many people were in the seats until our eyes adjusted to the low light. Not that I was looking around, because I'd seen the stage, where a small-looking man was manically thrashing away at his cymbals and tom-tom drums. Have to give it to him, Keith Moon was an incredible drummer. Even though they hadn't begun, he was making enough noise to fill the hall. The Who were beginning a full production rehearsal – and we're talking huge speaker stacks, flashing lights, Townshend's windmills, the works – and I got to within ten yards of the stage to watch them plough through tracks like 'Bargain', 'Pinball Wizard' and 'Won't Get Fooled Again'. My scalp felt as if it was electrified, my pulse raced, and I was as happy as I'd ever been. For the first time, without being able to put anything into words, I felt as if I

Never Boy Scout material, 1970.

understood... what? One of the lights that flashed across the audience during 'Won't Get Fooled Again' hit me like a lightning bolt, blinding me just as I realised that, from then on, somehow I had to become part of this world. It wasn't as clear or simple as wanting to be in a band, it was more of an understanding that this scene, this *thing* could help me make it through life without having to become an accountant or office clerk (and they hadn't even written *Quadrophenia* by then!). That day my world expanded, and I couldn't wait to explore more of it.

Over the summer I went searching for more of the same, attending free gigs in London's Hyde Park to see Humble Pie and Grand Funk Railroad, and at The Oval cricket ground to see The Faces and The Who again. On a quest for more rock enlightenment and experience I got to see acts like King Crimson, Little Feat, Todd Rundgren, Weather Report, John McLaughlin's Mahavishnu Orchestra and David Bowie on the final leg of his Ziggy Stardust tour in 1973. Seeing The Who that day played a big part in my deciding that I wasn't going to stay at school a day longer than I had to, as did my increasingly busy social life.

I attended school enough times in my final year to not arouse suspicion in my parents about my intentions, but long before the exams, I knew that I wasn't going to excel in them. Or even properly take them. I wasn't clear about much in my future, but I knew it wasn't right to be judged for the rest of my life on what marks I got in these exams. They took nothing about my real life into consideration – I'd just discovered sex, drugs and rock 'n' roll, for Chrissakes. Were logarithms or the linear coefficient of expansion really going to help me out there in the real world? I was adolescently outraged at the hours, days and years that school wasted in teaching totally useless crap. So, on my chemistry exam paper I wrote a short poem, which ran:

> a chemist I was not to be
> that I clearly state
> 'cos I got a splitting headache
> and I cannot concentrate.

For my technical drawing exam, I drew a nude woman and added the caption, 'curves are better than straight lines', and left the examination hall as if dancing on air.

That summer of 1972 I left home before the letter arrived telling my parents that I had passed only the biology and English language exams, and before my mother had the chance to throw me out.

For about eight weeks I shared a flat with Steven Mills, a white schoolmate in Wandsworth, before we realised that we had no idea how to survive on our own, so we moved in with my brother Desmond, in Brixton. He'd reappeared at the Letts' house two and a half years after 'leaving' and been reconciled with our mother and my father. Des lived with his girlfriend, had a job as manager of that record shop in Carnaby Street, and seemed a lot cooler to me than he ever had. I had no problem with him telling me what I should listen to and where to go – big brothers are like that, and I didn't have to pay much attention if I didn't want to, as Des didn't care.

In those weeks before moving in with Des, I thought a lot about where I wanted to go and what I wanted be. According to all the education I received at school, my history began with slavery and no Black man ever discovered, built or invented anything. Which was complete bullshit. Look at the sculptures and carvings of the city of Benin in Nigeria or the great 'lost' city of Zimbabwe in Southern Africa – both existed before any European set foot on the continent. I was taught about the abolition of slavery, but the key role slavery played in the British economy of the eighteenth century was too embarrassing to be included on the curriculum. Not only that, but although the majority of slaves went to the Caribbean and North America, some came to Britain and eventually married native-born Britons. There must be quite a few people out there whose great-great-grandfather was in fact an African slave.

So it was natural for me and others in the UK to find the Black Panther Party ethos alluring. American Black people were not taking any shit and at the same time looking really cool with their leather jackets, Afros, shades and open carrying of firearms in broad daylight in LA (which led to the repeal of the law allowing open gun carry in California in 1967). The mixture of soul music and militant right-on politics was a heady combination, and when the Angela Davis trial kicked off in 1972, I followed it as much as I could – I even had one of those great 'Free Angela Davis' posters on my wall. When she was found not guilty on June 5, 1972 we all raised a clenched fist in her honour.

Despite or perhaps because of what they'd suffered during the civil rights movement of the 1950s and 60s, Black Americans never really bought into the idea of a multicultural society. There's an equation between getting your arse kicked and getting your shit together, and clearly American Blacks were forced to get their shit together. They had to deal with motherfuckers running around with white sheets over their heads hanging Black brothers and setting them on fire. Eventually, a Black infrastructure developed in America that is economic, intellectual and artistic. In the UK we had institutionalised racism, but not legislated racism, which is much more difficult to tie down. So, there I was, an alienated first-generation Black British youth, with little choice but to the use the American blueprint. However, the social development of Black America did not really apply to the UK, the difference being that their forefathers had been dragged there kicking and screaming, but my parents had willingly bought a ticket to Britain from Jamaica.

Still, when I heard that there was a UK Back Panther Party and they were holding a meeting near my school in 1972, I got on a bus and went to Oval House in Harleyford Road, SE11. The place was a meeting hall and theatre space, some nights it held discos and the Panthers held fundraising reggae nights there. That night it wasn't packed but it was busy, and everyone was very serious. I took a seat not too near the front and listened to the speaker for a while, when the light started growing dim, the hall was becoming a tunnel, and... The next moment I'm wondering, why is everyone looking down at me, and why am I floating six inches above the ground? Apparently, I'd thrown a 'whitey' (as the stoners used to call it) and came to while being unceremoniously carried out of the hall. It must have been the 'too big to handle' spliff I'd smoked to muster up some courage before I got there. Too embarrassed to return once I'd regained my composure, I left and never went back to the Panthers. But I took from them the intention to lead my own rebel life, even if I couldn't see any role models to look up to. Jesus was apparently white, blue-eyed and blond-haired according to all the pictures in church and at school. White kids saw plenty of people who looked and sounded like them on TV, but if I ever saw a Black man on the telly they were usually American actors, figures of fun or white people 'blacked up'. For an insight into how we were perceived in those days, watch some of the popular British TV shows of the time like *Till Death Us Do Part*, *The Black and White Minstrel Show* (which ran from 1958 until 1978!), *Love Thy Neighbour*, or Jim Davidson's 'Chalky White' comedy routine – yeah, that's entertainment...

How could I find a role in a society where *The Black and White Minstrels* drew over ten million viewers at prime time on a Saturday night? The answer was not to bother, but, by looking outside the mainstream, among the alternative and underground scenes which required being 'different', become myself. In that I had a head start because I was immersed in truly alternative culture with *Trout Mask Replica* in one ear, and in the other all that great Black music coming from Jamaica and America. Being immersed in Black and white subcultures opened my mind to possibilities that existed outside the norm and was the beginning of my not wanting to be defined solely by my colour. I didn't understand the attitude or school of thought that dictated, 'If you're Black then you only listen to Black music and live Black culture.' The juxtaposition of Black and white cultures side by side made things more interesting for me.

Do It ('til You're Satisfied)

Interior. Nightclub with two glitter balls rotating above a dark, square, wooden dancefloor. Around the edges of the large, rectangular room are dark corduroy-covered sofas and low metal tables fixed to the floor. Worn-down leatherette-covered stools are scattered among the tables and sofas looking like misplaced pawns on the checker-patterned linoleum floor. Women in wide-bottomed, tight-fitting trousers and skinny tops perched on six-inch-heeled wedge sandals, and men in wide-lapelled two-button suits of man-made fibre, cheesecloth shirts and neck jewellery stand or dance around, together and near enough to pass as couples. In the middle of the dancefloor a young male wearing a bright blue-and-white Hawaiian shirt over dark blue peg-legged, pleated-front trousers with a thin, white, leather belt and flat-heeled black-and-white 'correspondent' shoes, his eyes shielded by dark aviator-style sunglasses, is dancing. He moves energetically, flashily but smoothly in the proximity of several women who cast looks at him which are in turns admiring, puzzled and impressed. They seem to be wondering, 'Why's he not chatting anyone up?'

They don't get that he is, but with dance moves and not words. There'll be plenty of chat later, once War's 'Me And Baby Brother' has segued into something less funky, like The Intruders' '(Win, Place Or Show) She's A Winner', when the dancer will take a breather, collect his three-button houndstooth black-and-white sports coat and move toward the bar opposite the DJ desk, taking one of the female spectators by the hand as he passes. She goes with him, smiling, uncomplaining, with only a hint of resistance. Once in the relative calm of a corner by the curved, Naugahyde-clad bar, the champion dancer leans into his trophy.

'So what's your name – Diana?'

'Huh?' She giggles and it sounds like ice tinkling in a glass.

'Diana Ross, right? You must at least be related to her.'

'Hey! Don't shit me, man, course I ain't related to Diana Ross!'

'You're American, huh? Now I know you're Diana Ross. Sing "Touch Me In The Morning"!'

More tinkling ice. 'No way, I wish I could sing like her.'

'Go on, give it a try.'

'Hey! What are you doing?'

'I'm trying to get you in the rhythm of "Touch Me", come on, swing those gorgeous hips with me, I'll start for you, just join in, ready...'

Tinkle. 'You mad, man.' Tinkle. 'Ain't you the guy who won the dance-off here last week?'

'You saw that? Yeah, that was me, you like my moves?'

'Yeah... but those other guys up onstage said it was a fix, man, yo' brother was the damned judge!'

'Yeah, but believe me, if it hadn't been for you and the crowd clapping me so hard, Desmond would have given it to some other dude, trust me. Ha, he hated giving me that prize.'

'Um, well, those guys didn't get any good moves on 'til "Kung Fu Fightin'" came on, s'true.'

'Oh yeah, but my Bruce Lee kicks were badder than the rest, right?'

A brighter tinkle. 'Well...'

'Touuuuuch me, in the mownin'...' I sing softly in her ear.

Now it's a full-blown, lazy laugh. This girl is gorgeous, and she really does look like a young Diana Ross. 'Come on, you're not trying. You gonna sing for Don?'

'You a Don? You don't look like no Italian.'

'Looks can be deceiving... You look like a Diana to me.'

'Well, ah'm not, ah'm Marilyn.'

With a swish of her long, loose hair, Marilyn slips under the arm I'd placed above her right shoulder braced against a pillar, and smoothly dances back to the floor. I don't immediately follow, of course. She'll wave me over soon enough, and if the tune's right, I'll dance her back to my place and into my life.

The next number does it: 'Rock Your Baby' by George McCrae. We leave the club wrapped in my big fur Biba 'Bud Flanagan' overcoat, heading for home.

At the time I'd been living in a room on the top floor of a large house in Mostyn Road, Brixton for almost a year, sharing with Desmond, his girlfriend of the time, Nana, and her aunt Betty who owned the house. I'd recently taken Desmond's front room and had the occasional overnight guest in my room, which I'd decorated but changed it almost every month as I went to more places, met more and different people and heard new sounds, saw different films. Not long after meeting Marilyn she moved in with me, making things very snug, but never really putting much of herself into the space. Which was how we both wanted it, I think.

Back then, Brixton was multiracial and pretty peaceful on the whole. Naturally, neighbours would squabble but we'd all join the same line at the dole office on a Thursday and moan about the same stuff between us. I didn't want to be on benefits, partly because it didn't pay enough for me to afford the cool clothes that I needed to make my entrance on the dancefloor noticeable, but mostly because I wasn't looking for any handouts. But it did until I could hustle a regular paying gig.

I was well into the soul scene and spent Friday and Saturday nights at places like the Q Club on Praed Street, Columbo's, Upstairs at

Ronnie Scott's, Trafalgar, Union Tavern, the Bird's Nest chain of clubs in Waterloo, Kensington High Street and West Hampstead, and once or twice the Lacy Lady in Ilford. My world revolved around Marvin Gaye's *What's Going On*, Curtis Mayfield's *Superfly* and Isaac Hayes' *Hot Buttered Soul*. I styled my hair into an Afro with a long blade comb sticking out of it and picked up the right kind of clothes where I could – a week's dole money stretched to an Italian shirt if you knew who to ask. I borrowed jackets from Desmond and worked up the right dance moves so I'd become the sharpest groover on the floor. All to get attention, both the right kind – from girls – and the wrong – from geezers who thought I was a flash git, showing off (and I was). I'd never go out dancing alone and was always in a group of friends like Leo, JR, T, and Desmond occasionally, because he and his mates knew how to handle themselves. The threat of violence was ever-present at clubs in the 1970s, whether from jealous boyfriends, over-eager racist bouncers or pissed-up out-of-towners in from the suburbs, looking for a fuck or, if that wasn't on, a fight. For me, dancing wasn't just a way to get that endorphin rush which raises the hair on the back of your neck and makes you want to move (the opening bars of Parliament's 'Up For The Down Stroke' or The Isley Brothers's 'Fight The Power' still do that). It was also a chance to show off and be noticed, which carried with it a frisson of danger from the Neanderthals who threatened to break a beer glass on your head if you look at them wrong. Most importantly though, it was about girls.

Disco nights were an essential rite of passage for young men in the early 1970s. After outgrowing youth club dances, we graduated to the paid-entrance discos to absorb essential cultural exchanges. The music was Black American-made, the fashions were European-styled, the décor purest cheap British glam. On the dancefloor the moves were home-made, practised in wardrobe mirrors of small bedrooms during the week and perfected on a Friday and Saturday night, with flash touches occasionally borrowed from other dancers. The disco was the place where boys learned how to communicate with women, visually and verbally. The style tribes of the first half of the decade were not to be found in discos usually, and I'd left the skinheads behind in the youth club, while bikers or heavy metal kids wouldn't be seen dead in a disco (thankfully). Discos were for working-class kids who enjoyed dressing up and showing off, getting off and getting down, where they could mix with lower-middle-class kids and young adults who were there for the sex, music, dancing and fashion. It was where future spouses were met – just like I did, as it turned out.

By the time that *Saturday Night Fever* was released in 1978, disco was almost a decade old and I'd been witness to the growth of the British scene as it emerged from the blues and sh'been scene in London, Birmingham, Manchester, Liverpool, Bristol and other major cities during the early and mid-sixties. The cult of the club DJ didn't develop in the UK like it had in America, though, where it emerged from an underground scene in San Francisco and New York. There, the upbeat, snare-heavy sounds of Tamla, Stax, Volt and small southern record labels were played back to back at 'rent' parties in lofts and at illegal warehouse parties. They were called 'rent' parties simply because everyone was charged a small entrance fee which meant that the occupants could pay their rent that month. At the end of the 1960s a handful of people who played the music at rent parties – none of them professional DJs – started playing album tracks on the home stereo systems turned up loud, because they lasted longer and kept the groove going. In 1971, War's *All Day Music* album included two tracks of more than seven minutes long, both of which had a dance groove: 'Slippin' Into Darkness' and 'Me And Baby Brother'. In the summer of 1972 I remember The Temptations' 'Papa Was A Rolling Stone' being the most played track in clubs in the UK (as it was in the US), because the album version at eleven-plus minutes was the longest, grooviest number around (Motown released a single version in September, but that was only six-plus minutes long, and you had to flip the 7-inch to hear it at full length). Because the gay scene in both New York and San Francisco was still pretty much underground until well into the mid-1970s, it developed a culture unchecked by commercial interests. Private parties in spacious lofts allowed gay men to dance together without hassle and they became hugely successful as the word spread, even among straight people with gay friends. A big part of the attraction of the private loft parties was that, while mainstream club DJs had to allow time for customers to get to the bar, keep the sound at regulated levels and let dancers have a smooch before closing at regular hours, loft parties played upbeat dance music as loudly and for as long as the 'guests' wanted. When the authorities closed down a lot of the 'private' parties because they had no licence to charge an entrance fee, some organisers were smart enough to turn private spaces into private members' clubs. That meant they could charge a 'joining fee' that covered equipment hire (and professional PA systems replaced home stereos). None of the new clubs sold alcohol and people could bring their own if they wanted, but generally speaking any stimulants in use were not legally available anywhere anyway.

Not having to follow any rules, inventive amateur DJs began making mix-tapes on reel-to-reel machines and cassettes, splicing middle-eight breaks into loops that went on for far longer than the original records. DJs on the underground gay scene could play what they wanted, unlike those at chain, Mecca-owned clubs in the UK who were usually given a playlist of popular chart and radio hits to play, the management having paid licences for them. In 1972, David Mancuso found Manu Dibango's *Soul Makossa* album in a West Indian record store in Brooklyn and started playing the title track at parties at his apartment. Then known simply as The Loft, it's widely credited as being the first gay rent party venue (opened in 1970). 'Soul Makossa' was so popular at The Loft that Mancuso looped it, and it played for up to twenty minutes at a time. It's come to be regarded as the 'first' disco hit and eventually formed the greater part of Michael Jackson's 1982 'Wanna Be Startin' Something' track, which, after a court case, is now properly credited as being a co-write with Dibango.

The music business took a big leap forward because of the growing disco scene in 1974, when a New York-based DJ and former record plugger named Tom Moulton, who'd become something of a star DJ on the gay scene when working at The Sandpiper on Fire Island, was given an acetate of a new Al Downing track which he liked a lot. As he usually did with pre-release records that companies trusted to him for making a club hit, he left 'I'll Be Holding On' with an engineer named José Rodriguez to be pressed onto a 7-inch single. But that night José didn't have any 7-inch discs available, only 12-inch ones. Tom wanted to play the disc that night, so told José to use a 12-inch, but the first attempt looked silly to Tom, having so little of the record covered in playable groove, so he asked José to extend the sound across the whole disc. Which he did, and by expanding the grooves he had to make it louder. Tom shrugged, grabbed the disc and ran to his gig. He ended up playing it almost continuously all night. After that, Tom pressed B.T. Express's 'Do It ('Til You're Satisfied)' on a 12-inch disc and it was a huge hit, while his extended mix of Don Downing's 'Dream World' (both for Scepter Records, 1974) became a disco staple of the era. So the disco 12-inch was born – coincidentally at around the same time that producers in Jamaica, who had been pressing tracks to 10-inch discs, switched to 12-inch for pretty much the same reason as José; they ran out of old-fashioned 10-inch discs and the results sounded louder anyway, so they stuck with it.

I didn't know any of this when I was on the dancefloor in London, though, as 'Bra' by Cymande (1972), 'Me And Baby Brother' by War (1973), 'Chameleon' by Herbie Hancock (1973) or 'Expansions' by Lonnie Liston Smith & The Cosmic Echoes (1975) – to name but a few great dance tracks – played, but I was more than happy it had all gone down.

Dancing wasn't ever going to get me off the dole, though, and because I was so into clobber, I spent a lot of time in the King's Road, looking for a job in a clothes shop. I worked briefly at Oggi e Domani, a high-fashion, Italian designer boutique which sold outfits similar to the early seventies *L'Uomo Vogue* style, but working there sucked, and I was really talked down to, so I left. Pretty quickly I got work at Jean Machine on the King's Road, a chain store that was considered a hip place where kids not into hippy style but with a bit of money to spend on clothes hung out. It seemed to me that all the staff in the shop, and its customers, wanted to be Warhol stars – they included characters like Andrew (Alternative Miss World) Logan and Piggy, Luciana, Michael and Golinda, who had worked at Biba and been a part of the glam rock scene. They were all freaks in their own right, particularly a six-foot blonde Monroe lookalike called Wendy. I was the sole South London kid, everyone else came from Chelsea and Kensington. The management hired only what they considered to be 'the beautiful people', not just for their looks but their attitude, too. The staff was made up of self-described loud queens, obvious dykes, part-time trannies, and me, with my Black and proud, exuberant style. It didn't take long to figure out that what they really wanted was someone with an Afro to complete the cast. For the first time I became acutely aware

On a Harley Davidson, King's Road, Chelsea, 1976.   DAVID PARKINSON

that among the beautiful people my colour was not only in vogue, but very much an asset.

For the customers there was undoubtedly a kind of scary excitement about coming into the shop. It must have seemed as if they'd passed from the normal world to a forbidden cave of big cocks, cool drugs and the best soundtrack. Of course, it was all bullshit, but it worked for us. We, the staff, had to become masters of bullshit to sell as many jeans as possible and earn our commission. There was a never-ending stream of women needing a hand to get into jeans that were a size too small (everyone thought they were smaller than they actually were), for which we developed a technique to help do the zip up which entailed lying the female customers on the floor. After such intimacy, getting their phone number was a cinch.

The gay scene was very much a part of Jean Machine culture, and I regularly used to go to a small but semi-legendary gay club called Sombreros on Kensington High Street, where Bowie was known to pop in to pick up fashion tips, before he became too famous. The scene was very hedonistic and devoid of politics, although that became political in itself. It was here that I became comfortable moving between different worlds and ways of thinking and hearing. From the disco to the gay club, from Brixton to the King's Road, from my all-Black mates to all-white workmates, from The Who and Led Zep to Chairmen Of The Board and The O'Jays.

That, I decided, was the way I am, and will be.

I also realised that I belonged on the King's Road, because it was a yellow brick road taking me and everyone else to a different world. Since the mid-1950s a lot of popular subculture has emerged from British boutiques. Mary Quant's opening of her Bazaar shop in 1955 put Chelsea, and the King's Road in particular, on the fashion map. In 1966, Granny Takes A Trip attracted people like The Beatles (see their shirts on the back of the *Revolver* album) and The Rolling Stones (see the sleeve of *Between The Buttons*). Pink Floyd were heavily into Granny Takes A Trip's clothes, as were regulars like Soft Machine and The Move, who played the UFO club in Tottenham Court Road as often as Syd Barrett's Floyd.

A few doors down from Granny's, at 430 King's Road, Hung On You (which moved from nearby Cale Street in 1967) sold kaftans and items of ethnic clothing. It became Mr Freedom in 1969, run by Tommy Roberts and Trevor Miles. When I first walked into Mr Freedom it was like entering a giant play area for kids, with a stuffed blue gorilla, a revolving silver globe hanging from the ceiling and jars of sweets behind the counter. The clothes were influenced by over-the-top fifties fashion and Hollywood. The shop was full of pop-art items like Mickey Mouse T-shirts, Superman jackets and fake leopard-skin everywhere. Peter Sellers, Mick Jagger, Malcolm Edwards, and later Malcolm McLaren, all shopped there.

After a while, Miles found that his clothes and ideas were being ripped off everywhere, most notably his extremely successful star T-shirt, and so when Tommy Roberts split to set up Mr Freedom in Kensington Church Street in 1970, Miles rechristened 430 King's Road as Paradise Garage and went for a different look. Best defined as 'Pacific Exotic', it had a distinctly American feel to it, with imported Hawaiian shirts and used jeans from New York. It did pretty well until he took off on his honeymoon, oblivious to the fact that the manager he left in charge was about to rent out some of Paradise Garage's shop space to Malcolm McLaren and Vivienne Westwood. While Miles was away, they set up Let It Rock, selling fifties records and clothes. Before his return (it was a very long honeymoon) they took over running the whole shop and renamed it Too Fast To Live Too Young To Die. There was something of a Teddy boy revival going on in England at the time, and even the fashion elite were into the fifties look – Bryan Ferry and the early Roxy Music albums are proof of that. Malcolm and Vivienne did well selling brothel creepers, houndstooth drapes with velvet collars and mohair jumpers when no-one else was. On any typical Saturday there'd be an assortment of drag queens, Teddy boys and artists shopping at Let It Rock. That wasn't my style back then, which I had enough common sense to realise. Instead, like my parents' generation who made the journey to Britain wearing smartly tailored suits with trilby hats, tailored coats and dresses, I chose clothes that fitted me properly and didn't hark back to an earlier time so obviously. I was interested in what they were doing, though, and had many a long conversation with Malcolm in 1975, during which he showed me how to join the countercultural dots. He defined what counterculture was, its tradition and lineage. He also helped me understand that if you were brave enough and had an idea then anyone could be part of this thing that was way out of the mainstream (and this was before punk happened).

It didn't take long working in a high street retail store earning commission to learn that I had to become someone other than Don from Brixton, I had to be THE Don from Brixton if I wanted to sell more clothes (and impress more girls). The confidence that came from earning money chatting up girls in-store extended to my disco nights out, and then I met Marilyn. We had a good few months together dancing and dating through to 1975 and David Bowie's switch from glam to funk with *Young Americans*. That was a marker of how the disco scene had become mainstream, and while the music was great, the soul scene had begun to leave a bad taste in my mouth. A kind of prejudice was building in the clubs, and the scene I'd been a part of became elitist and almost separatist, which I was really not happy or comfortable with. More people were coming to central London at the weekend from the suburbs and beyond, and some of the clubs began refusing entry to people who they decided weren't dressed properly, or they just didn't like the look of.

Marilyn, the first Mrs Letts, 1975.

Partly because I was seeing things differently after having discovered Rasta through reggae albums bought from places like Daddy Kool's shop, and because Marilyn was living with me, we stopped going out as much. In the time that we'd been together I'd definitely changed. It wasn't just that the soul scene was becoming old, it was also the Jean Machine scene and the people who shopped there. I felt detached from my life, and had a growing sense of dissatisfaction. I had sat at a Marvin Gaye gig at the Albert Hall thinking how it was great, but Marvin wasn't living my life and his message wasn't directed at me. Having had a kind of existential crisis at that gig, I started to play new reggae albums more often than soul records. Through that I was discovering a different identity. It was around then that Marilyn often didn't want to go places with me, especially the blues parties in basements of Brixton where the bass bounced off every surface and shook your ribs loose. She didn't join in with increasingly regular sessions at the house with Des, JR and Leo passing the chalice and reasoning on why things were the way they were. Sometimes Marilyn sat by my side and listened, often falling asleep as she did so.

One night she said that her visa had run out and she'd have to go back to America. Did I want her to leave?

'Not if you don't want to.'

'Well, if we got married, I could stay.' She looked up at me, her lashes half-hiding those big brown eyes.

Leo laughed, and said, 'Don, you gotta marry the girl!'

'Well,' I stalled for a bit. 'You know I don't believe in all that bullshit, Marilyn.'

Leo sucked his teeth. Des looked at me scornfully. 'Do it brother, be a man.'

Marilyn looked hopeful.

'Alright, if that's what you want, I'll fucking marry yer. Registry office next week, if we can get in.'

With a shriek Marilyn threw her arms around my neck and kissed me deeply.

We married with a shrug and two witnesses (JR and Michael Collins who later managed SEX), after which we went back to work. We had no 'reception', there were no presents, no flowers, no mum and dad. It was a sign of how little future we expected to share, which wasn't much, as it turned out.

Smarten Up!

Exterior. Day. Brixton Road, early February. A light rain is falling, creating a sheen on the pavement which reflects back the strip lights of greasy spoon cafés, electrical goods suppliers and other shops which line the street. Hunched against the rain, a man in a double-breasted light mackintosh, collar pulled up and belt tied tightly against the cold, walks down the street, past a dully lit womenswear shop, a greengrocer's with a single bare bulb hanging over crates of wilting coriander, yellow yams and off-orange sweet potatoes. At a butcher's shop, beefy men wearing striped, bloodied aprons throw trotters into white paper. Walking on, his attention is caught by something set back in shadow. He stops and looks as if he's sheltering from the rain, but in fact he's staring at a big, ancient-looking wooden door. Through an opening can be seen a large, cave-like, cold space with bare walls and ceiling, as if to show off the skilled work of Victorian bricklayers. Stepping through the gap, we see rows of dormant pinball machines, jukeboxes and one-arm bandits. Spots of light are cast by what look to be bedside lamps, fitted with at most 30-watt bulbs. There's a clear pathway through the machines, which leads to a warmer-looking, brightly lit cabin at the back of the cave. Into the frame of the door steps a dapper-looking white guy in what looks like a 1940s American, double-breasted, pinstriped suit. At his neck a silk, paisley Tootal scarf is tied like a cravat.

'Alright mate,' he says in a voice showing no kind of accent. 'Can I help you?'

'I dunno, what is this place?'

'What's it look like? It's a jukebox and pinball emporium, with a few slot machines thrown in for good measure. You want to rent one?'

'No, why would I? Is that what you do, rent this stuff out?'

'Well, I'd rather sell it, but there's no call for this stuff except as a rental. That way pub owners can let their customers wreck it and I have to replace or fix it.'

'That don't sound like a good business model, are you doing alright? Well enough to take on staff, maybe?'

With a snort that could either be a laugh or clearing his throat, the man in charge says, 'Not for this business, but I might have something else. Where're you working now – or aren't you?'

'I was at Jean Machine on the King's Road but I've had enough of that, and I'm looking for something a bit more interesting, if you get my drift?'

'Clothes retail, that's perfect old son, come on in,' he waved me toward him. 'What's your name?'

'I'm Don.'

'Alright Don, my name is John Krivine, and this place is called Acme, but I'm about to open another place selling different stuff, clothes and that. It'll be in the same neighbourhood where you've recently been employed, and I need staff for that...'

So it was, aged 19 and having left Jean Machine feeling restless and looking for something different, I wandered into the next, important phase of my life. The site of which was a stall John and his business partner Stephane Raynor had taken in Antiquarius, an indoor market on the King's Road. I'd be my own boss, John said, and sell second-hand furniture, photos, bric-a-brac, demob suits and Acme-branded new clothes in the form of electric blue zoot suits that he had made by some bloke named Vic, who, John explained, was also Let It Rock's cloth cutter. Oh, and jukeboxes, too. After visiting Antiquarius and clocking a stall playing a reggae album and selling bespoke T-shirts printed with political messages, I knew that this was a place where I could be myself. The stall with the T-shirts was owned by Bernard Rhodes, a very chatty bloke always ready to tell me his theories of life, politics, music and religion. He had some regular customers who soon started visiting my stall as much as his too, and they helped to get Acme Attractions a reputation as a hip and cool spot. True to his word, and I'm grateful to him for it, John left me alone to do things at Acme my way. Which included 'stock taking' by buying in new stuff and selling what we had at prices I thought I'd be able to get. There was no till at Acme, and all the money went into my pockets, from where it could be distributed as I saw fit (including to a skinny, starving American girl full of worries and woe named Chrissie, so that she could eat and wouldn't have to take demeaning jobs in order to simply survive).

The stall had an atmosphere unlike any of the others in Antiquarius and quickly attracted a certain kind of clientele, who liked nothing better than to spend all Saturday chatting and smoking, listening to

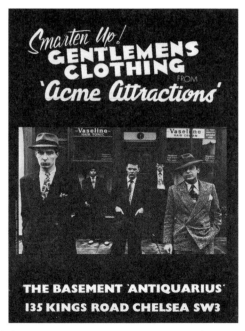

That's me, back left, with Acme co-owner Steph Raynor far right. Original photo by David Parkinson, 1975.

the sounds and blocking the path to other stalls. It wasn't long before the Antiquarius management had complaints from other stallholders about our customers getting in their way and so they offered John the chance to take over the basement to get rid of us, which he leapt at. The move turned out to be very much to our benefit, because it took an extra effort to reach us, and one that only the brave and adventurous would make. After the move to the basement I decided to become a dread. Although my hair was short and pretty much an Afro when I began work there, I was determined to grow locks. Within months, my look, complete with dark glasses (worn permanently to disguise when I was stoned, as well as to look cool), and the sound of dub playing (loudly) on the stall cast a definite vibe over the place. If you looked closely, you'd see I had triple-pierced ears and still wore what can safely be described as an experimental wardrobe. During the summer of 1975 I regularly wore winkle-picker boots, leopard-print waistcoats, wet-look peg-legged trousers and a long, see-through plastic mac.

Acme always attracted people searching for something different to chain-store fashions, and the larger space we had allowed us to stock even more stuff that you wouldn't find anywhere else. It also looked unlike anywhere else. We had a Vespa SS 180 scooter in front of a rack of mohair three-button suits, and Marlowe crepe-soled shoes that Steve McQueen used to wear. On the walls we had fifties prints of guys in Harlem wearing zoot suits with peg trousers hanging alongside classic fifties-era Elvis, Marilyn Monroe and Marlon Brando portraits. There were racks of old (what are now termed vintage) suits plus T-shirts specially printed for Acme. One-off second-hand leather jackets or overcoats were dotted around, hung between kitsch artworks and posters for 1960s gigs. The place came as close to a heaven on earth for me as I could imagine at that time. It was a real home from home.

Antiquarius was up the road from Too Fast To Live, which had been renamed SEX by this time. They were selling rubber fetish wear as well as their own designs because when the Teddy boy clothes stopped selling as well as they had, and in an effort to make some easy money, Malcolm bought a stock-load of rubber fetish wear from a bankrupt shop, because he knew there was a steady market for it (a desperate, tacky market, but still a steady one). The Edwardian gear was either chucked or adapted and restyled by Vivienne, who hung it alongside rubber gimp suits, whips, masks and latex wear and charged exorbitant prices for it. A huge, home-made sign stating 'SEX' was put up outside the shop and staff recruited in the same kind of way that I had been at Acme. The outspoken and totally unique Jordan (who'd stopped using her real name of Pamela Rooke when she was 14) was taken on two weeks after she'd somehow managed to get a job at Harrods. Even before punk happened, Jordan was wearing see-through skirts and no underwear, ripped tops, heavy black eye make-up and towering peroxided hair. We got on really well, and she used to visit me at Acme on her slow days.

SEX was an interesting place and I'd hung out there before getting the job at Acme and become friends with Vivienne and Michael Collins, and when Malcolm McLaren was in New York becoming manager of the New York Dolls (or not), Vivienne offered me a job. That was just after she took me to a Lou Reed gig, and we must have looked quite striking, me in my electric blue zoot suit and Vivienne in her see-through catsuit. I said no to the job, and the main reason was that I couldn't really see myself in black patent leather or rubber and high heels at work. I'd still nip in at times to see Michael and Jordan, and one time he gave me one of their rubber T-shirts. Not sure if it wasn't a touch too much even for me to be seen wearing in Brixton, I never wore it outside my bedroom. I tried it on but ended up having to rip the thing to get it off. It was very uncomfortable and hot, so I decided after five minutes to take it off – but it got stuck over my head. It wouldn't move past my neck and I began to have a panic attack. It was clamped on me like one of those face-hugging creatures from *Alien*, and I felt as if I was suffocating, so I hooked an edge of the T-shirt onto the bedpost and tried to force it off. When I eventually got my breath back the T-shirt was in a wet heap on the floor with a huge rip in it.

I didn't tell Vivienne about the job at Acme for quite a while (she didn't ask), but when she found out, I was banned from SEX. She demanded total loyalty and commitment from her employees and friends, and she banned her staff from visiting me. Vivienne didn't talk to me for thirty years (although there was a screaming match in 1978 on the King's Road), which didn't really bother me much at the time, though, because I was really enjoying working at Acme. The place had become an extension of my life.

Catch a Fire

Interior. Night. The Lyceum Ballroom, a large Victorian building with a domed roof about fifty feet above the dancefloor, July 18, 1975. The place is packed with bodies, with barely enough room to breathe easily. Strangers standing so close they unconsciously adapt their breathing to fit with those around them. The press of bodies and warmth of the night are added to by the amplifiers and lights on the stage. Multiple pin-pricks of glowing light dance through the crowd as scores of joints are passed around. Many of the audience have not been to the Lyceum since 1973, when the night's headline act first appeared there. Since 1968 the place had been a major venue on the capital's rock music circuit, with bands like Genesis, Pink Floyd, Alex Harvey, Edgar Broughton and Robin Trower attracting a different kind of crowd – tonight's headliners, who are being recorded for a live album release, are decidedly not a rock band. They are the foremost reggae act in the world, and their audience is definitely not a typical rock audience. The support act is Third World, and like the main attraction they are from Jamaica, and recently signed to the same British independent record label: Island. During the wait between Third World leaving the stage and Bob Marley & The Wailers taking their place, new people arrive and push their way into the auditorium. Among them are a couple dressed in clothes more suited to a night out dancing. They physically force their way between denim- and army-surplus-clad bodies to a spot in the middle of the floor, three-quarters of the way back from the stage.

'Can you see, Marilyn?'

'Enough,' she says, elbowing a guy who'd bumped her.

I'm here with Leo, JR and Marilyn to see the man whose albums have made a huge impact on us. Bob Marley brought the political to the forefront of reggae and almost single-handedly invented the militant Rasta rebel vibe. We'd missed Third World – deliberately, of course; support acts are for mugs – and almost didn't get in at all because even the lobby was heaving.

If I'd not got in that night, my life might have been completely different. As with The Who at the Young Vic in 1971, this was a defining moment and probably the single most exciting music moment of my life. It was the closest I ever got to a religious experience, and so packed that whenever anyone moved, I was lifted off the ground. When it began to 'rain' inside the crowded, high-ceilinged hall I wasn't the only one who thought that we were witnessing a biblical event. When I felt what I would have sworn were drops of rain land on my head, I looked up to see if someone had opened the roof – I'd heard about gigs at the Lyceum in the late 1960s when hippy bands played all night and the roof was rolled open as the sun came up so they could welcome the dawn – assuming that someone had let some badly needed fresh air into the place, but it was firmly closed. The stage at the Lyceum was high, and the floor not that sloped, so everyone had to crane their necks toward the spotlights in order to see the action. Looking around the room as much as I could, I was reminded of illustrations I'd seen in the books we were given at Sunday school, in which vast crowds stood at the foot of a hill, all looking upwards, toward Jesus. When the 'messiah' arrived onstage that night a sea of arms raised with a mighty cheer and The Wailers kicked into 'Trenchtown Rock'. The hairs on the back of my neck jumped to attention and stayed that way for the next fifty minutes. When it began to 'rain' just as everyone was singing along to 'No Woman, No Cry', a real sense of elation ran through the place, interrupting the crowd-chorus mid-flow. Listen to the Bob Marley & The Wailers *Live! At The Lyceum* album recorded that night and you can hear it in the background. Of course, it wasn't rain, it was condensation dripping from the ceiling and running down the walls, created by the sweating, heavily exhaling crowd, but no-one cared. That night Bob Marley looked tightly coiled, powerful, invincible. The band were note-perfect, tight and effortlessly groovy. They and Bob seemed infected with the same sense of optimistic enthusiasm as everyone in the crowd. As the music flowed and the singing grew in volume (you almost couldn't hear Bob during 'Get Up, Stand Up', the call and response was deafening), it seemed as if life was going to be alright, that everyone in that room was ready, willing and able to go out and make everything better no matter what it took. It wasn't spoken out loud and I didn't have that exact thought at the time, but I felt that something was happening, that here was a man who could teach me something important about the world. We'd been thrashing around with this British Black, Black British identity crisis and then the full impact and reality of what we had heard on his records came together in that show. It was no longer an abstract thing that you could interpret one way or another. Here was the man onstage delivering it live and direct, and giving me confidence to be me.

Until the early 1970s, reggae artists like John Holt, Dennis Brown and Gregory Isaacs provided the dominant sound – a precursor to lovers rock – but out of the sound systems came DJs like Big Youth, I-Roy and U-Roy who had a militant musical message which was far more relevant than anything else I was hearing. I went to sound system clashes in London and listened to the message from those guys (not forgetting Tappa Zukie), because they spoke about where I came from and what I had to offer. It seemed a whole lot more relevant to my situation in Britain where I was feeling alienated, downtrodden and oppressed, being pulled up every day on the streets by police who had the right to stop and search me just because they wanted to, and the law let them. The messages I heard through sound systems like Jah Shaka, Moa Ambassa and Coxsone were so compelling that my political and spiritual consciousness grew. This is what roots and culture reggae does – it's literally musical reportage. Sound system was a way of imparting information; spiritually, politically, culturally. It raises awareness in all those departments, and as young Black British guys, we were especially receptive to those messages and modes of communication.

When I discovered Rastafari, it was not a case of just buying the records and growing the dreads. I attended the Ethiopian Doctrine Church for a while, which was a serious commitment. But it was far too restrictive in the life journey that I had set for myself. A wise old dread once told me that there are two schools of thought – one says we are risen apes, the other that we are fallen angels – and Rastafari helped me identify with the latter. Our history predates Western history by thousands of years and it was not some mad old Rasta smoking weed who taught me that.

That night at the Lyceum I was a baby dread, struggling with the ideas of Rastafari and wondering how it could take me forward, but I was also confused by what I thought was some kind of a dogma. I have always taken what I need out of something and left the rest.

Listening to Bob Marley's album *Catch A Fire* (1973) as a 17-year-old was a revelation. Through it, I discovered the radical and political side to reggae music, that roots reggae had emerged as a response to the political battles between Jamaica's two rival political parties. The lyrical content of *Catch A Fire* was more conscious and sonically complex than a lot of reggae at the time. Island Records' boss Chris Blackwell brought in Wayne Perkins and John 'Rabbit' Bundrick to provide the overdubs and add touches to the songs that maybe Bob Marley & The Wailers would not have done, but – as I was to discover – Bob was nobody's fool. If he had not wanted them on the record they wouldn't have been there. Tracks like 'Concrete Jungle' referred to the state of urban poverty and 'Slave Driver' connected past injustices to the present times. It was definitely more an album than a collection of possible singles, like most reggae albums were at the time. The packaging, which was a passable imitation of a Zippo lighter (the flip top hinged to reveal the disc when opened), was completely different to most reggae sleeves, which looked like cheap Jamaican postcards. Bob Marley's 1974 *Natty Dread* was also important, and it too reflected on the political turmoil swallowing up Jamaica on songs like 'Rebel Music (Three O'Clock Roadblock)' and 'Them Belly Full (But We Hungry)'.

Bob Marley's records sent me searching for what else was happening on the Jamaican scene, and I found dub, which had then become a dominant sound, having developed out of a need to fill rocksteady single B-sides in the most cost-effective way. The word 'version' stamped on them described an instrumental version of the A-side, usually minus vocals, which had been recorded as a studio test for levels. Dub was the next logical step in the growth of reggae, born from a studio technique where drum and bass took centre stage. By utilising two-track, and sometimes four-track, set-ups, producers like King Tubby and Lee Perry used reverb and echo delay to shape the sound and took the giant step of using the mixing desk as an instrument in itself. Osbourne Ruddock (aka King Tubby), an engineer at Duke Reid's studio, began to cut dub plates of tunes with bits of the vocal left out to play on his sound system. He originally did it to offer his audience different versions of their favourite tracks. Fragments of vocals were 'flashed in' either from the A-side or a DJ would make an intro and then 'ride the riddim'. Their sound was pressed onto dub plates (one-off acetates) and played by the local sound systems through valve amps and towering bass bins, live and direct to the people.

Big Youth (Manley Augustus Buchanan), a former cab driver in Jamaica, served his apprenticeship with sound systems around Kingston before becoming known as the 'master deejay'. He addressed militant issues such as Garveyism (the return to Africa) and Rastafari through his music, his songs were spiritual, righteous, militant and culturally educational if you were Black and British. Big Youth, one of the first to include Rasta chants with his militant DJ lyrics, grew up in poverty in Jamaica, and when employed as a mechanic for the Sheraton Hotel practised his DJing skills in the empty hotel rooms. His break came when he became resident DJ for the Lord Tippertone sound system. His first recording with Keith Hudson as producer, 'Ace Ninety Skank' (1972), was a number one hit in Jamaica and when his album *Screaming Target* from '73 caught my attention, little did I know that Paul Simonon and John Lydon were also listening to it.

That Lyceum gig was such an intense experience that after the show I did something I'd never done before. I lost Marilyn, Leo and JR and followed Bob's coach back to his hotel where I snuck into the lobby with the band, roadies and helpers. The desk staff were clearly not going to stop anyone who looked like they might be a part of the entourage. Relieved to have made it through what passed for 'security', I followed everyone up to Bob's rooms and found a spot in the corner, watching the small crowd which ringed the man as he sat in a fake leather armchair, holding court, 'reasoning' and smoking with all the Rasta elders who made up the first ring of admirers, all of them from the different London Rasta communities. For a musician, Bob sure knew a lot of Rasta theology. I couldn't hear clearly what was being said for the first couple of hours, but I was just happy to be there, and breathed in the heavily perfumed air happily, passing the spliffs which came around regularly, nodding to the brethren, none of whom ever asked who I was. I felt accepted among a crowd of strangers in a way that was completely new to me. I'd never been to Jamaica, never left London in fact, but for a few hours that hotel was like a foreign country to me and, in my naivety, I imagined myself in Trenchtown. As the night wore on, elders left the debating circle to be replaced by others who wanted an audience, among them musicians, record company people, faces I vaguely knew or thought I recognised, all eager to 'reason' with Bob.

Finally, at around three in the morning, with Bob having out-'reasoned' and out-smoked everybody, he looked around the room and saw me with my baby dreads and little bag of weed. I was called to the table and 'reasoned' with him till dawn as he, naturally, finished off my herb.

Specifics of the conversation are lost to me now, but the sense and meaning of our discussion was to convince me that he was not just playing music, he embodied the Rasta ideology. For a young guy growing up in the middle of Babylon as I was, hearing his message was radical, hugely appealing and persuasive. He spoke about having pride without possessing or wanting the European aesthetic of beauty and values. Rastafari could empower but not define me, and besides the dreads and the ganja, Rastafarian ideology has much in common with the good parts of most religions. Rastafari blended the purest forms of Judaism and Christianity and accepted the Egyptian roots of both religions, without acknowledging the Catholic Church or the Council of Rome (especially because of Mussolini's invasion of Ethiopia in 1935).

Bob explained why the Rasta prohibition of combing or cutting of hair (as stated in Leviticus 21.5: 'They shall not make baldness upon their head, neither shall they shave off the corner of their beard') and smoking of ganja (marijuana), regarded as 'wisdom weed' because it was found growing on King Solomon's grave, are more than simply religious doctrines; they are socio-cultural tools which keep us separate from and in opposition to Babylon.

A lot of young people in the mid-seventies were drawn to Rastafarianism because the possibility of self-interpretation was one of the attractive things about it. Rastafari's refusal to be part of daily life and commerce in Babylon appealed to the destitute and alienated, giving them a kind of dignity in the process.

Bob Marley helped to shape me in many ways. He achieved status on his own terms, and not by straightening his hair or becoming Anglicised or Americanised. He was not trying to emulate things in the manner that my parents' generation did. It seemed to me that if you knew where you came from, then you knew what you had to offer. The interesting dynamic of Bob was that he had the roots consciousness on one side and the rude boy rebel on the other.

After our reasoning I was clear that I didn't need to debate whether I and my brethren were British Black or Black British – he gave me the confidence to be myself and all I could be. A couple of hours after sitting down with Bob, I emerged blinking into the light of a new day with a head full of righteousness and an intention to do *something*. Although a Saturday, I had to get to Acme, and had only enough time to get home, change and head straight there. All that the customers and other stallholders heard that day was *Catch A Fire*, *Burnin'* and *Natty Dread*, with maybe a spin or two of Tappa's *Man Ah Warrior* thrown in, too. Anyone who engaged with me got the Marley doctrine and nothing but the Marley doctrine.

A few days later I went back to the hotel hoping to get a picture of myself with Bob, before he returned to Jamaica. I took a Polaroid camera with me, not knowing that it would amaze Bob and the band. 'Bloodclaat! Instant picture,' he shouted when I'd pointed and snapped the first photo of him. Polaroid technology had not yet reached Jamaica, and everybody wanted a picture of themselves with Bob there and then. Ten photos down, I still had no picture of me and Bob. More film was sent for and soon enough another packet of Polaroids had gone, and I still had no picture of me and Bob. It took a third packet of Polaroids before I got my prize. That experience cemented our friendship – well, that and the Thai sticks I could get for him. From then on, he'd call me or come into Acme whenever he was in London,

Polaroid with Bob Marley, 1975.

and I took him to the Notting Hill Carnival that year where he asked me to score – and for Marilyn to stay and keep him company. He was a legendary ladies' man, after all.

Whenever we'd meet, I was never a filmmaker, and we couldn't have got to know each other if I tried to film him or get him involved in anything that I was doing professionally. That wasn't what our relationship was about. We knew each other well enough that the last time we met we had an enormous argument which wouldn't end it but define it. Before then, though, my life would take several twists and turns. One of the most significant came a few weeks after Bob chatted up Marilyn at carnival, when she and I split. It wasn't anything to do with Bob, or at least not personally. Marilyn and I had simply grown apart. We were young and still testing things out and we discovered that we wanted different things from life. Being American, Marilyn wasn't as concerned about the Black British question as me and my brethren. Happily, she had leave to remain in the UK because of our marriage, and we parted as friends. Not long after, I had another hugely important night out at the Lyceum.

R.E.S.P.E.C.T.

Interior. No natural light, the Lyceum Ballroom. It's a Monday, approaching midnight and the dancefloor is packed with people, some in couples dancing face to face yet apart, others restlessly looking for someone to dance with. Bodies shuffle and sway, gliding to and fro, sideways and around one another in an unchoreographed mating ritual to the sound of The Ohio Players' 'Skin Tight'. The moves are different, but the attitude is identical to that of the countless thousands of people who have danced across the floor of this former theatre since 1951, when it first became a dancehall jumping to the live swing sound of big bands. Two dark and unused tiered balconies lurk in the upper regions of the building, Grecian pillars stand at regular intervals, their tops invisible in the dark which sits above the disco lighting reflecting from the sole mirrored ball as it turns above the scene of the action. A stage at the opposite end to the main entrance is covered by a heavy, WWII-era blackout curtain with just enough room in front for resting dancers to perch at the edge, their legs swinging. Seated at the centre of the stage are two women dressed almost identically in pencil skirts, white blouses, stiletto-heeled shoes, their hair photo negatives of one another: a white-blonde and jet-black shoulder-length asymmetrical bob with a straight fringe, in a kind of grown-out Louise Brooks style. Unlike the other women in the room who wear clothes that are tight and revealing, flared and shimmering with colour, the two women look like they're going to a business meeting, all buttoned-up and kind of prim. Their kohl-rimmed eyes sweep across the dancers, their heads almost touching they seem to be critiquing the moves, fashions and haircuts on show. We watch them for almost half a minute as they stare in the same direction, their eyes locked onto an unfamiliar figure making its way toward them, shimmying around dancers with quick feet, shouldering aside the standing still. He reaches them just as the soundtrack switches to The Chi-Lites' 'It's Time For Love', the mood on the dancefloor chills and dozens of couples lip-lock. The man now in front of them is wearing a knee-length, see-through plastic mac over a cap-sleeved black T-shirt, and electric blue peg-fronted trousers which taper to black winkle-picker, crepe-soled shoes. His ears are studded with rings and his eyes as dark with kohl as the women he approaches.

'Excuse me darling, can I sit there a minute as my shoes are killing me?' I ask the dark-haired woman.

'How fucking rude!' she laughs.

'Sorry, I don't mean to be, but you look like a lovely and kind-hearted person who'd give a man a break.'

'Yeah, give him a break!' the blonde elbows her mate hard enough that she almost falls off the stage and they both laugh.

'No need to jump girls, slowly does it!'

With a raised eyebrow the dark-haired girl jumps down from the stage and I see that she's tiny. 'Blimey, who lifted you up here?' I ask as I boost my way onto the stage. 'I can only just get up on my own.'

'I did it without any help, thanks. I don't need any assistance with anything.'

'I bet you don't. What's your name?'

'Jeannette. And this is Angie. Who are you, then?'

'I'm Don, from Brixton. What do you do?'

'Do? What do you mean?'

'Are you an actress or something? I'm sure I've seen you somewhere before. Or maybe it was in my dreams?'

Jeannette's eyes roll back in their sockets and Angie snorts. 'Oh smooth, Don, very smooth. Where'd you get your mac from?'

'This? It's from my stall in Chelsea at the Antiquarius market, called Acme Attractions. Do you like it?'

'You must get really hot dancing in that.'

'I usually ask someone to hold it for me when I'm getting serious on the floor, but these bloody shoes are really pinching my feet and I need a rest. So, what do you do?'

'I'm still at school – or supposed to be. I finish in the summer.'

'Well, if you need a job, come and see me at Acme. I'm the manager and I could do with an assistant.'

'Well, that depends on what you need assistance with, but yeah, I might do.' She turns to her friend. 'What's the time? We'd best be going to catch the last tube.'

'Nah,' I offer, 'I can drive you home if you like, stay and have a dance when my feet are recovered?'

'Thanks, but no thanks. I'll see you next Saturday, maybe, at Acme Fashions.'

'Attractions! You do that. See you girls.'

Jeannette did come to Acme the following weekend, and she stayed almost all day. After that she kept coming back. When John moved the stall into the basement, I offered her a Saturday job which she took until school was finished, when she became a full-time employee of Acme Attractions. She'd said that she wanted one of the see-through macs on her first visit, but Jeannette always had her own style. Like me, she wore stuff that was distinctly not the same as everyone else on the council estate where she'd grown up. In Brixton I was considered a laughing stock for a while in my wet-look peg-leg trousers, winkle-picker boots and with all those earrings, even by Desmond, but I liked to think that people secretly admired my wearing things that other

Black people wouldn't, and going to clubs and places they didn't. That may have been wishful thinking on my part, but always being the odd one out was who I was. I loved the reaction and outrage caused by my appearance when walking through Brixton market. In Chelsea, though, wearing dark glasses permanently (being in a basement made it even cooler, bizarrely) and baby dreadlocks didn't outrage anyone, nor did I get shouted at or threatened with violence because of my clothes when walking about on the King's Road. By the beginning of 1976, Jeannette and I had developed a look and a crowd of admirers – or at least she had. There's a photo taken by Sheila Rock of Jeannette standing in the entrance of Acme wearing a wet-look mini-skirt, tight, cap-sleeved red jumper, high heels and dark glasses which perfectly encapsulates her glamour and allure, which was essential to the place. Men and women came to the place to see both of us as much as they did to buy stuff. For a while there, we were the golden couple of the King's Road. We were also in love, and shortly after starting at Acme full time, with Marilyn having moved out, Jeannette moved in with me. When she first visited me at Mostyn Road my room had a Warhol print on the wall and a massive lava lamp by the bed. There was a pinball machine, a one-armed bandit, an eight-track music player and 'every Rasta is a star' spray-painted on the ceiling. She described it as my version of a *Playboy* pad and told me that it was not what she expected to find in Brixton. There were records all around the room and on that first visit I asked her to think of one and I would play it. I was amazed when she asked for the latest Jah Woosh album, *Chalice Blaze*, which, luckily, I had. You could say that my room and Acme were interchangeable, and it wouldn't be strange to wander from one into the other, had they been next door. Which might be why Jeannette fitted in so well – it felt like home.

However, when the council served us with an eviction notice (although in the process putting my name on the Lambeth council housing list) we had to find a new place to live, and quick, which is why we ended up moving south-eastwards to Forest Hill. It was further away from Chelsea, but it was a big house. We were joined by three of my oldest mates, Leo, JR and Tony, and we still had a spare room. As it happened, Jeannette's friend Angie wanted to leave home, so we gave the room to her. Unfortunately, that proved to be a mistake, the consequences of which none of us could have predicted. The mix of four close, Black Rasta male friends in their early twenties who shared a wicked and sometimes dangerous sense of humour – Leo shot me with an air rifle one time after I'd threatened him with an air pistol, and my revenge involved putting gunpowder in an ashtray hoping it'd blow up on him, but JR got the small explosion in his face instead – with two young white women who were not inclined to join in with such stupidity was not always easy. Jeannette's relationship with me meant that she wasn't always there to be with Angie, who we soon discovered was going through a difficult time in her life. To me it seemed she was going through that teenage 'nobody loves me, everybody hates me, what am I gonna do with my life' stage, and I wasn't too understanding or supportive of her, I'm sorry to say. Angie could bring the mood down in the house with a look and she gave off negative vibes so strong that, try as I might, I couldn't deal with her being in the room when everyone was trying to chill. We were pretty much a happy bunch, though, and

With brother Desmond and his Che Guevara beret, 1976.

because we had known each other for so long, me and the brethren would often do stuff together and Jeannette was usually happy to be a part of what we did.

In those days we drove around in a Ford Zodiac I'd bought and christened the Red Shark – Desmond loved it, and unknown to me used to drop by and take it on trips to 'liberate' electrical goods when I was at work in Acme. It was huge inside and had an enormous boot. The paint job was pretty flash, too. It was great for taking trips with our crew down to Brighton or Hastings if the weather was good.

One Friday night, everyone agreed that we should load the car up, take a bag of drugs and drive to the country the next day. Except Angie, that is, who stormed off to her room after I snapped at her for being so fucking miserable, suggesting that she should go back to her parents' house if she couldn't get with the programme – I came to regret my words later but had reacted instinctively. We didn't see her the following morning before driving off and she didn't respond to shouts of 'goodbye', so I figured she was asleep or still mad at me. When we returned to the house late that night everyone was nicely chilled, and despite a funky smell hanging around the place, we were so tired that we put it down to the bins or blocked drains and all crashed out. The next day everyone lay in bed until late – as much to avoid having to wash the dirty dishes which had piled up over the past few days and deal with the smell as anything else. But when we did get up we all piled into the Red Shark for another road trip, and stayed out all day again. When we returned later that night everyone crashed again, even with the smell having got worse.

By the middle of the following day, pretty much everyone was up and trying to find the source of the smell that had become too fucking strong. We'd emptied the bins and checked the sink and bathroom drains before noticing that Angie's door was shut, which was not that odd since we assumed that she'd gone to her parents, but the smell seemed to be stronger near her room. Feeling kind of guilty at having shouted at her, and at the same time worried about what might be behind the door, I shouldered it open with a shove just as Leo, JR and Jeannette were coming up the stairs. The door swung back against the wall in the room, and I gagged as the most sickening smell I had ever encountered hit me. Because the curtains were drawn, I hit the light switch and there on the bed was what looked like a body covered entirely by a sheet, with two deep red spots around the area of the nose. In my head I screamed and rapidly pulled the door shut. Everyone was freaking, Jeannette was crying, Leo and JR were cussing and bending double, steadying themselves against the wall with the hand which wasn't covering their nose and mouth. I fought the need to vomit and breathed deeply, waiting until everyone was calm. Someone, it was agreed, had to go back in and see if it was Angie in the bed and, if so, what was wrong with her. Jeannette couldn't go, and somehow feeling responsible, I decided to do it. Thinking that perhaps the smell wasn't as bad low down near the ground, I went into the room on my knees, crawled up to the bed, and raised the sheet. Under it lay Angie's naked body, the upper part snow white but the part touching the bed a sickly blue. Working up all my courage I touched her side, expecting her to be ice cold, but she was warm. Confused, I reversed out of the room as fast as my hands and knees could carry me.

With more confused cussing and crying we tried to figure out what to do and what might have happened. We were almost shouting at each other when Tony came bounding up the stairs to find out what was going on, and to tell us that he had guests downstairs. Obviously, they had to leave. What else to do? Call an ambulance, call the police . . . police? Ah, shit, clear out all drugs and lose any obviously stolen gear (Des would leave some of his stuff in the car if he didn't have a buyer), because the police would be very suspicious on finding a dead white girl at the home of four Black men. Our act of self-preservation in clearing up involved numerous phone calls to friends to come and take away any contraband. When the police and ambulance were finally called, with the flat looking tidier and cleaner than it had since we moved in, we all retreated to my room, where we sat nervously awaiting the inevitable interrogation from the law.

Which never happened, amazingly. It took about half an hour for the police to tell us that Angie had left a suicide note and taken a fatal mix of Tuinal (barbiturates) and alcohol in a fit of depression. In our mad panic we'd missed the note. Horribly, because she'd left the electric blanket on, Angie's body had been kept warm for two days. We never found out what she'd written in the note, and perhaps the not knowing ramped up the sense of guilt among us, with each thinking that perhaps it was something that we'd done, or at the least there was a lot we hadn't done to help her. For about two months after Angie's death, something – a collective sense of guilt? irrational fear of Angie returning to haunt us? – made it essential that everybody sleep in one room – mine – so everyone dragged mattresses in and arranged them around the floor.

Despite what others think about suicide being a horribly permanent solution to short-term problems, it's not at all: it's a waste, a terrible blow to the family and loved ones of those who commit suicide. It leaves terrible emotional scars on the living. I can't imagine how Angie's parents must have felt, and we never met them – unsurprisingly, perhaps, we weren't invited to the funeral – but as a parent of teenage girls I know that I couldn't begin to deal with the idea of my daughters being so miserable, desperate and alone that they'd do anything like that. We were young and unwilling to think that death could touch us back then, but Angie showed us how fragile life can be, and at the same time how mundane death is. A while later her room was let to Joe Strummer, although the distance from The Clash's rehearsal space in Camden and Mick's and Paul's places in Westbourne Grove meant that he was rarely there, so he moved closer to where the action was – having first decided to liberate some of my precious reggae records. That was when Chrissie Hynde moved in. She used to joke about 'seeing' Angie hanging around the place, which never failed to freak us out even as our lives returned to 'normal', and the house became a centre of after-hours punk activity.

I Wanna Be Me

Interior. Night. The Nashville, an old gin palace of a pub on the Cromwell Road in West Kensington, April 3, 1976. Pan around to see the sticky, swirl-patterned carpets, walls covered with lots of wood panelling, windows of ornately etched glass. There are huge mirrors hung around the bar, reflecting back the dark wood bar and its pillars. Scattered around a space in the corner of the bar, near a raised stage backed by long, pleated curtains, stand two mismatched groups of people, who eye each other with mutual distrust. The Nashville has a reputation for hosting the city's leading R&B-based pub rock bands, but while tonight's headline act, the 101'ers, are very much in the vein of Dr Feelgood, Roogalator, Ducks Deluxe and Kilburn & The High Roads, the support act are a very different-looking bunch.

The Sex Pistols amble on to the small, dark stage looking like a bunch of scruffy school kids. The smallest one, really not much more than a boy, climbs behind the drum kit, jaw clenched and half a smile showing in his raised eyebrows. The guitarist, who looks like he'd just come from a building site, smirks and leers at scantily dressed women at the front of the stage. The friendly looking bassist shakes his shaggy head and looks to the drummer. An emaciated, wild-eyed kid without an instrument steps stiffly to the microphone and stares unblinking at the back of the room, his profile repeating weakly in the fading mirrors facing the stage, all the while giving the impression that he'd rather be somewhere else, possibly tearing the wings from butterflies or torturing kittens. About thirty people are in front of them, an odd mixture of long-haired, leather-jacketed drinkers, bored football fans and about a dozen extravagantly dressed band followers, all either brightly coloured or starkly black and white. Despite the time (8pm on a warm April night) there is an almost physical sense of anticipation and expectation in the room. The musicians in the band look as if their singer is about to tell a joke – a big, unbelievably funny joke. Instead, he turns his back on the crowd. The bassist nods and the guitar rings out loudly, phasing in and out with a brutal edge. The drums clatter and the bass booms.

As the band kicks off, the peacocks at the front of the stage jerk about awkwardly while looking around to see who is looking back at them. The singer turns on his heels, grabs the microphone stand with his right hand on the top and left in the middle, to emit a raucous whine. 'Eyedontmindthefingsyousay...' The effect is instant, I can't quite catch my breath and Jeannette looks at me with an unbelieving smile on her face.

'Yeah,' I shout at her, 'me too.'

As usual, I was the only brother in the room. In among the crowd that night were plenty of people who decided there and then that punk was where it was at – including me. Seeing the Pistols that night made me realise what that *something* I was looking for after leaving Bob Marley's hotel nine months earlier might be. And it had only cost me 50p, the price of entry. When the Pistols hit that first chord, it was as if someone had dropped a lit match into a box of fireworks, and the rockets going off were not just onstage. At one point, Vivienne Westwood began pushing a long-haired guy around, shouting 'hippy' or something at him. Seeing that, Malcolm McLaren, of all people, began laying into the poor guy, which naturally had the pub staff rushing over, and a proper fight broke out. It was all over in thirty seconds, and the band carried on playing with barely a break in tempo. The crowd went back to staring or doing their odd dance. At that point, barely six months after their first gig, the tendency toward violence among Sex Pistols' crowds had followed the band everywhere, unfortunately, and it was mainly because, as their manager, McLaren did his best to play up their yobbish, working-class roots and fuck-you attitude to the music press. The result was that those who didn't know better believed punks to be nasty, vicious, violent thugs.

Mick Jones and Paul Simonon had gone along that night to see the 101'ers' frontman and singer Joe Strummer, sent by Bernard Rhodes, who was 'managing' their band, London SS. It was the first time I'd seen Joe onstage, and while he tried his best, the pub rock outfit he was fronting couldn't understand, let alone show the energy and anger that the Pistols had. The result was that, while Joe burned up his small bit of the stage, those around him seemed wet, lead-footed and ordinary. Later Joe would say that night persuaded him that everything he was doing was wrong, and when asked by Mick and Paul to join their punk band, he didn't take too long to say 'yes'. Which is pretty much what happened to me, I guess. No-one asked me to join a band (at least not then) but I was inspired by the sound and fury of the Pistols' performance that night to want more of it, and less of what had gone before.

Ultimately, the reason I was at the Nashville that night was because, as 1976 progressed, our end of the King's Road began to see more and more people who were travelling up to Chelsea from the suburbs just to buy the new clothes that John Krivine had commissioned from Vic, who'd become so fed up with having to deal with Malcolm McLaren and Vivienne Westwood that he wasn't working for them any longer (which made Vivienne even more mad at me). Vic's clothes fitted perfectly with Acme's vintage stock since they were almost caricatures of classic styles – shirts with big collars, trousers with too many pleats or too many zips, T-shirts with plastic panes over the breast area, huge fluffy angora sweaters in bright colours, sandals made from clear moulded plastic, jeans in coloured vinyl. In 1976 Acme was all about multiculturalism, while SEX was more exclusive and Eurocentric – definitely not in tune with the multicultural way the city was headed. They were not into that whole reggae thing that brought a lot of working-class kids into Acme. At SEX the jukebox played only 1950s- and 1960s-era rock music.

The two shops became different and sometimes opposing camps that year. Jordan drew a group of people into SEX every Saturday from

Bromley, and they later formed the hardcore Pistols fanbase, dressing up (and down) for every gig the band played, making their own way to wherever it was, spreading the word by look and deed. They'd been at the front of the stage at the Nashville. The Bromley contingent, as they became known, ended up being photographed almost as often as the Pistols. A few of them made their way to Acme, without telling Vivienne or Jordan, and one of them who called herself Siouxsie Sioux, along with her boyfriend Steve, became mates.

Not all of the SEX crowd came into Acme, though. Local likely lads Steve Jones and Paul Cook, who had a knack for 'finding' musical instruments and amps, were more Malcolm's crowd. Especially after he had expressed an interest in the music business and they'd asked him to manage their band, The Strand (after the Roxy Music song), early in 1975. Malcolm agreed but then took that two-month trip to New York. While he was away, Bernard Rhodes, who'd known Malcolm since the late 1960s, took on the management of The Strand. When he found out that Glen Matlock, a Small Faces fan and Saturday boy at SEX, played bass, he got him to join Cook and Jones and then changed their name to Kutie Jones & His Sex Pistols. They were on the lookout for interesting characters who might take the job as singer when Bernie spotted a thin, dishevelled-looking kid in a graffitied Pink Floyd T-shirt (he'd scribbled 'I HATE' above the name) on the King's Road in August 1975. Bernie asked him along to SEX to audition for a band, and after John Lydon sang along to Alice Cooper's 'I'm Eighteen' on the jukebox, he got the job.

When he'd returned to London after the Dolls split up and before he could get any further than telling people he was their manager, Malcolm was determined to style a band along New York Dolls lines and become a music mogul. Once Lydon had been found, and despite the two not getting on, Malcolm decided that the Sex Pistols (renamed because 'Kutie' Steve Jones was no longer the frontman) were the ones for him. They played their first gig at Saint Martin's School of Art on the Charing Cross Road (where Glen was a student) on November 6, 1975 and took along the Bromley contingent.

Now, Acme was not a typical shop, but it wasn't unusual on the King's Road, where black-market culture reigned, and where people from different shops in the street would swap merchandise (one gave us smoked salmon and caviar in return for clothes), and that suited me perfectly, being a class act even then. I acquired my entire record collection (apart from the reggae) at Harlequin Records on the King's Road. Once I had the job managing Acme, money became no problem. Jeannette told me that she thought Acme was a quite hostile environment with me and my dark glasses looking intimidating when she first came down the stairs, but when she was hired it became a friendlier place and people started to visit her more than to see me or the clothes. It soon became more than just a clothes shop, but a kind of private members' club, where people could meet and hang out. Or at least the people we wanted to. Among those were friends and customers of SEX, like John Beverley (aka Sid Vicious), who was clearly in love with Jeannette, and despite Vivienne's 'orders' – or more likely because of them – John and Glen became regulars at Acme, and we became friendly (John would do anything to piss off Malcolm and Vivienne). They were the reason Jeannette and I went to see the Pistols at the Nashville Rooms, after which my world took another radical turn.

Photographed for the *Evening Standard* as part of a story about Black London, 1975. EVENING STANDARD/HULTON ARCHIVE/GETTY

Not long after that gig I was asked by an Italian magazine to talk about my Beatles memorabilia collection, which had grown to become the second largest in the UK. During the interview, though, I began thinking 'this is complete bullshit' and stopped it. The next day I swapped my entire collection (except the records) with Steph Raynor for a real fuck-off car, a metallic blue Plymouth Satellite (registration UWN 125K) which had been done up like the *Starsky & Hutch* Gran Torino, complete with massive back wheels and white stripe around the back window and along both wings. I also got rid of a lot of great music that I was listening to for the same reason, albums by Bob Dylan, Led Zeppelin and Pink Floyd among them. Just like Joe Strummer had done after seeing the Pistols, I wiped the slate clean and began again. Joe got his hair cut, left his band – which meant also losing his 'home' because they shared a squat – and ditched all the records that he'd learned to play along to. But then, all of us got rid of our record collections in 1976, although now I think how interesting it was that we had them in the first place, and that most of us ended up buying those records back eventually – well, I did. All counterculture becomes appropriated until the next movement comes along to react against it. It becomes this thing that the next lot have to rebel against; you almost need it to happen. Sometimes you have to get ill before you find the medicine to get better.

Despite shedding all the rock and pop records I'd collected, along with posters and photos, books and other crap, I held on firmly to my reggae collection. I was fired up by what the punks were doing, but I wasn't going to become one. Their argument and problems with Babylon were only partly the same as mine – they could choose to look like outsiders.

Police on My Back

Exterior. Aerial shot. A blindingly bright, sunny day, mid-morning, summer 1976. We're looking down on Atlantic Road in Brixton, SW9. Cars are parked either side of the road, half on the pavement – there are early 1970s Ford Cortinas, Triumph Heralds, Opel Kadetts, Austin Princesses and the occasional Mini, all in eye-popping shades of red, orange, blue or yellow, interspersed with older Austin 1100s, Commer and Transit vans and even a rusting Ford Popular looking like something left over from WWII. Car windows are wound down, men in vests or untucked white work shirts, jeans and shapeless mismatched suit trousers and jackets lounge against their cars, chatting and smoking while women with colourful headscarves wearing loose maxi-skirts, sandals, T-shirts or light-coloured blouses make their way in and out of the grocer's, butcher's and other shops. No-one pays much attention to a large, left-hand-drive American car in electric blue with white trim as it cruises slowly toward the corner with Coldharbour Lane. Showing no sign of noticing it, everyone is aware that close behind the Plymouth Satellite is a light blue Austin Allegro with the word POLICE written on each white door of the panda car. As the vehicles reach the junction of Atlantic Road and Coldharbour Lane, the driver of the Plymouth nods to a couple of men with dreads under yellow and green woollen hats standing in the doorway of Desmond's Hip City, the first Black-owned record shop in London, and then stops the car without warning. There's a small screech of brakes from the panda car, and the street becomes still, almost silent for half a second. Then the large cylindrical blue light on top of its oblong POLICE sign starts to flash, and a loud ringing sounds from somewhere under the bonnet.

The left-hand door of the Plymouth is thrown open and the driver snakes out of the car, looking back to where two uniformed men are getting out of the Austin. One officer is wearing a flat, peaked cap, but the other is adjusting the chinstrap of an almost comically large, pointed helmet.

The policemen close their doors, leaving the light flashing, and walk toward the Plymouth driver who is dressed in a plain black cap-sleeved T-shirt, black peg-legged trousers, pointed-toed loafers with white socks, shades and dreadlocks. As the police advance toward him, he throws his arms wide, and shouts.

'Look, what do you want? You make me really nervous when you are behind me, you are going to make me crash, let's get it over with.'

'Now, sir, don't get... what are you doing?'

I've pulled the T-shirt over my head and dropped it onto the driver's seat. Still talking loudly, I start to flip my shoes off each foot.

'Yo, what are you guys trying to do, crucify me?'

They've stopped advancing and look uncertain. 'Sir, why are you taking your shoes off? What...'

With my shoes off, I use the driver's seat to climb onto the roof of my car. 'What's it look like, man?'

Flat cap is doing all the talking. 'Sir, come down from there, don't take your trousers off or we'll arrest you for indecent exposure.'

I've undone the button and zip of my pegs, which are resting on my hips and threatening to reveal my thankfully clean underwear (Mum would be proud, I think), and have formed a crucifixion stance.

'See I got nothin' to hide!'

I don't believe this, but the copper in the pointed hat has taken it off and is scratching his head as he stares up at me, like some cartoon character. Naturally, given the scene, everyone on the street is also looking at me, and at the police – which is exactly what I wanted.

'So, y'goin' to arrest me, officers? Wanna search me? What did I do? I know I ain't broke no speed limit, you're so close behind me I thought someone stuck a photo from *Z Cars* on my rear-view mirror, and ain't no-one out here gonna say we were speedin'.'

'OK,' says flat cap, 'That's enough now, come down, put your clothes on and move this car off the highway, please. You got the MOT and insurance for it?'

'What d'ya think? Course, officer, in the glove compartment, all present and correct. I don't need to come down, you can reach in and get it. I'm a whole lot safer up here where everyone can see me.'

There's now quite a crowd of people gathered around us, circling both cars. A couple of Rastas are sitting on the panda bonnet, arms folded, half-smiling at the scene in front of them. The police are clearly beginning to feel really uncomfortable, and not just from the heat of the day. Flat cap doesn't make a move to my car. Instead he turns back to the panda, and waves away his new bonnet mascots, who don't move. Both cops make toward their car and have to physically push past the crowd to get in it. The blue light stops flashing. The Rastas slowly get off the panda, and it rolls away, heading down Coldharbour Lane, flat cap gives me a long, hard stare as he passes.

A couple of middle-aged women cluck their tongues as I climb down and button and zip up my trousers. The Rastas give me a nod and head back into Desmond's Hip City, and everyone else goes back to the same, slow day as it was before the entertainment broke in on them.

A Black man driving a flash car getting pulled over by the cops in broad daylight wasn't unusual to residents of that area. But it was becoming too fucking usual for my liking, and despite loving the Plymouth, the attention it got me from the Old Bill made it impossible to hang on to it for long. Even the bright red Ford Zodiac got me too much attention

Trying to be helpful with the Met, 1977.

from the police. I was driving it in Chelsea once when I got pulled over and told that, 'People with red, gold and green hats shouldn't have enough money to drive flash cars.' It got to the point where if I wanted to be anywhere at a certain time, I'd leave thirty minutes early because I'd inevitably get stopped and searched while on my way there.

Police harassment of young Black males was endemic in the 1970s. The almost entirely white Metropolitan Police had the power to stop and search anyone that they 'suspected' of concealing illegal drugs, weapons or just the wrong attitude. I came up with the idea of taking my clothes off when pulled by police after one too many stops while walking in Brixton market one day. I figured that since they made you empty your pockets, take off coats, jackets and shoes while they searched them whatever the weather anyway, as soon as I was stopped, I'd save time and attract as much attention to what was going on as possible. I'd heard too many stories from brothers who had suffered bruised kidneys and balls while under a sus search, had their toes 'accidentally' trodden on when shoes were removed, had 'fucking nigger' spat in their faces and a rib cracked with a truncheon while 'resisting' the search, to trust any copper not to do me damage if they thought they could get away with it. As blatantly bent and racist as they were, no cop wanted to be seen beating up a suspect without obvious provocation. As events at 1976's Notting Hill Carnival demonstrated, the time had come when a bunch of brothers seeing one of their own being hassled and beaten by the police would react violently.

Of course, driving a flash car – and both the Plymouth and Zodiac were flash – attracts attention and you're easily remembered. Luckily when pulled over I was never in possession of anything which would get me properly busted, but the car was a police magnet. Eventually I replaced it with a slow, old and almost invisible Morris Minor. That was the kind of car that Miss Marple would drive through the English countryside of the 1950s, and small enough that I couldn't give lifts to the increasing number of people who were demanding I take them places. The Morris fitted four people at a pinch, where the Zodiac and Plymouth often had twice that many crammed in there – offering another reason for the police to stop me, of course.

The first time I was caught with weed I was on foot, walking down the King's Road with a friend, smoking a spliff. Sensing that something was wrong, I looked around and saw a plain-clothes cop behind us, so I took off running. My friend was not as quick as me, though, and got caught. I went back and said it was my first spliff, ending up with a conviction for possession of a Class B drug. The second time I was watching a late-night Clint Eastwood triple bill at the Scala cinema in Kings Cross with my Rasta bredrin'. We watched the first movie, smoking spliffs. Then the second one, too, passing joints along the line. Before the third movie started, though, there was a break, so we went to the canteen. Where we were met by fifteen Old Bill who arrested us before we could see the last film. It turned out that a gang of off-duty cops had sat behind us for the first movie and then called for reinforcements. Made me wonder if the cops related to *Dirty Harry* in the same way that I did...

Because it's impossible not to mention it, yes, tensions in the city in 1976 were greatly increased because of the unnaturally high temperatures and lack of rain. Tarmac did actually melt, and people fried eggs on car bonnets for tabloid photographers. Every day from late June until mid-July the temperature was never lower than 27°C (80°F) and often more than 30°C, prompting all the tabloid newspapers to print headlines with the word 'Scorcher' in them. Not that I saw a lot of the sun on those sunny days, what with being hunkered down in the basement of Antiquarius with two fans blowing hot air around me and Jeannette as we perched behind the 1930s display cabinet which doubled as a shop counter. We weren't complaining, though – I loved being with Jeannette and she seemed as pleased to be there as I was – and we played reggae and dub records constantly. In my mind, the sounds combined with the stifling heat and pungent aroma of burning herb to conjure up an atmosphere that approximated a store in Kingston, Jamaica. Regular customers who not only bought gear from us but exchanged stuff were the best kind as far as we were concerned, and they understood the Kingston vibe. Part of which was knowing the worth of that most precious of cultural currencies, the mix-tape. It was a mix-tape that got me onto the stage of the Hammersmith Odeon, performing in front of several thousand screaming people.

Ain't It Strange

Interior. Night. A large, 1930s-built theatre with banked seats stretching away from a wide stage and a single deep balcony. The Hammersmith Odeon is packed, the house lights are down, all light is coming from the stage. It's October 23, 1976 and the auditorium is filled with people excitedly shouting at the stage, where a band of long-haired white, male musicians are chugging out a reggae rhythm. Out front stands a dreadlocked Rasta in dark glasses, leaning into a microphone stand and bouncing lightly up and down. At his feet a woman writhes, as if in ecstasy. To his right stands another Rasta holding a Fender Stratocaster guitar. He is laughing.

What a laugh, I think. Or maybe a dream?

From this side of the monitors everything is small except the music. Out there among the shapes of people, the sound – as I know from experience – is big and messy. But here, in front of the footlights, with banks of lights behind me bouncing colours off the inside of my shades, making it impossible to see anyone, just a swaying, moving mass of people, the sound is shattered, coming from all sides, including the front. First and foremost, Lennie's guitar is clanking against Ivan's, both making a harsh rhythm clash, while under that somewhere Jay Dee and Richard are keeping the 'reggae' beat going in a rock-unsteady manner. I can feel that as much as hear it.

Turning to my left, Tappa is fake strumming at Patti's guitar. Tappa don't play guitar, but she'd dragged him onto the stage half a minute

75

earlier from where we were standing with Jeannette and jammed it into his hand. He gave me a terrified 'what do I do?' look, so I made 'air guitar' moves and he took the hint, breaking into the best air guitar I've ever seen. Then as Jeannette and I are laughing at his predicament Patti suddenly walks over and pulls me out to join him! I'd never been on a stage in my life, and hope my dark glasses are hiding the terror I feel. Then Patti gives me the microphone and I think, 'There's no such thing as air microphone.'

Fuck it. I decide to put on my heaviest Jamaican accent and start babbling.

'Babylon is a whore, bloodclaatt, getupstandup, skanga... skanga.' Pause.

Shit, they love it. I can hear cheering.

'Cramp and paralyse them and those who worship Babylon...'

I look at Tappa again and he's rocking out. I look down and Patti's writhing on the floor. She might even be moaning, but all I can hear is the screech of guitars and a plumping, awkward bass.

Then I look at the audience and they're loving it.

Jah Rastafari!

Now I know why they're called 'Rock Gods', because this is making me feel as big as one and twice as happy. The Hammersmith Odeon is full, and 3,000 people are cheering me as I chant the first things that come to mind.

Up until the band began 'Ain't It Strange' they'd played a mostly OK and straightforward rock 'n' roll set. It began with the Velvets' 'We're Gonna Have A Real Good Time Together', which set the tone and suited the bunch of long-haired men onstage, all of whom looked like any other American rocker of the time with their flared jeans, T-shirts, scarves and posturing. The British press might have lumped Patti Smith in with the punks, but no-one seemed to have told the band. Only she wore tight jeans, which had what looked suspiciously like a purposely ripped left knee.

Patti liked punks, though, and her show at the Roundhouse in May 1976 had attracted pretty much everyone who was part of the scene (not that there were many), including me and the Pistols – John Lydon was not impressed. Not many of the punk elite turned up at the Odeon, though, partly because the venue was the 'home' of the rock acts that punks despised, and partly because the support band for the show were The Stranglers, a British pub rock band who'd jumped onto the punk bandwagon as it rolled through the music press that year and were dismissed for doing so by the Bromley contingent.

I'd met Patti because one of my reggae mix-tapes had been given to Lenny Kaye (Patti's guitarist, co-songwriter and band leader) by Chrissie Hynde, who I'd met at Acme. When Chrissie first came down, we talked about the New York punk scene and she said she knew Richard Hell and Lenny Kaye. When she told me that she had just arrived back from Paris after living with the journalist Nick Kent, the *NME* writer who worshipped Keith Richards so much he dressed like him and tried to do the same amount of drugs, I realised that I'd seen a few of her gig reviews in the paper. After she split with Kent she had nowhere to live so I offered her the room in Forest Hill. She worked at SEX for a while and then became a cleaner but was paid so little that I'd give her cash so that she could eat. She also had a talent for drawing and made some T-shirts for us to sell. She was always at Acme and often with Judy Nylon and Patti Palladin (who went on to form Snatch together before Patti began working with Johnny Thunders & The Heartbreakers). Chrissie would meet up with most visiting American punks in London, and that year she'd seen Lenny Kaye and given him one of my reggae compilation cassette tapes, and he decided to search me out. He had a deep interest in US garage rock and psychedelic bands of the mid-1960s, which you can hear in his songs and in the cover versions they played, like The Kingsmen's 'Louie Louie', Velvet Underground's 'Pale Blue Eyes' and the Stones' 'Time Is On My Side'. Anyway, that Saturday afternoon in October he made his way down the stairs into Acme, closely followed by Patti Smith. I was playing Tappa Zukie's version of 'Don't Get Weary' (or 'Don't Get Crazy') at the time, and Patti started jumping up and down on the spot, jabbering 'Oh, oh, oh, I know that voice!'

Naturally, I pretend I don't know who she is, and stare at her, expressionless. Lenny leans across the old draper's display case behind which I'm sitting, with his hand out.

'Hi, I'm Lenny Kaye,' he turns his head toward Patti, who's now sort of dancing on the spot. 'And this is Patti.'

She shouts at him/me: 'It's Tappa, man! Do you know Tappa?'

I briefly touch Lenny's hand, nod, and turn to Patti (thinking, 'Of course all the brothers know each other').

'Course I do.'

'Really? Well can you get him to come to my gig tonight? You too, right?'

'I can ask.'

(And I'm thinking, doesn't Tappa stay with Militant Barry when he's in London? Is he in London?)

'I know Tappa's in London,' Patti half-shouts, as if she can read my mind and then lunges at me. 'Hey, man, look.' She sticks her skinny arm in front of my face to show off a shiny Cartier watch on her wrist. 'Just like yours – two of a kind, eh!'

I pull my sleeve over the Cartier watch I'd acquired on the Acme black market a few weeks back, say, 'Well, what do you know?' and think 'I don't think so, love.'

'Where you playing?' I ask, stalling for time, knowing the answer.

'We're at the Hammersmith Odeon man, can you guys make it? Call him up, call him, get him to say yes and we'll put your names on the list.'

Patti's real excited at the idea of meeting her newest idol. She's met all the rest, excepting poor dead Jim Morrison and maybe Bob Marley, who she'd taken to namechecking whenever asked about music lately.

'Lemme see,' I say coolly picking up the big red telephone receiver and putting my fingers in the ring dial (hoping to fuck that he's at Militant Barry's).

Pause while the phone rings.

'Yo, Barry?'

'Yeh man, who that?'

'Don Letts from Acme. Is Tappa with you?'

Patti has moved around behind the jukebox to squeeze against me and is trying to listen to the phone call, her head close enough to mine to feel her quivering through her leather Schott Perfecto.

'Yeh man, why you wanna know?'

'There's an American singer here, name of Patti Smith, and she wants me and Tappa to come to her gig tonight at the Hammersmith Odeon. You ask him?'

'A'right.' I hear the phone dropped, the receiver banging against the wall in the hall of Barry's place as his footsteps move away.

Patti's moved away, too, as if she's just remembered to act cool. Lenny's engrossed in the records stacked by the player. I wait, doing my best to look bored for at least a whole minute, then hear footsteps return to the receiver.

'OK, him say come get 'im from my place and see you later.'

Click, brrrr.

Patti and Lenny leave Acme happy, Jeannette and I smile at one another and know what we're doing that night.

With Tappa and Patti Smith onstage at the Hammersmith Odeon, 1976.

The punk scene had grown rapidly that summer. In July I saw the Ramones supporting The Flamin' Groovies at the Roundhouse, an old train depot in Camden, and everyone who'd seen or simply heard about the Pistols was there to see the American support act (few bothered with bottom-of-the-bill Stranglers). The Clash had played their first ever gig more than 160 miles away, as support for the Pistols at the Black Swan pub two days earlier, and both bands saw the Americans the following night at Dingwalls, where the Ramones were headlining and promoting their first album release. Among the Ramones' Roundhouse audience were a smattering of people who'd seen the Pistols in places as far from London as Middlesbrough and Manchester. Buzzcocks' Pete Shelley and Howard Devoto made the trip south and called it a 'defining moment' for the punk scene. They'd almost single-handedly started the Mancunian punk scene that summer, and when Buzzcocks played at the 100 Club Punk Festival on September 20 and 21, 1976 they had a fair few fans with them. That 'festival' was held on a Monday and Tuesday night because they were traditionally the quietest days of the week for clubs and the management thought it a chance to make some money – they certainly got a lot of press, although not much of it good. The Pistols headlined on Monday, with The Clash on just before them, but that night is best remembered for being Siouxsie Sioux's stage debut, as singer for The Flowers Of Romance, who jammed their way through twenty minutes of the Lord's Prayer with Sid Vicious on drums and Marco Pirroni on guitar.

That spirit of trying anything, regardless of skill, training or experience, was what was most attractive about punk. Bands formed with members not having even the rudiments of knowledge about how to play or even what they were playing, but they got onstage and made a noise anyway. Sometimes it was thrilling, often it was torture, but it was always energetic, positive and anti-authoritarian. I took my recently acquired Super-8mm camera to the Screen on the Green in August to film the Sex Pistols with no clear plan in mind other than to film something of what was happening and what turned me on. I only got a few numbers filmed, though, before Malcolm had me ejected.

Malcolm had been making increasingly ludicrous statements about the Pistols to anyone who'd listen for months. He also put some in the mouths of band members – although never John – for interviews with the music press (Paul would never have thought to say something like 'We're not into music really, we're into chaos,' for instance). John refused to say or do anything he was told to by anyone, so he came up with his own outrageous statements.

After signing to EMI in October the Pistols released their first single, 'Anarchy In The UK', a month later. As part of the press campaign to promote it, on December 1 they appeared live on a London ITV teatime show and swore at the presenter, Bill Grundy. At a time when using 'bloody' was banned on TV before the 9pm watershed, Steve's calling the host 'You dirty fucker' caused so much fury among viewers that a lorry driver in Kent was driven to kick in the screen of his TV set (according to a newspaper, that is). The following day the tabloid newspapers reacted as if the band had murdered Grundy live on screen, and headlines screamed about 'The Filth and the Fury!' Malcolm was delighted and set out on a long-planned punk package trek around the UK, titled the Anarchy In The UK tour, with the Pistols, Clash and former New York Dolls guitarist Johnny Thunders and his band The Heartbreakers sharing a bus. The Damned – who'd released the first 'proper' punk single a couple of weeks before 'Anarchy' – travelled separately; either because they were so disliked by the others on the bus, or because their record label (Stiff) wouldn't pay Malcolm for the thrill of travelling with him. So The Damned used their own van and stayed in B&Bs, not at McLaren-booked hotels. Mind you, The Damned only travelled on the first six or seven dates, playing twice, before they disappeared from the tour altogether – and no-one has ever agreed on the exact reason why they left.

As it turned out, most of the hotels booked for the Anarchy tour cancelled their bookings after the Grundy TV show, as did most of the venues, some only hours before the gig was due to take place, and only seven of the planned twenty-four gigs actually took place. But the bus travelled to more than a dozen of the cancelled gigs with everyone expecting to play.

The furore that the Pistols created made it difficult for all punk bands to get gigs, even in London. But punk was all about being inventive, doing things for yourself and not waiting around for something to happen. Most long-established music venues only booked bands from agents and with promoters who knew that they'd get people through the door because their acts had record deals and fans who'd pay to see them. Plus, the average gig-goer would stand or sit nicely as the music played; there was little risk of a fight or riot breaking out, even at a Dr Feelgood gig. Punks, as the tabloid and music press kept telling everyone, were violent, rude, disrespectful, angry and dangerous – Sid Vicious ended 1976 in a remand centre, having been convicted of throwing a glass at The Damned during their set on the second night of the 100 Club Punk Festival in September, hitting a girl in the crowd instead, blinding her in one eye (that was the last punk show at the 100 Club for a few years). In the weeks following the moral outrage caused by the Pistols, only brave venue owners dared to book them or their kind.

Which is why, in December 1976, Acme's bookkeeper Andrew Czezowski (who also managed a punk band called Generation X, fronted by Billy Idol), Sue Carrington and Barry Jones decided to take up a short-term lease on a shabby club on the ground floor and cellar of an old vegetable warehouse in Neal Street, Covent Garden. At that time Covent Garden wasn't the high-class shopping and tourist centre that it's since become; it was in a kind of limbo state. The old fruit and veg market, which closed in 1974, was being redeveloped and the whole piazza was a building site. The streets that ran around and off it were a mixture of collapsing buildings and empty shops waiting for regeneration and gentrification (not that anyone called it that in 1976). Lots of places were let on short leases just to keep the buildings occupied and some money coming in, regardless of what the space was to be used for. Number 41–43 Neal Street had become a late-night gay drinking den called Chaguaramas Club when the market started to close down, and it had a drinking and late-night music licence (although there were only a few months left on both). The setting was perfect for a punk club. There were no neighbours to get annoyed by noise, no expensive cars in the surrounding streets to get scratched, and the dark, dirty buildings looked as if they had no future (and many didn't).

Because of his work for Acme, Andrew knew about the reggae I was playing there and maybe he thought it gave the place a sense of continuity – Chaguaramas had been owned by reggae singer John Holt's producer, Tony Ashfield – so he asked me to DJ at what he was calling the Roxy on a regular basis, even though I'd never DJed anywhere in my life, and didn't have any aspirations to, either. Before I took the job, I thought I'd see how the first night went, which wasn't a proper opening but a money-raising exercise intended to fund the restyling of the club, on December 14, 1976. The basement, with its tiny stage and low ceiling, was grimy, cold and barely habitable, but it suited the mood of the people and bands who turned up. Naturally, Generation X were the main act, and the place was full of faces I recognised. The following night The Heartbreakers played headline, because the Anarchy tour gig in Glasgow they were supposed to be at had been cancelled, and it was great. They rocked like motherfuckers, and if it hadn't been for the smack they brought to the scene (along with Nancy Spungeon), they could have been truly great. I was unsure about how long the Roxy would last but told Andy I'd be his DJ – after all, I could still work at Acme during the day. I tried to persuade Desmond, Leo and JR that they should join me and work the bar and security at the Roxy, but they laughed and took the piss – until I got them to come to the Siouxsie & The Banshees (formed by Siouxsie and Steve Severin after the 100 Club Festival, without Sid Vicious) and Gen X gig there on December 21 and explained that they could sell ready-rolled spliffs to the 'customers' at the club because, as they could see, none of them knew how to roll properly. When it officially opened on New Year's Day 1977, the Roxy had the Forest Hill Rastas working the bar, the door, security and sounds. That night The Clash headlined, with Joe Strummer wearing a white shirt with '1977' stencilled in big numbers across his chest. As the lyrics of the song so prophetically put it, there was 'no Elvis, Beatles or Rolling Stones' that night.

100 Days

Interior. A bare, shabby nightclub in a cellar painted black. Pillars around the room are there to stop the ceiling falling in. Stark white lights glare onto a stage and spill onto the dancefloor in front of it, where a small crowd of people are jumping up and down and into one another. Many are wearing large white shirts with pencilled slogans and words, spray-painted, deliberately ripped and held together with safety pins. One girl with a black ponytail that reaches her waist has smeared heavy black eyeliner and scarlet lipstick on her face, which is very white. She wears a loosely hanging black tie inside the collar of a baggy white men's shirt with a belt that cinches it around her waist, a couple of badges pinned in odd places, and black leather gloves. Underneath she's wearing black fishnet stockings, large black silk drawers and four-inch stiletto heels. She's barely visible because she's outside the pool of light from the stage, happy to dance on her own, not being a part of the crowd, which has become a scrum of boys in school blazers throwing each other on the floor. Off to the side of the stage a man with a camera is filming the melee. Next to him stands an angular woman with a black Cleopatra haircut, a cap-sleeved red T-shirt worn over tight, straight-legged white Capri pants holding a heavy-looking arc light by her side. She thumps the cameraman on the shoulder and points.

'Hey, Don, over there...'

I swing the camera away from the bundle of boys, and my lighting assistant raises the light, which throws the white-shirted dancer into stark relief.

'Thanks, Jeannette.'

It's a Friday night at the Roxy and onstage a bunch of school kids from Finchley who called themselves Eater are making a racket which Jeannette is obviously pained to be listening to (a few times I asked Chrissie Hynde to work the light to give Jeannette a night off, but she didn't much like the bands). Jeannette's great at spotting subjects for my camera and the white-shirted dancer can't avoid her light, which sways around a bit at times ('This is fucking heavy, Don!') so she starts dancing for the camera. I'm trying to concentrate on the dancer, wondering if she'll do something that she thinks is outrageous, when I catch a glimpse of red, white and blue on my left.

A London-Irish public schoolboy, Shane MacGowan, wearing a jacket made from a Union Jack flag, a black shirt and jeans, his hands tucked inside his front pockets, rocked toward Jeannette's light in a Status Quo-style stomp. I pan toward him and Shane twirls for me. As I swing back toward ponytail, she pulls her shirt apart, flashing her breasts. I keep filming. Inspired, Shane takes his hands out of his pockets, throws his arms about and makes a running kick at a beer glass on the floor. Enter my frame from the right a boy wearing almost the same white shirt as ponytail; he grabs her and pogoes on her back. She laughs and tries to throw him off. They tussle and end up on the floor, laughing: the picture of young punk love in 1977...

After a friendly fashion editor on glossy magazines and regular at Acme Attractions named Caroline Baker (she'd worked at *Nova* in the 1960s and then *The Sunday Times Magazine*) gave me a Super-8mm cine camera, I'd taken it everywhere and pointed it at anything which caught my eye and imagination. I filmed parties at the flat in Forest Hill, the Notting Hill Carnival, the streets of Brixton and punk gigs around the city. Caroline was smart enough to recognise that something new and special was happening on the punk scene and that while she was never going to be a member of the core movement and couldn't get the insider view, I was and could. We'd chat about fashion, punk and movies whenever she came into the shop, and she knew that I wanted to do something on the scene, so she helped me out. Seeing

The Harder They Come (1972) made me want to become a filmmaker, but I thought that the way things worked in the film business made it a ridiculous idea – you had to be a member of the right club, and I wasn't. But when punk came along it inspired me to take Caroline's camera and, even though I'd never held one before, do something with it. As soon as I started using it, I felt completely comfortable and it became my punk 'instrument'. I didn't read the instructions but it didn't matter – in fact, it was part of the prevailing attitude. I knew that a lot could be gained from the blind 'fuck you' energy of just going out there and doing it, without any preconceived notions or value structures. That was the most important thing I'd learned from mixing with the punks, the whole punk DIY ethos, a blueprint for the working class to create their own art outside the class system and ignoring the closed-door, old-boy network which ran things in the music, art and entertainment world just like it did in every other part of life.

When I began to film bands performing at the Roxy I didn't give too much thought to method. But as I got into it, and prompted by the cost of buying film and getting it processed, I started to question the artistic process. What justifies picking up a camera in the first place? Am I aware, deeply aware, of what constitutes good picture composition and framing of the subject? Obviously, I wasn't, but I began to take my new role seriously and documented all the events that I thought were either interesting or ridiculous. As it turned out, I got a lot of film that was representative of the whole movement. I was in the right place at the right time, and had the sus for filming what was important, rather than just tabloid punks trying to grab some screen time (although I got a bit of that, too).

I worked out how to load the three-minute film cartridge it used, how to focus, pan, zoom and record as I went along, but took a more 'Fred Flintstone' approach to editing sound and film, which needed more time. After I was spotted filming The Clash and The Slits at the old Roxy Theatre in Harlesden, the following week I read in the *NME* that 'Don Letts is making a film about punk rock'.

'That's a good idea,' I thought, 'I'll call it a film,' and before long people were asking me when it was going to come out. I filmed for four months and the thing took on a life of its own, even the title – it became *The Punk Rock Movie* because that's what everybody was

My first front cover and the start of the 100 days
at the Roxy, 1977.

calling it. I got a lot of the Forest Hill party footage because, after the Roxy shut, Chrissie Hynde, some of The Slits, The Clash, Generation X and the Pistols would want to keep things going, not wanting the night to end. They also wanted to watch me putting *The Punk Rock Movie* together and check their moves onstage. If you look at the credits for the film, it says, 'scissors and Sellotape' and that's exactly what we used to edit the film. Jeannette and JR helped me to literally stick it together. Fortunately for me, punk bands seemed to cram everything into about two-and-a-half-minute-long numbers, and most punks ran out of things to say after about three minutes, which meant sections were self-edited, in a way. Between my eye for action and the need to save on the costs I learned to edit 'in camera'.

Because the Roxy crowd knew and trusted me, I managed to film what mainstream TV cameras couldn't – the real background, the real truth. Every time someone announced that London Weekend Television or the BBC were coming to film at the club – which happened more often as punk spread across the country – all the really important people stayed away. The other kids stuck on more safety pins and extra make-up to jump around in front of the professional cameras. Which meant that all the mainstream media got was a distorted idea of the scene, while I managed to capture the essence of punk at its rawest.

I became friends with journalists like Vivien Goldman, Tony Parsons, Caroline Coon, Janet Street Porter and John Ingham who hung at the Roxy. They were all influential in helping to break the punk movement (and were also all massive reggae fans) in music mags, and as well as pushing punk through the door of *Sounds* and the *NME*, Vivien and Caroline in particular gave me a leg up by writing about me, which resulted in me having a profile and something of a vibe grew about the movie. The one thing that the movie doesn't get across is the influence that the records I played had on punk. I couldn't film when I was being DJ – there was only one deck which meant I had to concentrate on getting discs swapped as quickly as possible – and no reggae bands played there. When the club started the only punk records to have been released were 'Anarchy In The UK' and 'New Rose' by The Damned, which is why I played what I was into: serious dub reggae. I've always liked writer Jon Savage's view that the reggae made a welcome sonic, tuneful break from the loud, fast, often not very good bands. However, I also slipped in some MC5, Stooges, Ramones and New York Dolls because most of the upcoming punk bands owned the first two Dolls' albums and many learned to play by listening to the Ramones' debut album. Plus, speed (amphetamine sulphate or Dexedrine pills) was the drug of choice among the punks, who were either playing or pogoing. As there was only one deck, in the gaps between records I could feel the vibe of the room and choose tracks which were right for the moment, for when the heavy bass of a Prince Far I track like 'Heavy Manners' was needed; then the bar staff did great business in spliffs. I never played requests. Why hear something you've heard before when you can hear something new? To most punks, King Tubby's 'Bag A Wire Dub', 'Fisherman' by The Congos and the mighty 'MPLA Dub' by Tappa Zukie were all new. Being well aware of the Jamaican sound systems tradition of delivering information that was spiritual, cultural and political, and as a young Black British guy, I was sensitive to the messages in songs like 'Burn Down Babylon', 'Need A Roof Over My Head', 'Money In My Pocket', 'Police And Thieves' and 'Two Sevens Clash'. As it turned out, the punks were very receptive, too. Reggae spoke with a currency that the punks could identify. It was the anti-fashion fashion, the rebel stance, and, importantly, a kind of musical reportage, talking about things that mattered. Which struck an obvious chord with them. As, of course, did the weed, which was a big part of the serious cultural exchange going down.

Slogans that The Clash painted on their clothes like 'Hate and War' and 'Under Heavy Manners' came directly from phrases they'd heard Tappa Zukie, Prince Far I and Culture using. The 'White Riot' picture sleeve (designed by Sebastian Conran of the Conran design family, by the way) deliberately resembled the cover of Joe Gibbs & The Professionals' *State Of Emergency* album sleeve, where the band is lined up against a wall with their backs to the camera, being frisked by police. The Clash and Johnny Rotten (as he was then) understood and aligned themselves with reggae's revolutionary stance and relentless hatred of the establishment.

Still, those who 'got it' really got it. I spent many smoky nights wedged up against bass bins in the Four Aces reggae club in Dalston in 1977 with either John Lydon, Joe Strummer or Ariane (Ari Up) from The Slits. It was a dark and tiny room with speakers up to the ceiling and every second someone used to drop from a combination of the weed, the drink, the heat and the bass. It was the heaviest reggae club in the country and Lydon, Strummer and Ariane would be the only white faces in the dance, for which they got a lot of respect, because they had the balls to walk in the club in the first place. Ariane and I went to many reggae clubs in those days, and sound clashes like Coxone vs Saxon that used to happen at local town halls. If I was going to a reggae show and John or Joe were around, I'd invite them along.

The cultural exchange between the punks and dreads continued through 1977, and all over the country things were happening. Local reggae bands and performers gained reputations and a fanbase which would grow as they toured the UK staying true to their roots, playing the same kind of places which had hosted the original punk bands. David Hinds put Steel Pulse together in the Handsworth area of Birmingham in 1974 against a backdrop of dole queues, police harassment and the collapse of the area's main employer, British Leyland, which mirrored what happened with the motor industry in Detroit. Although Steel Pulse were initially refused permission to play in Caribbean venues in the Midlands because of their Rastafarian beliefs, the link between punk

Dread at the controls, Mk 1: the Roxy, 1977.   ERICA ECHENBERG/REDFERNS

and reggae brought them support slots for The Adverts, Generation X, The Stranglers and XTC, and I have to say they blew the headliners off the stage every time. Eventually they opened for Burning Spear on a nationwide tour, signed for Island Records and released *Handsworth Revolution* (1978), which was a major landmark in the evolution of British reggae. They also became an important part of the Rock Against Racism movement.

London-based bands like Black Slate and Ladbroke Grove's Aswad also started out in the mid-1970s, and while the Aswad I loved was during their *Warrior Charge* period (1980), that was when the only airplay they could get was on pirate radio stations, like Dread Broadcasting Corporation (aka DBC), which beamed a weak signal from the top of whatever W10/W11-area tower block they could gain access to, playing roots and dub reggae records. (Of course, it wasn't only Black music that couldn't get mainstream or widespread exposure. Anti-establishment music which had no current pop sensibility always had a hard time getting widespread exposure, which was needed to generate funds enough to keep going.) Aswad were not really getting their dues, so I can understand why they made the change that they did in 1988 when they recorded a Tina Turner B-side, 'Don't Turn Around'. It went to number one on the national pop chart and they got to appear on *Top of the Pops*. They lost their core audience but gained a new, larger one. Sometimes you cross over and can't get Black...

Also on the UK reggae scene in 1977 were Misty In Roots and Dennis Bovell with Matumbi, who'd been around since the start of the seventies. Engineer and producer Dennis Bovell collaborated with I-Roy, Steel Pulse, Errol Dunkley and Johnny Clarke, and produced Janet Kay's massive hit 'Silly Games', which kick-started the smoother-than-roots-reggae 'lovers rock' genre. Dennis and his Dub Band also worked with Linton Kwesi Johnson on his albums. Although musically punk drew more from reggae than reggae took from punk, reggae undoubtedly benefited from the increased exposure that came from the loose alliance, since it enlarged the audience enormously, if nothing else. There were some truly great British reggae records made in the late 1970s, especially by Aswad, Steel Pulse, Delroy Washington and Reggae Regular. All of whom had it rough and suffered from an attitude among some people that 'If you ain't from Jamaica then you are not real', which was bullshit. The punk attitude that 'anyone can do it' worked equally well for reggae musicians, as did the shared antipathy to authority and the status quo, combined with a need to find an identity and voice that were not borrowed from anywhere else. It all sparked creative interplay between punks and Rastas.

So it was that, by the time Bob Marley was giving me grief in spring 1977 for wearing bondage trousers, asking, 'What ya deal wid Don Letts dem nasty punk rockers, you look like a bloodclaat mountaineer!' I had to tell him, 'Dem crazy baldheads are my mates,' or words to that effect and explain the punk–reggae crossover that was going on all over the country. He must have reconsidered his opinion, because in June he recorded 'Punky Reggae Party'.

By the time Bob's single was released I had a whole lot more film footage in the can, and my life had changed considerably. I left the Roxy, as did all the original team who ran it. Maybe it was the appearance one night of Led Zeppelin's Robert Plant and Jimmy Page that did it (Desmond wouldn't let them in at first, enjoying fucking with them), but the landlords must have thought that the place could make some real money and so demanded too much rent from Andrew to renew his lease. When he and his partners left we went with them, because he wasn't just our boss he was also a mate, and we were loyal. New owners took over the running of the club, but it was never the same again.

Acme Attractions was also about to move. Propelled by the reputation and money we'd earned at Antiquarius, John and Steph took a lease on a shop in the King's Road and asked Jeannette and me to run it. We said yes, but not with great enthusiasm.

Burning Down the House

Exterior. A dark pre-dawn, wide street of shops glowing in the yellow light of street lamps. Traffic is light, a bus pulls away from the stop outside a laundromat and two people who've got down from it move toward number 153 King's Road. The building – a shop on the ground floor next to the laundromat on one side and an optician on the other, a restaurant above the shop – is dark, its windows unlit and seemingly blank. It's uncertain what the shop sells.

'Have you got the key, Don?'

'Yeah, it's... here. Lemme get the door open.'

After some fiddling with the lock, turning one way and then the other, the plain white door with no glass finally gives way, and I use my shoulder to push it open.

'What the fuck's that smell?' I want to back out, and hold Jeannette back a bit.

'Smells like something's burned,' she says, wrinkling her nose.

Holding mine, I lean into the shop and feel for a light switch. 'Let's have a look... Fucking hell, who's done that?'

The lights reveal burn marks on the walls and ceiling of the shop, all of them obviously new, and probably done by a blowtorch. 'Fucking Steph, what's all this about?' The interior of BOY isn't much bigger than the space we'd had in Antiquarius, but it's a lot less interesting, to me.

93

'I like what he's done with the place,' says Jeannette, laughing.

'This shit ain't cool. Why are there boots nailed to the walls, and where's the rest of the stock?' A couple of racks of T-shirts and bondage trousers stand in the centre of the space, obviously there to avoid them being scorched in the 'decorating'.

'And what's in the window?' I turn back to look at where there should be a display rack of some sort. Instead four boxes hang on chains, each one too small to show off anything that we'd sold at Acme, even in the recent months when all the interesting bric-a-brac and vintage clothing had been replaced with Gary Gilmore T-shirts, bondage strides (I was wearing a pair the day that I debated the punky reggae party with Bob Marley) and other punk-related stuff.

'I'd better get on to Steph or John and find out what the fuck we're supposed to do with this crap,' I grump at Jeannette, and pick up the phone.

When Jeannette and I arrived at BOY at 7am to finish getting everything ready for the big opening on March 12, 1977 at this new location (we were no longer a subterranean secret club), I hadn't known what to expect. John, Steph and the 'designers' of the new interior had spent the week redecorating. After Steph arrived about an hour later, he told me that 'Little' John Harewood and Peter 'Sleazy' Christopherson had blowtorched the walls and ceiling the day before. Because, he explained, they wanted to generate some controversy and publicity they'd allowed Little John and Sleazy to make something that would illustrate a concept that Steph called 'Boy Arsonist Killed in Shop Attack'. On the walls were framed 'newspaper' pages with the 'Boy' in the headline of each one. All the 'stories' were about murder, terrorism or children in trouble. When I got a proper look at the window display Steph had to explain the 'concept'. The whole space was taken up by three Formica cabinets with glass front and backs, inside of which were the remains of this imaginary 'boy arsonist'. In one was a Doc Marten boot with a stump of leg sticking out, which looked very realistic. In the next was a bit of waistband of blue jean with 'skin' attached, while the third had a 'finger' with a cheap ring on it, plus an 'ear' with hair attached. All made from what Little John and Sleazy claimed was called 'Revoltex', laughed Steph.

John and Steph had decided to close Acme Attractions and leave the basement in order to open BOY, which stood halfway between Sloane Square and World's End, to cash in on the tabloid-fuelled, growing punk phenomenon. I wasn't totally happy about the move, nor the commercial direction. Acme had been my living room for two years, and I'd spent more time there, surrounded by my stuff – posters, records, furniture – than I had anywhere else. It had been the happiest time of my life up to that point, and I'd met more interesting people and learned more in that time than I had in five years of schooling. Still, Jeannette had said give it a go, so we did, and initially we carried on selling the newer, punk-related stock from Acme as Steph and John made plans to turn the new place into proper competition for Malcolm and Vivienne's Seditionaries (as they renamed SEX in December 1976). Two brothers, Jay and Phil Strongman, who'd been long-time Acme customers and almost lived in the basement for the last couple of months, were hired to work in BOY, and they were into the new place in a big way. Although John and Steph had originally wanted to take out the front window of the building and have a sheet of rock installed with holes cut into it for things to stick out, the landlord wouldn't allow it, and it would cost too much anyway. New stock was added to the pictures of American serial killers and mock-up death masks of Gary Gilmore printed on T-shirts and jewellery made from hypodermic syringes and assorted punk paraphernalia were brought in while the second-hand originals that I loved were faded out. From what I could see, the plans for a grand reopening were not promising to be a continuation of the original Acme spirit. Essentially, Steph and John were copying the punk rock uniform, and it just wasn't going to work for me.

After the Pistols' Grundy TV interview (in December 1976), the whole country had heard about punk because they'd read about it in the tabloids, all of which ran along the lines of the 'Filth and the Fury' headline of the *Daily Mirror*. After that, every tabloid in Britain sent reporters along to cover the Pistols' Anarchy tour, which began two days after the broadcast, and because so many gigs were cancelled, Fleet Street journalists followed every rumour about a Pistols performance but most of them were also cancelled. That didn't stop the tabloids

The outfit that upset Bob Marley, 1977.   SHEILA ROCK

from running punk stories, of course, none of which were written by music journalists but by old-style newspaper reporters who knew how to produce copy which would send their readers into a self-righteous frenzy of indignation, and in time-honoured tradition create new urban folk devils. Which inspired their sons and daughters to want to do the same by getting into 'punk' and wearing the 'look'. I thought it amazing how ugly people could make themselves look even uglier by putting on the punk uniform, but there you go. There were increasing numbers of 'weekend punks' – so-called because they got dressed up in pantomime punk gear to parade along the King's Road on a Saturday – who looked fucking ridiculous in outfits they'd read about in national daily newspapers. Tabloids were obsessed with punk because it was visually and 'morally' so outrageous, and they kept running photos of punk women wearing ripped stockings, with safety pins through their cheeks, lips and nose adding a little bit of sado-masochism to the titillation. But the inner circle of punk that I knew was very stylish, and nobody had safety pins in their noses, nor did anyone wear plastic bin bags as dresses. That didn't matter, though, because by the spring of 1977 'punk' had become clearly identified as a craze to be exploited. I understood that it made commercial sense for BOY to cash in. I wasn't into the blatant commercialism of the place, which made me feel less than proud of running it for the short time that I did, nor the fact that I was essentially a part of the atrocity exhibition which BOY styled itself as ironising – no-one was getting the irony, believe me. The stuff we were selling just wasn't cool.

I understood why Little John and Sleazy had been employed to do something that would take attention away from Malcolm and Vivienne. Little John had appeared in Acme with John Krivine's friend the photographer Sheila Rock one day, and she introduced him as a 'designer'. He and Sleazy had a lot of the same friends, all artists and photographers or filmmakers, all very 'out there' and creating 'challenging' work – most of which verged on the obscene. Sleazy, the son of a Cambridge don, had been at university in America until 1974, and when he got back to London worked on a few things with the hippy album designers Hipgnosis. He took photos for Pink Floyd's *Wish You Were Here* in 1975 and their *Animals* album, which had come out in January 1977. The Pretty Things' *Savage Eye* artwork looked like something he'd do too, but none of that bothered me. I just wasn't too sure about someone who'd earned his nickname from Genesis P-Orridge and Cosey Fanni Tutti of Throbbing Gristle. They were the people (then calling themselves COUM Transmissions) who'd put on a show at the ICA in October 1976 titled Prostitution which included the same kind of Formica cabinets with glass front and backs as in BOY's windows. But inside of theirs were a clock filled with used tampons, a Venus de Milo with tampons for arms, a box of maggots that turned into flies and a bunch of used tampons in a bowl. The show also included a lot of pornographic photos, which was unsurprising because when Sleazy photographed the Pistols in the early days, Malcolm refused to use them because he thought they made the band look too much like male prostitutes. Whatever the merits of Sleazy's work (and he created the BOY logo as well as the window display), it was certainly lifelike, as I was to discover only a few hours after opening the shop. It didn't take long for a crowd to form outside with people trying to get a good look at the exhibits in the window. People strained to see what everyone was looking at and a crowd built up, spilled into the road, and stopped buses from getting past. When Chelsea police station got complaints about the traffic problem, they sent some constables down, and they were met by two nurses who swore to them that we had human body parts in our window. Being the manager, I was arrested and taken to the station and thrown into the cells. They then sent some officers to BOY and removed the cabinets, which they stuck in their evidence room, I guess. Jeannette called John Krivine and, to his credit, he telephoned the inspector in charge and told them that he was the person they should have in the cells if anyone, and not me. The Old Bill took their time, but I was let go without a charge – as much because they couldn't figure out what it would be as anything else – and cautioned not to leave town. The cabinets were not returned, according to John, who went to the police station on the following Monday to be interviewed by an Inspector Rice. John said that the inspector was polite, almost apologetic in fact, and that they hadn't yet decided what to charge him with. The police also asked who'd made the display, because they'd been compared with details in a book of forensic medicine and found to be of excellent quality. John gave them Little John's name and number, which must have annoyed Sleazy because he'd have loved the notoriety, I'm sure. About six months later John was taken to court and charged under the Vagrancy Act of 1824; originally brought in to stop veterans of the Napoleonic War from displaying their wounds for money, it hadn't been used for 150 years. He lost, was fined, and got a criminal record. The London *Evening Standard* published a small news item on page six and everyone forgot about it.

My few hours in the cells annoyed me, though, and I began to think about doing something other than working at BOY. I felt it was time for a change, for something that'd take me away from BOY, if only for a while. Within a few weeks I got an offer to see parts of Britain that I'd never heard of, let alone visited, and thought that was just what I needed – a long bus ride around the country with a gang of argumentative, sarky, snarling, smart, funny, squabbling, revolutionary women. Oh, and a bunch of all-male punk bands, too.

Typical Girls

Interior. Day. A long shot of a single-deck, early 1970s-built coach, parked in a layby on the A72 about ten miles outside Edinburgh. Some of the seats, which are covered in a striped, horsehair-like cloth of various browns, have padded headrests, but not all. They are mostly set in pairs either side of the central aisle, but there are a few tables at the back and in the middle rows of the coach, with seats facing backwards and forwards. The seats with tables in the middle are occupied by members of The Clash, all dressed in black leather jackets, washed-out T-shirts, black straight-legged jeans and an assortment of biker boots and brothel creepers. Ranged around the bus are other punks, members of Subway Sect and various roadies and mates, plus four young women. Everyone is seated, slouched or lying across seats except for a young girl with mussed hair, wearing a leather jacket, bright pink tights, satin-sheen hot pants. She has a very loud, insistent voice, and is running from the back to the front of the bus, stopping at points to shout or argue with someone. The windows of the bus are rattling, partly from her physical antics and partly because of the diesel engine idling at the rear of the vehicle. The bus driver, a middle-aged, paunchy man named Norman, is standing outside the open coach door, gesturing at the manager of the all-girl band whose singer, Ari Up, is causing havoc on board the coach.

'Listen mate, I don't care what you say, I'm not taking this bus anywhere with her and her mates on board, got it?'

'Yes, but no, OK, listen, she'll calm down, she's just excited,' I tell him.

'And that's what I'm complaining about, her being excited!' Norman points inside the coach. 'She's going to make me drive off the bloody road if I have to watch her running about in my rear-view.'

'She won't be running about, I'll settle her down,' I tell him, trying to think of something, anything, short of an enormous spliff which might do that.

'Yeah, but you said that back in Edinburgh and what happened? She didn't last more than ten minutes before she was all over the place, acting up with the boys, showing her arse in that get-up. If she were my daughter I'd knock her bloody block off.'

'Yeah, but you're not her dad and neither am I, but...' I don't get to finish the sentence because Ari's stuck her head out of the door and yelled, 'Don, I'm fucking hungry, you got anything for me?'

'Listen young lady...' Norman moves toward her and Ari runs to the back of the bus laughing, so he turns back to me. 'I'm sorry, but it's not worth my job to drive on with her in that state, larking about, causing a fuss, I'll crash the bloody bus, I'm telling you.'

Norman's use of the word 'worth' is the first inkling I get that there's a way around this.

'OK, Norman, what would make it worth your while carrying on to Manchester with all of us on board?'

'What do you mean?' He looks suspicious.

I take a quick look around, pull a bundle of cash out of my pocket, peel a few tenners off the bundle and move closer to Norman. Slipping the £10 notes into his waffle cardigan pocket, I tell him, 'I'll get her settled at the back of the bus and keep her quiet-ish until we get to Manchester. When we get there, I'll make other plans for us to get to the rest of the gigs, not on this bus with you, OK?'

'Humph.' Norman feels the cash in his pocket and nods once. 'But that's it,' he warns. 'She's quiet until Manchester and then off my bus, right?'

'Right.'

With that, we climb back on board. Norman takes his seat, closes the door, gets the thing in gear, indicates and we move off. I've walked down the coach, picked up my ghetto-blaster and taken it to Ari, who's barely 'hiding' on the back seat.

'Ari, listen, take my deck and here are some mix-tapes. And here's a smoke, just sit back here, don't fuck about and hopefully we'll get to Manchester without being kicked off the bus, OK? It's just cost me a few quid to keep us all on here, and I don't want to waste our money, do you?'

'Ah Don, you're lovely! I'll be good, promise.'

Somehow, we made it to Manchester.

When The Clash released their debut single, the brilliant 'White Riot' c/w '1977', they were booked to play a forty-date UK tour starting May 1 (imaginatively titled the White Riot tour), with a support package of punk bands. It was some line-up, designed to take the sound of punk around the country, and included The Jam (who dropped out after only nine gigs), Buzzcocks, Subway Sect and The Slits, who joined the tour in Edinburgh on the seventh night. The Clash demanded that The Slits come along, despite the girls not having played any full gigs with the present line-up of singer Ari, bassist Tessa Pollitt, guitarist Viv Albertine and drummer Palmolive. The Clash knew them as well as I did, and we were all hugely impressed with their attitude and true punk sensibility. They were mates and we looked out for our mates, especially in such dark times as those. Because the tour would be the first time The Slits had done any regular gigging and they had never been out of London, and because every other band had one, they decided that they should have a manager. Since I'd helped them out with some funds from BOY to get on the tour, they asked me. I said yes, glad to get away from BOY, packed up a few clothes and my camera and travelled north with them on a train.

On May 7, 1977 Ari was 15 years old. Born in Munich she was the daughter of a German musician father named Frank Forster and a music promoter mother named Nora who moved to London in the early 1970s with Ari after she'd split with Frank. Nora was dating Chris Spedding when he worked on the Pistols' first recordings, which is how she got into the scene. Nora and Joe Strummer got on well and sometimes he found a temporary home with her and Ari. Which was kind of unexpected because Ari's godfather had been prog rocker Jon Anderson, frontman for Yes, and Nora had known Jimi Hendrix, or so it was rumoured. Nora, the daughter of a rich German newspaper owner, clearly preferred punk company to old rockers by 1977, when she and Spedding were introduced to the Pistols by Chrissie Hynde. Nora went on to marry John Lydon and they were still together at the time of writing.

At 15, Ari was precocious and loud, full of energy and punk attitude. She made Joe teach her a few guitar chords while he stayed at her

With Ariane (and the heater she just wrecked)
in Forest Hill, 1978.   RUDOLPH

family home, and then talked Palmolive (Paloma McLardy) into forming a band with a couple of other friends, Kate Korus (Korris) and Suzy Gutsy (Webb). The first line-up never played any gigs, only ramshackle rehearsals that invariably ended up in an argument. Viv Albertine and Palmolive, along with Keith Levene and Sid Vicious and others, had been in The Flowers Of Romance, whose reputation has persisted solely because of the people who were 'members'. Around the same time Tessa Pollitt was going through the motions with all-girl group The Castrators. I first saw The Slits play at the Roxy Theatre in Craven Park Road, Harlesden (not to be confused with the Roxy Club) in December 1976 when the line-up was Tessa on bass and Kate Korus on guitar. They were on the bill with Subway Sect, Buzzcocks and The Clash, which was a great punk line-up. Shortly after that Kate moved on briefly to join The Raincoats before forming the Mo-dettes, so making way for Viv Albertine to complete what became the now-classic Slits line-up.

I'd known Viv for a while by then because she used to come down to Acme regularly. Later she and Mick Jones of The Clash had a thing going and they would often come to my place in Forest Hill after the Roxy closed for reggae and spliff along with lots of other punks who'd chat and swap ideas, get stoned and chill.

I was hugely impressed by The Slits' sound, which had a disjointed rhythm packed with maximum energy and determination: Palmolive destroying the drums, Tessa's heavyweight bass and Viv's spiky, choppy guitar chords delivered like broken glass on top of Ari's swooping and screeching vocal style. They sang about shoplifting, dumping boyfriends, the boredom of straight life and told women to rebel. They were rough, rugged and they rocked. They had an attitude unlike anything I'd ever seen before, male or female, and I filmed them countless times as they rehearsed, while they were on tour and generally every time they played live – you just couldn't tell what might happen at a Slits gig (see *The Punk Rock Movie*). In her autobiography *Clothes, Clothes, Clothes. Music, Music, Music. Boys, Boys, Boys* (2014), Viv describes her first performance with The Slits as being a kind of smash-and-grab of the stage at The Pindar of Wakefield pub in Islington, where they smuggled their guitars in and then physically pulled an all-male band offstage before plugging in to their amps and using their drum kit (a couple of cymbals are knocked over in the seizing of the stage, but 'Palmolive doesn't care, she doesn't use them anyway') to race through 'Let's Do The Split' ('I shit on it!') before being hauled offstage. That was a week before the beginning of the White Riot tour, and only two weeks before they joined it.

The Slits had a well-earned reputation for being unpredictable, chaotic and downright scary onstage. Despite the music press constantly namechecking them during and long after the tour, A&R men who appeared sporadically at their gigs were clearly scared stiff of what they saw. But The Slits inspired and empowered legions of young girls up and down the country who were fed up with the options open to them at that time. The Clash didn't just take them along because Mick's girlfriend was a member (their relationship was not that constant anyway, even though Mick did have to tune Viv's guitar for her back then), but because they were genuinely impressed by their performances. However, it didn't take me too long as 'manager' to realise that I wasn't destined to be the British Clarence Avant (look him up) and my first doubts crept in when we got to the hotel we were booked into in Manchester. Just as I was signing the check-in, with the band slumped into the reception area, looking unlike anyone who had ever stayed there before, I could hear Ari hawking up what was sounding like a large and nasty gob. I'm scribbling away and thinking 'No Ari, don't you do it, don't...' when she spat on the carpet. In the lounge. The concierge, who'd already looked dubious about booking us into our rooms, saw and heard it and immediately ordered us to leave. We were kicked out before we could check in. There was no way the hotel could be persuaded to change their mind, so I had to trawl the streets of a city I'd never seen before – it was dark, wet and windy – trailing a motley bunch of underdressed women behind me, mostly getting refused entry to hotels by doormen who didn't like the look of any of us, one after another until finally finding a cheap, not-so-cheerful bed-and-breakfast place with two rooms which smelled of bacon and cabbage, Players No. 6 and tomato ketchup, for which we were charged far too much. That was to become a regular occurrence of the tour. Hotels would take one look at The Slits with their wild hair, torn clothes and fuck-you attitude, then they'd see a smiling Rasta wearing shades whatever the time of day or night claiming to be the girls' manager and... 'Sorry, we're all full and your rooms are taken.'

My role as manager came to an end before the tour finished. 'Don tries to control us but it's impossible,' writes Viv in *Clothes, Music, Boys*, and that's putting it mildly. Bands fighting each other was one thing and not unheard of; Chrissie Hynde tells a story in her autobiography *Reckless* (2015) about seeing Mitch Ryder & The Detroit Wheels play live in the late 1960s and being amazed and excited when a fight broke out mid-set, and the band carrying on. She went back for the following night and the same thing happened in exactly the same place in the set, which was when she realised that it was all set up – they weren't really fighting, it was part of their act. But when The Slits fought onstage it wasn't rehearsed or part of the act, it was for real and spontaneous. They'd fight the same way offstage too and at all times of the day or night. The thing about The Slits was that they were Slits twenty-four hours a day, not just while they were onstage performing. It wasn't an act. Viv's version of The Slits story gives an intimate and personal perspective on the chaos that was The Slits, and it was never contrived nor planned. Malcolm McLaren would have loved to have 'managed' them and try to turn them into a female Pistols-type outrage, but no way would Ari, Viv, Tessa or Palmolive ever let any man, not least Malcolm, tell them what to do or take credit for their actions. I once filmed a Slits show at Ari's school in Holland Park (which was the only way anyone could get her to attend), and predictably the gig ended in a near riot. It was mayhem. Someone let off a smoke bomb and kids were throwing butter and eggs. I was there trying to capture all this on film and loving every minute of it, even if I was worried about the safety of the camera. The scenario made the original *St Trinian's* films look like documentaries.

The Slits had plenty of support from people who could see and feel their potential, though – John Peel championed them (listen to *The Slits: The Peel Sessions*) and Derek Jarman put them in his film *Jubilee* (they destroy a car), for instance, and it wasn't all outrage and chaos. They broke new ground without really trying. Musically, lyrically, stylistically, everything was different, which was partly why they were the last of the first wave of punk bands to get signed. However, after parting company with Palmolive, who ended up playing for The Raincoats, and replacing her with Budgie (he later joined The Banshees and Creatures), The Slits got a record deal with Island Records. Not that their debut album, *Cut* (1979), one of the first great post-punk albums and a sonic delight produced by dub master Dennis Bovell (Matumbi/Janet Kay), made it clear that there was a male band member since it came in a sleeve which had a photo of Ari, Tessa and Viv naked but covered in mud. Long bored by what punk had become by the time they got to make an album, The Slits were one of the first bands to embrace reggae, and later African rhythms, and use it in their own particular way. It had been their love of reggae that brought us together as friends, and when we went to reggae clubs every eye in the house would be focused on Ari, as she whipped up a storm on the dancefloor. Ari became interested in more than Jamaican music, and engaged with the whole Rasta culture. She loved coming to Sunday lunch at my parents' house (I used to take lots of people there in 1977 and '78, mainly because that way I didn't have to talk to my mum, never knowing what to say to her). Ari loved the food, my mum and dad's stories about Jamaica and embarrassing me in front of them. She was curious about the philosophy of Rasta, so I took her to a meeting of the Twelve Tribes at the Tabernacle of Rastafari House, 28 St Agnes Place, Kennington. The Twelve Tribes is the most mysterious school of Rasta thought, relating to the twelve different star signs, and is perhaps better described as a society within a religion. I don't know what possessed me to take Ari to this meeting, because I knew exactly what she was like and what kind of response she was going to get from the elders, all of whom were there when we arrived – Ari was confrontational when she was 15 and remained so throughout her too-brief life (she died from breast cancer in 2010) and I must have been fucking crazy. When the Rasta elders gave me the chalice, I passed it to her, which according to the fundamental aspects of Rastafari, and like most belief systems, was a big no-no, because women are not allowed to take part in the ceremony (like many belief systems) and definitely not smoke the chalice. I didn't have the same gender problem as the elders, though, and considered Ariane as one of my brethren, which meant she should be included. There was a big argument and we were kicked out of the building. Ari didn't care, of course, because she was Ari, and I loved her because she was always true to herself. She was a real inspiration to many people, me included.

I really enjoyed filming that tour, and very glad that much of the footage made its way into William E. Badgley's 2017 documentary *Here To Be Heard: The Story of The Slits*. If I hadn't filmed them in 1977 it would have been a true loss to the cultural history of punk and the feminist involvement, and that's because no-one else was willing or able to film them, not because of any great skill on my part. It's thanks to Ari and The Slits that a new form of music film developed, because although music promo films were a growing trend in the late 1970s, me and a guy called Mick Calvert from Bristol realised that bands like them and The Pop Group, who were friends of his, were never going to get the sort of budget that other bands would for a promo video. We had the idea of asking for ten grand from the record company and shooting a short film, not just a music promo. The plan was that we'd make a half-hour documentary-style film which would include promos for two songs and could be shown on TV or made commercially available alongside albums and cassettes. Mick had come up through the punk scene in Bristol filming bands who had a similar approach to music and politics to The Slits – they and The Pop Group later 'shared' a double-A-sided 45 rpm single release on The Pop Group's own label, Y Records, in 1980: 'In The Beginning There Was Rhythm' / 'Where There's A Will There's A Way'. Mick and I made *Slits Pictures* with Island Records money in 1979, and it captures some of the sheer energy and desire with which The Slits created great music (check out 'Typical Girls') and why they are one of the most significant female punk bands of the era.

Mick and I met in Bristol on the White Riot tour on May 26, 1977, which was the first time I'd visited the city. In fact, it was the first time I'd visited any of the places on that tour and, as such, was a real education. After Edinburgh and Manchester, we returned to London and a gig at the Rainbow Theatre (on May 9), and although the next day we were supposed to be in Stourbridge, at the town hall of all places, that had to be cancelled because Mick Jones damaged a finger at the Rainbow. The gig in Nottingham two days later also had to be cancelled, so everyone chilled in London before driving south-west to Plymouth (on May 15). First impressions of the Fiesta Suite were that it had clearly seen better days. A large, sticky dancefloor faced a wide, not-too-deep stage opposite the bar, which owed a lot to late 1960s sci-fi B-movies in design with gold-painted, studded surrounds to serving hatches that were guarded by steel shutters. Like a lot of British venues of the 1970s it had been plenty of things in its existence, from music hall to wrestling arena and discotheque. In 1977 it was a live music venue, but probably became a bingo hall at some time. By the time the doors opened and people started arriving it was clear that the punky reggae party hadn't reached that part of the country. All the gigs on the tour were well-attended, but while at the universities (Swansea, Leeds and Brighton) the crowd was mostly made up of curious, long-haired students with a handful of short-haired, safety-pin-studded local punks making up the numbers, the crowds at places like the Fiesta Suite contained a lot of denim-wearing, long-haired heavy metal fans curious about this thing called punk, mixed in with skinheads and football hooligans looking for action, soulboys with wedge haircuts wearing Bowie trousers and jelly sandals, and wannabe punks dressed just like they'd seen in the *Mirror*, *Sun*, *NME* and *Sounds*. Thankfully there were always people waiting to be sneaked into the gigs by The Clash through side doors and windows in the 'dressing rooms', when they had any. The Clash did the same everywhere they played, from Middlesbrough through St Albans, Stafford, Cardiff, West Runton, Leicester, Chelmsford and Dunstable, and there were always plenty of mostly school kids at every back door and window at every venue. Unfortunately, some of them arrived dressed in identikit punk uniform, and they pogoed and spat at the bands, which was pretty disgusting and annoyed everyone onstage. I purposely filmed from the back of the room and the side of the stage, where I could keep away from the hails of gob.

Toward the end of the tour, one night when I wasn't filming I stood at the back of the venue alongside Clash manager Bernie Rhodes. We were leaning against the wall, and all around us was calm, but in front of us there were hundreds of jumping, spitting, shouting and singing people worshipping The Clash. I was troubled by something and hadn't figured out what until I looked sideways at Bernie who stared, stony-faced at the stage, not a trace of emotion showing. He was wearing his trademark Lewis leather biker jacket, T-shirt, jeans and brothel creepers, his thick glasses perched on the end of his nose. Then I looked at myself in my leopard-print waistcoat, white shirt, leather trousers, sneakers and dark glasses, with my dreads – only shoulder length by then – loose. I looked back at Bernie. Then me, again. And I thought, 'Nah, this isn't for me.' Which is why I spent the 'summer of hate' on the King's Road, back at BOY.

Action filmmaker... 1977.

JANE ASHLEY

Punks vs Teds

Exterior. BOY, 153 King's Road, London SW3. Mid-afternoon, the street is filled with people walking, shopping, talking. Along the road slow-moving cars – racing green Rovers, pop-art-coloured Minis, bronze, red and black vinyl-roofed Ford Cortina Mk IIs and IIIs, Hillman Hunters in bright yellow, dark Rolls-Royces, purple Vauxhall Cavaliers – battle with red Routemaster double-decker buses. The pavement outside BOY narrows slightly because of the bus stop just outside the shop next door (now empty), and people sometimes have to step into the gutter to pass one another. Throughout the morning a steady procession of shoppers has made its way past BOY, few of them showing more interest than a glance at the huge letters suspended above the window. As the day has worn on various young people wearing too much make-up, exotically decorated clothes and dyed hair have made a beeline for the widow. One in four or five entered, those who emerged carrying a BOY bag showed it off as proof of their punk cred. Inside, looking out, a couple of regular customers sit on their haunches watching the world pass by.

'Look at that kid,' one of the regulars says, interrupting my rolling. I look up and see a boy of about 16 wearing a BOY Gary Gilmore T-shirt underneath his school blazer, which has badges and a safety pin in its lapels. He's holding up a copy of a punk single – I can't see what – and grinning, still walking, not looking where he's going. I wave a hand and go back to my rolling.

'Fuck!' Steve Roth, who looks like a real hard nut but is as gentle as a butterfly normally, jumps up and makes for the door, his mate closely following him.

'What's up with him?' asks Jeannette.

'What?' Putting my skins down, I stand up and crane my neck to see what's going on. 'Shit – stay here!'

Outside, Steve and his mate are standing over the punk kid who's lying on the pavement, having not seen a gang of Teds who'd obviously punched or kicked him down. About six Teds step back a bit, clearly not knowing if Steve and his mate are mad and bad. I guess Steve thought the best form of defence was attack, because he steps forward and headbutts the nearest Ted. His mate takes a swing at another one, and as they all move a half pace back, I drag the punk into the shop.

'Steve, get in!' I shout, and after a couple more lunges at the Teds, he and his mate run back inside. Me and Phil slam the door behind them and barricade it as best we can. The Teds attack the shop, throwing bottles at the door (which was solid wood, luckily) and kicking the plate-glass windows. As we try to keep the door shut Jeannette stands at the counter, turning steel coat hangers into weapons. We don't need them, though, because the Teds soon get bored and wander off in search of easier prey.

It's just another Saturday afternoon on the King's Road in the summer of 1977, and I'm getting mighty sick of it.

The three weeks in May I spent with The Slits and The Clash on the White Riot tour was the longest period of time I'd ever been away from London and it hadn't been a holiday. Every town we visited seemed to be still living in the 1950s. Shops in the town centres closed for lunch, and the only places to eat were Wimpy bars, Chinese or Indian takeaways and pubs offering cheese sandwiches and pickled onions in the snug (a small room at the side of the main bar, usually filled with old folks). In rougher parts of town – and they all had them – there were pubs advertising strippers at lunchtime. People in the streets who looked older than 30 were all dressed like my parents, the men in flares, fat ties, Burton's suits and wide-toed shoes, their hair worn well over the collar, split ends waving in the wind, dandruff powdering their shoulders. Young women wore maxi-coats, platforms and flared trousers, their hair flicked into waves and perms held firm by whole aerosol cans of hairspray. When we got to Brighton, we found a load of shops closed for the afternoon ('half-day closing', they called it). The best thing about most of the towns and small cities we visited were the kids who came to the gigs whether they had a ticket or not, simply to speak to people who they thought knew how they felt – these kids were bored, itching to get away, hungry for new music, new experiences, open to new ideas and energised by what they heard in punk and reggae. There was always at least one kid with a pile of their

We could be heroes... King's Road, Chelsea, 1977.

freshly Xeroxed fanzine who'd be looking for an interview. It was an eye-opening experience, although usually I was the only brother in the room at the gigs and on the streets before and after performances, which created a permanent sense of unease with the threat of violence.

Being back at BOY kept me in touch with the Chelsea scene while earning money. I didn't have a great time on the King's Road that summer, though, and neither did a lot of punks.

As stories about punk 'outrages' became increasingly common in national newspapers, readers across the country who'd been barely aware of what was happening at Seditionaries and BOY and who favoured the Teddy boy apparel and attitude of their fathers and uncles decided that punks needed a bit of 1950s-style 'community counselling'. It began one Saturday in May, when a gang of self-styled Teddy boy vigilantes marched down the King's Road looking for punks to chastise with fists, boots, chains and flick knives. Malcolm and Vivienne hadn't helped matters by putting some old Too Fast To Live stock of Ted gear on sale in Seditionaries (John Lydon looked great in it, by the way), which meant that punks were wearing drape jackets and brothel-creeper shoes with obscene T-shirts and bondage trousers to create a look which was a red rag to a bull for naturally conservative 1970s Teds and their dads. Soon enough, Teddy boy versus punk battles became a regular tourist attraction on the King's Road. After Elvis Presley died in August, old-school, 40-something Teds started rocking up on Saturdays with their teenage sons dressed as mini-mes. Many a time I saw a bunch of Teds chasing a lone punk and would run out of the shop cussing heavily in Jamaican to deflate the situation. I couldn't bear to watch shit like that going down. Mind you, at the same time, if I saw a Ted being chased by a load of punks, I'd do the same thing. I can't remember how many people I chased down the King's Road waving whatever home-made weapons I could find and swearing in Jamaican as loudly as I could.

Which might sound brave and exciting, but in truth I was becoming stressed and angered by such scenes. As summer came to an end, so did my association with BOY.

Pressure Drop

Exterior. Day. A small London music venue is lit by two professional arc lights, unshuttered and casting an unforgiving glare around the shabby, sticky interior. The stage is bare of band equipment, but filled with comically made-up punks, some of them with safety pins fixed in their cheeks. They're almost all extravagantly kohl-eyed, their hair in Vaselined tufts. Most wear freshly and deliberately ripped T-shirts with band names inexpertly felt-tipped across them, under school blazers with chains of safety pins hanging from the lapel. School ties hang knotted loosely around necks that aren't already occupied by studded dog collars. Girls wear ripped fishnets and pointed stiletto heels, boys wear a mix of straight-legged women's PVC trousers, nondescript black trousers or jeans with flares pinned to make them look like 'straights'. Facing the assortment of cartoon punks is a camera, boom operator and director, talking with a late 20-something, lanky, buck-toothed woman with dyed red hair and over-large spectacles wearing a pristine T-shirt tucked into red straight slacks.

Shaking his head, a sunglasses-wearing man with short dreadlocks, in a white T-shirt and black straight jeans, walks past the camera toward the doors leading out of what the buck-toothed woman has referred to in a short piece to camera as 'London's premier punk pub' with the gurning faces of smooth-cheeked punks behind her clearly in shot. She reaches out and physically stops the man heading out.

'Don, can we interview you?' she says in a poshed-up Cockney accent.

'What do you want to interview me for?'

'Haven't you been filming this place? We'd like to include some of your footage if we can, and it'll be good publicity for the movie.'

'Nah, sorry, but I've never seen this bunch before in my life,' I jerk a thumb at the crowd of rent-a-punks, 'and I really don't want to be seen with them, thanks.'

'But,' she persists, clearly thinking I'm stupid or not understanding the 'opportunity' that she's offering, 'this'll be on television!'

'Yeah, I get it, but no, thanks.'

With that I shake her hand off my arm and exit, stage right.

A week after Richard Williams wrote about my making *The Punk Rock Movie* in *Time Out*, someone at the Institute of Contemporary Arts in London made contact and asked if they could screen it like a 'proper' film in their cinema. No way could I refuse that, so it opened the week of the Notting Hill Carnival, and then ran at the ICA for six weeks, breaking all their box office records. *Time Out* (issue #387, August 26–September 1, 1977) interviewed me and used cut-up film reels from the movie on the cover with the headline 'Punk's Home Movies'. On the contents page under a heading 'The Beautiful & The Damned', a blurb reads: *'Before the commercial film industry has had time to capitalise on punk rock, one of its own DJs has come up with a "home movie" film that captures all the excitement and exhibitionism of the Roxy during its fabled 100 days. Dave Pirie reports and DJ Donovan Letts talks…'* That week, *Time Out* also ran reports on a Hackney bookshop being burned out and London's 'Sink Estates', while the major feature article was a eulogy for Elvis Presley's first four years of success (he'd died a couple of weeks earlier). I'd knocked The King off the front page.

Fittingly, the 'run' at the ICA was a very punk affair. Because it was shot on Super-8, there were no negatives, so I had to run the original in their cinema for them. It didn't have any titles – it was just the raw film stuck together, and very much in the punk school of filmmaking.

On any given night the film would break, or the projector bulb would blow. On several occasions I had to shout to the audience, 'Hold on everybody,' and run up to Piccadilly to get a new bulb to finish the screening. Surprisingly, most people would hang out to see how it ends. (Wonder why I never had a spare one on me?)

Original poster for the first Don Letts film, 1977.

Leader of the primary school gang, circa 1967.

My father, St Leger 'Duke' Letts, and his Superstonic sound system, early 1960s.

Kung fu moves would win me dance competitions (and the girls) in years to come, mid-1960s.

Rude Boy dress. Crombie coat, Ben Sherman button-down shirt, Sta-Prest and the rest, 1970.

Say it loud. Heading for the Black Panther meeting in Kennington, South London, 1972.

At my parents' house, with my dad's hi-fi, mid-1970s.

Original Roxy poster advertising the gigs for March 1977.

Jeannette Lee and me at work, in the basement of Antiquarius, welcoming customers to the original Acme Attractions, 1976.
SHEILA ROCK

SUS in action, 1977. I always tried to help the police with their broad daylight searches by taking off some clothing.

Verité filming at the Carnival, early 1980s.
ADRIAN BOOT/
URBANIMAGE.TV

New York, just like I imagined it... On the subway with sounds, 1981.
LISA JONES

A meeting with destiny – Grace – in New York, 1986.

With Joe Strummer and Mick Jones at Trident Studios, London, recording *No. 10, Upping St.*, 1986.

Don Letts – Film-maker and Musician, 1990, oil on canvas by Caroline Coon.

With Himba women in Namibia while making a film to celebrate the country's independence from British colonial rule, 1990.

With the stars of *Dancehall Queen*, Audrey Reid (left) and Patrice Harrison, 1996.

Stussy 40th anniversary portrait, 2020.
MARK LEBON

That was a state of affairs that couldn't last, of course, due to the fragility of the film, and if it was going to be shown anywhere else it needed to be blown up to 35mm, with titles added. That was done in 1978, but I cringe when I see it now, because the techniques for blowing up film in those days were pretty primitive and while it works on the small screen, it's torture for me to watch *The Punk Rock Movie* on a cinema screen. Still, despite that, there was a lot of prestige about it having a proper theatrical release and there were guys from the movie business telling me that it could be done. I was thinking, 'Here I am, a kid from Brixton, who am I to argue with them?' It had a (limited, arts cinema) nationwide release and made me a British filmmaker in the public eye. But it wasn't easy being an aspiring filmmaker, especially when you're left of centre, and being Black sure didn't help. During the late 1970s one interviewer said to me, rather than asked, 'Aren't you doing well for a Black man.' Without thinking, my reply was, 'What the fuck are you talking about? I am a manifestation of my heritage and this is only the tip of the iceberg, dude.'

There was no clear infrastructure for Black filmmakers in the UK, though. Funding was a problem and remained so for a couple of decades, because there was a generally held perception that movies about Black people only appeal to Black people, and the audience won't return a big investment. Of course, Black films could be marketed outside Black communities but that would cost money, which may never be recouped... In the USA, emerging Black directors had support in New York and Los Angeles from other filmmakers and the community who'd come up through the industry, but I never felt like I had that.

British mainstream cinema did produce a couple of movies which dealt with the social ructions between the recently arrived West Indian immigrants and locals in the late 1950s, and they included important parts for Black actors. *Sapphire* (1959) starred Earl Cameron as the doctor brother of a woman found murdered on Hampstead Heath, while Paul Danquah played the sailor father of Rita Tushingham's illegitimate baby in *A Taste of Honey* (1961). But the history of Black directors making movies in England began with a couple of short films that made some waves. In 1963 one of them had a limited cinema release, the twelve-minute short drama *Ten Bob in Winter* funded by the BFI and written and directed by Lloyd Reckord. A Jamaican playwright and actor, Reckord became infamous for kissing white women in theatre plays and TV dramas in the very early 1960s, and he liked challenging bigoted opinions in his work. In 1965 he directed another BFI-funded short, *Dream A40*, about a gay man coming to terms with his sexuality. Reckord never got to direct any feature movies, though. Neither did Lionel Ngakane, a South African who came to Britain in 1950 to escape apartheid, became an actor and appeared in British TV shows like *Z Cars* and *Dixon of Dock Green*. In 1965 Ngakane got hold of a 16mm camera and made a documentary about his homeland titled *Vukani/Awake*, which became the first film about South Africa made by a Black African. He followed that with *Jemima & Johnny*, a thirty-minute drama made in London, which became the first Black British film to win an award at the Venice Film Festival. It took the Trinidadian Horace Ové, who began making documentaries in London in the late 1960s, to become the first Black feature film director of British-made movies. Ové moved to England when he was 21 in 1960, and by the end of the decade he'd made a documentary with James Baldwin and Dick Gregory in London, and put together a great documentary shot partly using a hand-held camera on the streets of London and Kingston, which was intercut with live performances from the Caribbean Music Festival held at Wembley Empire in September 1970. Titled *Reggae* (1971), it has some great live footage of performances by Desmond Dekker, John Holt, The Heptones, Symarip, The Maytals, Bob & Marcia, Laurel Aitken, The Pioneers and others who were then being released in Britain on Trojan Records. It's not a straightforward concert film, though, because Ové's time in London had politicised him and he mixes commentary from white men talking about reggae in pompous, patronising terms and film of Enoch Powell's 'rivers of blood' speech, with the founders of Trojan Records and producers like Junior Lincoln, plus Darcus Howe talking about why reggae is so big in England and should be in America. There's also footage of original Black and white skinheads dancing and being interviewed. The film was briefly shown in cinemas in England, but more importantly for him the BBC showed it and then hired Ové to make other documentaries, and even a *Play for Today*.

Just before punk happened, Ové shot what was the first all-Black British feature film, titled *Pressure* and funded by the British Film

Institute. The storyline follows London-born teenager Tony as he drifts through West London trying to find his way in life and constantly being knocked back – he can't date the white girl he likes, can't get or keep a job and is hassled from every side, including by his older brother, Trinidad-born Colin, who bullies Tony to join him in the Black Power movement. Because of some realistic scenes of police brutality handed out to brothers in the film, the BFI held release back until 1977 when it had a small cinema release, got some great reviews and then disappeared. *Pressure* was shot in the streets of West London, in markets and on street corners with the locals as unpaid extras giving it a documentary feel. In some ways it was not unlike *The Harder They Come* (1972), which was the first film I saw that gave me a sense of true empowerment. The first film project produced by Island Records owner Chris Blackwell, and directed by white Jamaican Perry Henzell, it's a brutally honest story about ghetto life in Jamaica with no attempt to romanticise it. Jimmy Cliff, the star of the film, was not a trained actor, which adds to the realism of the movie that was shot in places we had never seen before – the ghetto and shanty towns. *The Harder They Come* stays away from the postcard Jamaica sold to tourists as the perfect getaway destination. Henzell had been influenced by French new wave films and their use of flash frames and cross-cutting, which he employs in his first feature film work to great effect. *The Harder They Come* taught me a lot about my culture, much of which I had been unaware of. I'd already grasped the musical element of life in Jamaica, but the marriage of soundtrack, imagery and narrative in Henzell's movie made a huge impression on me, and it's been a constant inspiration for my filmmaking. Even as I shot *The Punk Rock Movie* I had the idea of doing something like *The Harder They Come* one day.

That dream came closer in 1979 when I got to make *Rankin' Movie* using pretty much the same methods as I had with *The Punk Rock Movie*, only this time with reggae artists – Linton Kwesi Johnson, Culture, Prince Hammer, Big Youth, Prince Far I at Dingwalls with his Chelsea FC bag that he claimed was filled with ganja, and Dr Alimantado bursting into a full performance of 'Born For A Purpose' in the middle of Steve Barrow's Daddy Kool's reggae shop on Hanway Street, London. It wasn't just a live performance film because I also shot and edited into it verité footage of Jamaican police shaking down a carload of Rasta brethren in Kingston and of the Notting Hill riot in '76. I filmed U-Roy with his chalice and Tappa Zukie in Rema on his motorbike with a gun-toting brother who was shot dead a couple of weeks later. Which to my mind makes it a natural successor to Ové's *Reggae* (had it ever been officially released). There was no conventional movie narrative to *Rankin' Movie*: it was a documentary on reggae culture at the end of the decade which had begun with Ové's film, held together by the reggae performances. Most of the performers saw me as someone who could help their career by putting them on celluloid, and they hadn't been filmed before. I'm glad I did it, as most of those guys died before their time.

When the ICA showed *Rankin' Movie* in the summer of 1979, they also screened Bajan director Menelik Shabazz's documentary *Breaking Point*, which had been shown on ITV the previous year and helped raise public awareness of the racist sus law. Two years later Shabazz got to make his first feature film, *Burning an Illusion* (1981), which joined the list of movies that made me want to direct, to tell stories about my experience and culture in film.

After the release of *Punk Rock Movie* and *Rankin' Movie* I was determined to make a feature film and worked up a script titled *Dread at the Controls*, with which I approached the producer Michael White — he'd had a great run of success with *Monty Python and the Holy Grail* (1975), *The Rocky Horror Picture Show* (1975) and *Jabberwocky* (1976). Given the slightly surreal nature of the story, I figured he'd be the man most likely to make it. It was intended to be a modern reggae Western set in Brixton, centred around a mini-cab office, where dreads drove cabs instead of riding horses. It began at the cab office and ended with a race riot in London and was directly inspired by Linton Kwesi Johnson's 'Five Nights Of Bleeding', which he recorded under the pseudonym of Poet & Roots on the 1978 *Dread, Beat An' Blood* album for Front Line, produced by Dennis Bovell. LKJ's poem summed up life as a young Black man growing up in the decaying and violent inner cities of Britain, and I wanted the movie to do the same. Michael White bought the script, although he wanted to change the title to *Dread*. In the end it never got made, but it was kinda cool to think that I came so close. We even got as far as casting the actors but were beaten to the punch by Franco Rosso's *Babylon* (1980), set and shot in South London. That starred Brinsley Forde, Aswad's singer and former child actor, along with *Not the Nine O'Clock News* comedian Mel Smith as his racist, garage-owning boss. Dennis Bovell wrote the score and put together the soundtrack, which included Aswad's 'Warrior Charge'. The story – Brinsley works as a mechanic by day and runs the Ital Lion Sound System at night, gets sacked, beaten up by the police, and goes on the run after stabbing a racist neighbour – is well worked. But even though it was a great film, *Babylon* did not make much money either at the cinema or in video rental, so *Dread* was shelved. There'd be other scripts.

Orson Welles said that if you want to make an original film, don't watch films, but I learned the technical aspects of filmmaking from watching some classic, some trash and a lot of underground movies. From an early age I went to the cinema whenever I could afford it or find a way in without paying. I also watched a lot of movies on the black-and-white television that sat on a chest of drawers in my parents' bedroom. I'd bounce around on their bed with Norman and Desmond taking parts we saw on the screen, acting out our own version of events – in which Norman always got 'killed'. Watching those Westerns, war films and sword-and-sandal adventures I learned about morality, heroes, losers, death and redemption. Without realising, I took in aspects of moviemaking that would come back to me much later in my life when I got the chance to make movies.

Because I wasn't ruled by one genre or style, nor any particular directors or actors, I was always willing to try something I didn't know when suggested by people I thought had good taste. When John Krivine turned me onto the movies of John Waters and the arthouse circuit of the mid-1970s I was hugely impressed with the subversive DIY feel to John Waters' *Pink Flamingos* (1972) and *Female Trouble* (1974), especially because they were independently made films which gained a cult status without anybody being able to see them. You had to be a member of a cinema club or invited to late-night 'private' screenings at places like the King's Cross Scala or Independent Filmmaker's Cooperative in Primrose Hill, because Waters' films were un-certifiable and as far removed from family viewing material as you could get back then.

Around the same time I discovered Melvin Van Peebles' *Sweet Sweetback's Baadasssss Song* (1971) which, in a similar way to the John Waters films, built a reputation so quickly that once word got around, if you had not seen it you really had to check it out, despite it being independently made and released and impossible to find in chain cinemas. *Sweet Sweetback's Baadasssss Song* was one of the first blaxploitation films to break out and gain a multiracial audience, and despite Van Peebles having no money to buy advertising, it became the highest grossing independent film of 1971. He was helped by having Stax Records release the soundtrack album by Earth, Wind & Fire before release, because that got him the advertising he couldn't afford. That move was later copied by major studios who wanted to get into the same market, which had pretty much been 'discovered' by Van Peebles' film. Like *The Harder They Come*, it was shot in the streets and includes a line in the closing credits that reads: 'Starring the Black Community.' Because he'd used a multiracial crew to make the film, Van Peebles had to tell the various industry unions that he was making a porn movie, and not a 'legit' feature film, otherwise those unions would have shut him down for breaking all kinds of bullshit rules. Unsurprisingly, *Sweetback* is an angry film, but one with such a high level of energy that even the Black Panthers were down with it. Legend has it that *Shaft* was originally going to be a white movie with a white lead actor until *Sweet Sweetback's Baadasssss Song* came along. *Sweetback* made being revolutionary and politically informed attractive and important and it played at cinemas around the world. Without it there probably wouldn't have been *Black Caesar* (1973), *Cleopatra Jones* (1973), *Truck Turner* (1974) and many others.

The reason that I got to see such a wide range of films was because not all cinemas were owned by chains, and small, independent places screened movies which their managers thought would bring in an audience. They also showed as many films a day as they could, and when they started showing movies after 11pm as 'Midnight Matinees', chain cinemas soon followed suit. The arts cinema and midnight matinee circuit allowed people like me to see things that would otherwise have never been shown in the UK. No Russ Meyer film (*Faster, Pussycat! Kill! Kill!* [1965], *Vixen* [1968] and the *Beyond the Valley of the Dolls* [1969/70]), for instance, would have been seen in the UK before the invention of video players. As a teenager I got to see Cocteau's *Orphée* (1950) and Gillo Pontecorvo's *The Battle of Algiers* (1966) and loved both of them, as I did the work of the great Alejandro Jodorowsky, whose *El Topo* (1970), which he wrote, directed and starred in, somehow manages to mix Spaghetti Western sets and quasi-mystical plotlines with Christian and Ancient Greek mythology, topped off with Jungian archetypes, and starring a severely disabled cast of extras.

I saw the groundbreaking Sergio Leone Westerns *A Fistful of Dollars* (1964), *The Good, the Bad and the Ugly* (1966) and *A Fistful of Dynamite* (1971) on late-night shows. Martin Scorsese movies *Mean Streets* (1973) and *Taxi Driver* (1976) were constants on the mid-seventies art cinema circuit. They've been a huge inspiration as well as providing snatches of dialogue and soundtrack to my work in B.A.D. *Mean Streets'* use of doo-wop, sixties girl groups, Motown, rock and opera as the action moves from scene to scene, and the fact it had been shot on a hand-held camera for flexibility and to save time, were enormously influential. Like Scorsese, who was always namechecking them, I loved Powell and Pressburger movies, particularly *The Red Shoes* (1948), which Marty became obsessed with at the age of 9. The films of Michael Powell and Emeric Pressburger are hugely impressive – check out *A Matter of Life and Death* (1946) and *Black Narcissus* (1947) – with their perfect examples of brilliantly choreographed tracking shots which show how the way the camera moves can smoothly guide a story. Because of their oddness and saturated colour they were perfect for late-night audiences in the seventies. As were the works of one of my favourite filmmakers, Nic Roeg. Not every movie made by Powell and Pressburger or Martin Scorsese is totally successful or perfectly done, but they say the true sign of genius is inconsistency, and that definitely applied to Roeg. His trademark use of colour, intercutting scenes, a willingness to be experimental and an attention to detail make all his movies worth searching out, from the first movie he co-directed (with Donald Cammell), *Performance* (1970), through *Walkabout* (1971), *Don't Look Now* (1973) and *The Man Who Fell to Earth* (1976) to *Eureka* (1983).

Cinema was as important to me as music, and the brief cinema release of *The Punk Rock Movie* meant a lot to me. I didn't have a clear plan of how to capitalise on it but knew that I had to keep taking the camera with me wherever I went.

Chalice in Ganjaland

Exterior. Day. View from the air. A bright blue sky with a relentless sun beating down turns the tree-top foliage a deep green. Blue mahoe and dogwood trees line and almost completely cover a dusty road as it snakes up a hillside. Through the foliage a white Cadillac can occasionally be glimpsed as it rumbles over potholes, swerving to miss the deepest ones, crossing an imaginary line that would separate lanes barely wide enough to allow two mules to pass without touching. The shot pulls wide to show a clearing at the top of the hill on which is a haphazard arrangement of roads and alleys between shacks, some with corrugated iron roofs, some with tree branches woven into a covering and others with a tarpaulin thrown over three walls of brick and cement. The car stops in front of a trio of men sitting on boxes in the shade of a tree. One of them steps to the driver's window and points up the hill; the car moves slowly on. This happens three times more at different houses before the camera swoops down to meet the Cadillac as it pulls up in front of a shack with a small garden stacked with boxes of mangoes, breadfruit and yam. One of the rear windows rolls down and a skinny white man with sharp cheekbones, matted hair poking from under a black, wide-brimmed hat and a lopsided grin peers out. He has a toke on a messy, unrolling joint, blows smoke out through his nose and cackles.

'Fuck me Don, is this it?'

'That's what the driver just said.'

Stepping out of the air-conditioned car, the heat wraps around me like an electric blanket on full whack. Was this it, I wonder? My roots grew here, in this small garden where my mother dug up vegetables as a kid? The directions we'd been given to the place were crude to say the least – take the third turn on the left on the highway where the Kentucky Chicken sign used to be, go up the hill and then ask. But here we are, in the back end of nowhere, me in search of my roots and Johnny Rotten, the most infamous man in the Western world, riding shotgun in a fuck-off white Yank-tank, parked in a clearing like something out of a Western made by Jodorowsky. Unlike most of the shacks on the way up here, this one has a closed door and no-one leaning out of a window staring. It was only three or four steps to the door, but it felt much, much further, more like a fall into a chasm I hadn't known was there. I knock nervously, not too loudly (hoping no-one will be home, perhaps, or if they are, that they won't hear me), and after a couple of loud heartbeats an old lady opens the door and stares up at me; this tiny old woman, I guess, is my grandmother. Without thinking I blurt, 'It's me – your grandson from England.'

She looks at me as if I'd said something else altogether, not moving or answering and probably not understanding. She certainly shows no sign of knowing who I am, nor why I'm there, but then how could she? No-one had bothered to write or call ahead telling her that a dreadlocked grandson she'd never met before, speaking the Queen's English, will be turning up one day in a massive, chauffeur-driven white car. Deciding that this is embarrassing for everyone involved – even John has ducked back into the dark, cool interior of the Caddy – I'm thinking that of course the poor woman is surprised, confused and may well get angry. Still she doesn't move or answer, just watches as our driver starts loading the trunk of the Caddy with various vegetables from the garden. Pulling some notes out of my pocket and adding it to the letter that my mother had asked me to give her, I hand everything to the grandmother I'd never know and retreat to the car, hurrying the driver to get us back to Kingston.

I never go back.

In January 1978 the Sex Pistols imploded while on their first American tour. John had been very happy about going to America, which was unusual at the time because very little in England was making him happy. His relationship with Malcolm McLaren was toxic, he hated Nancy and what Sid had become by then – a smelly, lousy junkie either nodding out and semi-comatose, or a snarling cartoon version of himself, too ready to pull a knife on anyone who Nancy told him to 'get'. John's relationship with Sid hadn't improved after he'd bunked down at a place in Sutherland Avenue, Maida Vale with Sid and Nancy for a few weeks at the end of 1977. That really didn't make for a peaceful or harmonious scene. John had stayed at a flat in Chelsea before then which Malcolm had borrowed from someone he knew, but John left after a few weeks because he hated it, which is odd, because he then bought a flat in Gunter Grove, a major road running through Chelsea from Earl's Court to the Harbour. Paul and Steve were miffed about John getting his own place while they were still dossing around at mates' places, pretty much. They only saw John and Sid at rehearsals – and many of them Sid missed – or onstage, where Sid might as well have been absent, since he couldn't keep time or stay in key. Just before Christmas '77 the Pistols played a shambolic gig at Brunel University in front of more than 2,000 people (Jeannette and I travelled there in a Rolls-Royce), which John still says is the worst he's ever done. It wasn't just Sid's fault, although he was out of it, but because Malcolm hadn't paid for a decent PA no-one could hear anything. Mind you, everyone had great fun at the last-ever Pistols' gig in England (not that anyone knew it then, of course) on Christmas Day. It was in Huddersfield, a benefit for striking firemen and their families. A matinee for the kids turned into a huge food fight with cake and jelly thrown at the band. As John tells it in his last autobiography (*Anger is an Energy – My Life Uncensored*, 2014), with cake flying everywhere, Sid's face covered in it, everyone laughing, the band were then 'probably the closest we'd ever been'. That didn't last much past the outer suburbs of Huddersfield in the bus on the way back to London, of course, but still, they were all really up for the American tour in January.

I would have been just as excited, and not just because I'd never been on a plane to anywhere further than Greece before (a week's holiday on Mykonos with Jeannette the previous summer, when I'd

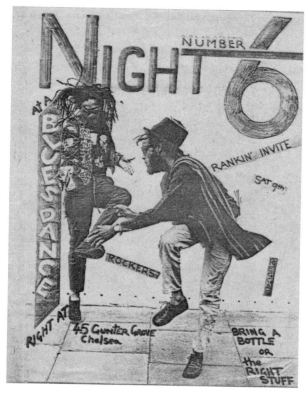

Handmade and Xeroxed invite to a party at John Lydon's place, 1978.

taken acid and decided that I was going to be a film director). None of the Pistols had ever been on a plane journey further than Scandinavia, and their idea of what other countries were like came from the same source as mine: watching television. Like all of us, the Pistols thought they were going to walk into an episode of *Kojak* when they got to New York, or *The Streets of San Francisco* when they got to the final gig in California. Not that they got to New York until after the tour and band had finished, though, because for some reason Malcolm only booked them into clubs and places in the southern states, where I guess he thought they'd cause most offence and generate headlines (which they did, naturally). By all accounts the tour was a disaster for fans as much as for the band. The band all started out travelling on the same bus in Atlanta on January 4, but by the time they'd been through Memphis and San Antonio, Steve and Paul were flying separately and staying in different hotels to John. Sid had been absent, robbed, beaten up, arrested or carved up at pretty much every stop before they got to the final gig at the Winterland Ballroom in San Francisco on January 14. That was the one that ended with John asking everyone – not just the fans but the band and himself too – 'Ever get the feeling you've been cheated?' In the aftermath of the band split following the gig, Sid was ferried to New York by Malcolm and set up in junkie paradise on West 23rd Street (aka the Chelsea Hotel), while Paul and Steve flew to Brazil to record with Great Train Robber on the run Ronnie Biggs. John had to borrow the price of a plane ticket to New York from photographer Joe Stevens, who also put him up for a week. By the end of January, without a band, pissed off and spoiling for a fight, John was back in London and, after starting a legal case against Malcolm, moved into Gunter Grove properly. He'd bought the top two floors of the four-storey house, and they soon resounded to the mighty sounds of dub long into the night and all day, as friends and enemies alike made their way to 'reason' with him. It wasn't long before neighbours started complaining about the noise and comings and goings, and while it wasn't all bad news – he bought the rest of the house when the downstairs neighbour became too pissed off – it brought even more attention on him from the police and tabloid newspapers.

So, when Richard Branson's number two in charge of Virgin Records, Simon Draper, offered him a chance to get away from London for a while, John took it. An irregular visitor to Gunter Grove, Draper was fully aware of John's interest in and knowledge of reggae, which was becoming of greater interest to British and American record companies (Mick Jagger and Keith Richards had been sniffing around in JA and were rumoured to have signed Peter Tosh to their own Rolling Stones Records), and Draper thought Virgin should get into the market, too. Which was why he asked John if he wanted to go to Jamaica and help Branson find artists for their reggae label, Front Line. Of course he did! Being smart, John thought that he should take a couple of friends along with him who might 'fit in' better than he would. So, he asked me and the photographer Dennis Morris (who'd taken some great photos of Bob Marley and the Pistols), as well as *Sounds* magazine's features editor Vivien Goldman, who'd written more about reggae in the British music press than anyone else and knew everyone on the scene. I'd never been to Jamaica, and everything I knew about it came from *The Harder They Come*, but there was no way I was going to turn down the offer of a free plane ticket and hotel in Kingston. I told my mum I'd be going, and she said I may as well visit her mother, gave me the address, such as it was, and a letter. Perhaps, Mum suggested, I could let my grandmother know that I existed, and maybe give her a run-down on what her daughter had been up to in the quarter of a century since they'd last spoken. 'Yeah, of course, no problem,' I told her, doubtfully.

We had to get to Jamaica first, though, and that wasn't as easy as it should have been. When I turned up at Gunter Grove to get the car to the airport with John, I had my passport, a plastic bag and one pair of underpants. Because no-one had told us that we were on a transfer flight and would have to switch planes in Miami, none of us had a visa, not even Viv. When it was discovered that we couldn't hand a visa to the stewardesses as we came in to land, we were held back on the plane while everyone else got off. It felt like hours before we were allowed to disembark, and then had to have an armed guard to take us to the transfer plane gate. Welcome to America! My first time on American soil and I was under close arrest, or something like it.

When we finally reached Norman Manley International Airport (named in 1972 for the country's first premier and founder of the People's National Party) I thought I was pretty well prepared for what I was about to experience. The heat was a physical shock, but at first little else was. Despite my parents rarely talking about their roots or experience in Jamaica – they couldn't afford to look back, they had to keep moving forward, I thought – the place didn't feel 'foreign' to me, probably because the Jamaican roots scene in the UK was so strong, and I'd been a part of it for some years by then. With my dreads, dark glasses and deliberately unflashy clothes, the locals clearly thought I was just one of them. It was only when I spoke that they could tell I wasn't from Kingston. Well, that and my inability to walk on the scorching ground in bare feet.

Because Richard Branson was in town, we were booked into the Sheraton Hotel, the same place that Jimmy Cliff dreamed of staying at, and the epitome of having made it as he saw it in *The Harder They Come*. The place wasn't quite as sparkling and glitzy as it looked in the movie when we got there, though. A high-rise block sitting on a hill in New Kingston, the 'posh' part of the city, it had seen better days. Now parts of the exterior walls were cracked, the carpets worn, an escalator on the ground floor had become a metal non-moving staircase and the lift threatened to stop several times between floors before we made it to the one which Branson had booked the whole of, and from where he'd hold court. Still, the swimming pool (a huge 'S' painted on the bottom was visible from our rooms) glittered in the sun. White plastic tables and umbrellas pitched around the pool edge were served by waiters from the bar. That, we decided immediately, was where we'd do 'business'; not on the tenth floor with Branson in an

With John Lydon at the Sheraton Hotel, Kingston, Jamaica, February 1978.

adjoining room, but out in the open, getting the sun – although John always kept himself fully covered, and wore his wide-brimmed hat constantly, often paired with Ray-Ban sunglasses, because he wasn't a suntan kind of guy. Actually, being out in the open wasn't a brilliant idea, because as we'd found at Heathrow when leaving, the tabloids were following John everywhere, and the paparazzi knew the value of a photo of Johnny Rotten lounging in the sun, being waited on hand and foot, to the tabloids. They tried to take pictures of him using a telephoto lens, but we usually spotted them and actually grabbed one and threw him into the pool.

'Business' for the first two weeks consisted of us entertaining the best musicians Kingston had to offer, and at various times, as Viv wrote in *Sounds*, she saw, 'at least one superstar on a stool per three hours. Very occasionally Peter Tosh, frequently a sprinkling of Gladiators, The Abyssinians, I-Roy, U-Roy, Tappa Zukie & The Tamlins, Jah Lion, Prince Hammer, Johnny Clarke, John Holt, the mighty Culture with the other two Cultures, Robbie Shakespeare, Sly [Dunbar], Chinna, Bim Sherman, Prince Far I, Lee Perry, Inner Circle (alas, Jake 'the Killer' Miller was chowing down in New York at the time), Prince Mahmoud, Big Youth, The Congos – it got to feel like you were wading through your singles collection every time you went to get a glass of water.' Not everyone came to see us, though, and one afternoon John and I took a trip in the Cadillac with Viv to visit Peter Tosh at home, where she was going to interview him. He refused to let John and me in, though, because we were 'heathens', he said. He had a point.

The arrival of so many Rasta musicians at the hotel was something of a shock to the staff, because Rastas were not allowed in the Sheraton. They'd always been considered rebels, they were the voice of the people and their Black power doctrine angered the local Black upper and middle classes because it said they were attempting to deny their Blackness. Rastas reminded them of where they had come from, and consequently were considered a definite no-no around 'polite' society – and the Sheraton was polite central. It was only because Branson was paying for it all that the hotel management turned a blind eye to Rastas at their bar. Yet, until Bob Marley became an internationally famous Rasta, it was almost illegal to openly show dreadlocks in JA, and I mostly wore mine under a hat, no matter who we were meeting with, because I had to stay at the place so I'd see the staff every day and eat the food they prepared for me.

The food was another reason for the Rastas to visit Johnny Cool (as they called John). They all wanted money, of course – Tappa Zukie said he wanted a contribution to help toward building a community centre in Rema, the ghetto where he lived – but they also, more pragmatically, wanted to sample the free food and drink on offer at the Sheraton. That was an aspect of JA that I hadn't expected. Although we'd imagined these artists to be big in their own town, the reality was quite different. Even though some of them had a huge cult following in the UK, more often than not they would be seen as yet another hustler on the streets of Kingston, someone who happened to have made a record for some unscrupulous producer.

Most meetings involved eating, and although the Rastas' doctrine included a set of dietary laws which meant no alcohol, tobacco, meat or shellfish – anything that was not 'ital' (the Rasta term meaning 'pure') was not allowed to be eaten – I didn't follow that doctrine. The first time Prince Far I visited us, he looked on disdainfully as John and I tucked into some lobster with melted butter. The hotel staff looked at me in shock.

'Rasta eat lobster!'

I told anyone who cared, 'Check out my accent; I am from England – different kind of dread.' Having decided long ago that I would not blindly follow anything, I always found a degree of self-interpretation a necessity if I was to enjoy life and not be trapped by dogma. Within a few days Prince Far I also seemed to have learned this lesson, and could be seen sipping champagne with his lobster and fries by the hotel pool.

It didn't take long for the Rastas to love John. To them he was the 'punk rock Don' from London. They were aware of all the trouble he'd stirred up and they were into what he stood for and they dug his stance. They saw him as public enemy number one in the UK, and the Jamaicans love a bad man. One night following a power cut at the hotel (they were frequent) we were sitting outside by the pool looking up at the stars – John, me, Vivien, Ashanti Roy Johnson and Cedric Myton of The Congos – when a police helicopter came flying over, low and noisy. John said something about the police just wanting to keep the people scared so they could control them, and Cedric said, 'Johnny knows.'

To which Roy said, 'Johnny *Cool*, y'know.'

Earlier that day The Congos had asked John and me to go with them and Dennis for a photo session at a quiet cove, on a beach far away from tourists. It was beautiful, and even John took off some of his clothes, it being so hot and no chance of any paparazzi being close by. The longer we were in the city (the pre-planned two weeks turned into three), the more we saw of Kingston, the further we ventured from the Sheraton.

John and I quickly became friendly with U-Roy, who we recognised as the man with the best herb, and more often than not if we weren't at the Sheraton we could be found giggling behind a cloud of smoke in U-Roy's backyard. His posse were really impressed by John's apparently ever-expanding lungs, as he could draw on the chalice along with the best of them. It has to be said, though, that I was far more modest. One morning (the days began at 8, when the sun was up and breakfast was served by the pool at the Sheraton) John and I smoked a chalice with U-Roy in his yard, and he invited us to one of his dances, miles out in the countryside. We went along on what turned out to be a long journey by car, following the gargantuan Stur-Gav mobile disco piled onto the back of two massive trucks, Jamaican-style. His numerous sound guys were hanging onto the equipment for dear life, because they all knew you could 'drop a bwoy, but you can't drop a box', and the roads up country were often not tarmacked but lined with potholes and ditches.

When we reached the spot where it was to take place after weaving our way through some truly glorious countryside, it was little more than a clearing among shacks, but it had the essential element of a power pole, from which dreads strung up the sound system, clipping cables direct to the supply on the top of the pole (I borrowed the idea for a scene in my feature film debut, *Dancehall Queen*). As they worked setting up the sound system, John and I decided to burn some herb. It seemed like no time before the show kicked off with some earthquake dubs, and that sound system was LOUD. The next thing I remember is some dreads shaking us awake.

'We're ready.'

'Uhhh...' I slowly came around. 'Ready for what?'

'Dance done.'

We'd smoked and crashed out where we we'd been sitting six hours earlier. With a groan and a moan, we crawled back into the hotel Cadillac for the long ride home, having missed the whole show.

Another afternoon we visited Lee Perry in his studio, where assembled musicians and singers had been hired to record reggae versions of 'Anarchy In The UK' and 'Holidays In The Sun'. We had no idea why, except that these guys had to somehow make a living and Scratch (who'd produced The Clash's 'Complete Control' in London a few weeks earlier) clearly thought he could make some money out of Branson releasing reggae versions of punk songs. We sat in the smoke-filled control room listening to cheesy reggae versions that Scratch's bunch of hired session men were banging out while drawing on the best herb that Branson's money could buy. It felt more like bread than dread at the control. John and I ended up giggling like girls at the absurdity of the scene and the truly awful renditions of the music.

In an almost complete contrast to that visit and the one I made to my grandmother's place, we'd noticed that Joni Mitchell made visits to the Sheraton for a swim (wearing a black-and-white, polka-dot micro-bikini) and we'd been introduced by a mutual friend, Dickie Jobson, director of another fine Jamaican-made movie, *Countryman* (1982). Possibly intrigued by John's reputation she invited us both to visit at a house she owned up in the hills. Naturally we went, and after eating burned some herb (in a previous age it would have been cigars, I guess). Joni put music on, slightly too loud to be just 'background' sounds. I couldn't help but listen, and it was not dub, rock 'n' roll or soul music. I couldn't make much of it, and after a few passes of the herb, burst out with 'What is this shit we're listening to? Take it off!'

Joni calmly replied, 'It's my new album, actually.'

Back-pedalling furiously (and, I thought, coolly aided by my ever-present shades) I foolishly replied, 'Well it's not "Carey", is it?'

I'd just demonstrated that I'd heard nothing the woman had recorded since 1971. It was pathetic, but for the life of me I couldn't think of a better comeback. Once again John sat giggling on the sofa as the rest of *Don Juan's Reckless Daughter* played, and small talk resumed without me.

Although I knew enough not to have taken it with me to Joni's place, throughout our visit while John was doing his stuff, I hung around with my Super-8mm camera, capturing as much of the action and inaction as I could. Some of the best – and rarest – footage I got on our trip came courtesy of Tappa Zukie, who took me and John to Rema, one of the heaviest parts of Kingston (they used to call it 'Jungle' and it was a no-go area for the police), to see where he wanted to build his community centre. A dread with a camera was as rare in JA as it was in London, but because we were with Tappa, we could walk through the desperately poor, barren streets with me filming without too much comment. After a bit John said, 'What's the big deal, where are all the guns?', and a guy stepped forward and asked, 'Do *you* want to see a gun?' Without waiting for an answer ('YES!') he reached into his back pocket and whipped out a massive fucking handgun. That did it – suddenly there were guns all around us, and me and John were shitting ourselves. Three days later the guy who I filmed holding his gun as we walked in broad daylight along a highway was dead.

By the middle of the decade gun crime in Jamaica was so prevalent that Prime Minister Michael Manley (son of Norman) created a special prison camp that came to be known locally as 'Gun Court', although its real name is South Camp Adult Correctional Centre, on Camp Road, Kingston. Manley also brought in a new set of laws designed to put away anyone caught with a gun quickly, and without a proper trial. The laws were passed in 1974 and Gun Court, essentially a big fortress, quickly filled up with rude boys who'd been convicted and imprisoned indefinitely without trial by jury after a closed hearing (no spectators allowed). The legend of Gun Court quickly grew in the yards and ghettos of JA, and it became the only place where a rude boy could earn a rep. No self-respecting gunman could get a name for themselves until they'd been held there for at least a week, and naturally it became a subject for songs and stories about bad men. Manley tried to make people fear Gun Court and had the prison camp painted red, because as anyone who'd seen Clint Eastwood in the film *High Plains Drifter* (1973) knows, 'red is dread'. Consequently, every self-styled outlaw gunslinger in JA took it as a challenge, not a threat.

Back then, Jamaica was still totally into Westerns and there were recording stars called Clint Eastwood, Gregory Peck, John Wayne and Dirty Harry (and because they also loved kung fu there was even an artist called Bruce Lee). To the rude boys of JA the movies were real life, and for a while in the 1970s they'd shoot real bullets at the screens in cinemas when certain movies were showing. Perhaps some cinema owners might have thought about replacing the wrecked screens and stop showing Westerns, but Jamaican cinema owners couldn't afford to not show them, so they simply replaced the screens with white concrete walls and projected onto them instead.

Intrigued by the idea of Gun Court and thinking I might be able to use the footage at a later date in something, one hot and sticky afternoon I decided to film the exterior of the place. After a brief ride out toward the airport in the white Caddy, I got the driver to park up around the back of the camp, so that I could walk around to the front and get an idea of what might look good on camera. I didn't lift my Super-8mm to my right eye until I got to the heavily guarded front gates, though. I'd barely started when two soldiers ran out of the barbed-wire-ringed gates, grabbed me and my camera, and holding an arm each, marched me through the gates and into the first yard of Gun Court. Without stopping they made for a door in an otherwise blank wall, opened it and threw me into a small, cramped, bare cell. For the first time on that trip I found myself actually glad to be English. Having slammed the door shut behind them as they entered the cell with me, they stood five feet away, their guns still holstered, hands behind their backs.

'You cannot film round here, you know.'

With my best English accent, I replied, 'I certainly won't do it again, officer. I'm on holiday from England, I didn't realise what I was doing.'

'How do we know you are from England?'

It must have been the dreadlocks, I thought; they're used to seeing people from England dressed like the English in linen suits or shorts and Hawaiian shirts, hair cut short and parted in the middle.

'Listen to how I speak!'

'Hmmm, true, true... but...'

Unconvinced, or maybe enjoying scaring an English 'Rasta', they continued to question me and came up with the bright idea of testing my knowledge of the UK's geography.

'Where's Durham Prison?' asked one of them. I wondered if it was a trick question for half a beat before suggesting that it was, in fact, in Durham.

'And where's that, then?'

'In the North East, a damned cold place, near Newcastle.'

Giving the correct answer wasn't quite the end of it, and it took two hours of non-physical interrogation, interspersed with my being left alone in the cell to sweat on what might happen next, before they were convinced that I wasn't a local and let me go.

Making my way back to the Caddy on shaky legs, I thought perhaps my generation of Blacks in England who were empowering themselves by emulating their Jamaican brothers needed a reality check.

Living in Babylon meant frequent police hassle, but in Kingston we saw roadblocks everywhere and they were all manned by police or soldiers with guns and big sticks. People they stopped were made to stand up against a wall, backs to the police who'd search them, hit them upside the head, or whip them across the back of their legs with the sticks, and no-one passing by said or did anything about it. That was normal, everyday business, just some harsh justice being handed out. We were stopped and searched on four different nights during the three weeks we were in JA, and while we didn't get a knock, kick, whip or rap, we were made to line up facing the wall, hands above our heads as the taxi we were travelling in was searched for drugs. None of us were dumb enough to carry anything with us between the hotel and clubs or people's houses.

But, despite the heavy manners, my first trip to Jamaica was a great experience, and it made me realise that although I didn't feel like a total alien when I first landed in Kingston, I was different to the family living on the island who I'd never known, or could ever know, but that was OK with me. Because of that trip I became friendly with Prince Far I, Tappa Zukie, I-Roy, U-Roy and Big Youth. It didn't quite work out the way that Virgin hoped, though. I got the impression that they'd gone to Jamaica thinking that it would be just like it was in America when they went looking for Black artists across the Atlantic. They didn't understand Jamaica or know the Jamaican music scene. People like Far I and Keith Hudson could be very scary if you caught them on a bad day, and they had a different way of doing business. Far I fell out with Branson and later released a track on Adrian Sherwood's On-U Sound label called 'Virgin', which included lines about the Virgin boss being a pickle that the singer didn't want on his plate. Punks loved it when I played Far I's

'Deck Of Cards' at the Roxy because his voice sounded like he gargled with bleach. A lot of the JA artists were consummate rude boys, not bad people, just tough. Far I merely saying, 'Good morning,' in his heavy Jamaican dialect to the staff at the record company could sound intimidating. Although Virgin's Front Line label released some great albums and singles, it didn't last very long and was closed down after a couple of years. But John and I had helped to get a lot of the artists in the door with Virgin (plus some much-needed financial assistance) and probably helped a lot of people to hear records that may have never made it out of Jamaica, or at least no further than the specialist shops in the UK.

Arriving home from Jamaica early in March 1978 I took a walk along the King's Road and came upon an almost surreal scene. Seditionaries stood boarded up, with some really lame graffiti written all over the front in red paint, mainly slagging off John for going to Jamaica as well as some mad stuff about him being Irish and Haile Selassie being a Catholic. I started to film it on my Super-8mm camera when Vivienne came running out of the shop and attacked me. I had to physically pin her to the wall to try to get her to chill out. A Black man doing anything to a white woman in public, particularly on the streets of Chelsea, was a dangerous move and I was shitting myself, but I had to calm her down. I wasn't violent, I simply held her, pinning her arms by her side for half a minute until she calmed down enough for me to be able to walk away.

Haile Unlikely

Interior. Night. Early autumn. A party is happening on the first floor of a flat-fronted four-storey London townhouse. Two windows face onto a busy main road (Gunter Grove, SW10). Both are half open. The lights are low, close to darkness, with only a smutty yellow sulphur glow from a streetlamp outside casting shadows on walls dotted with posters. The gloom is pinpricked by a steady flow of joints being passed around a crowd of dreads and punks standing and skanking to a deafening dub soundtrack. Others sit, crouch or lie on a couple of battered, low-level sofas with no backs, covered with blankets. A 21-inch, lumpy television squats on a board on bricks between the windows. Toward one end of the room a set of open, wooden steps leads to the second floor (and the roof, reached via an access gate) of the early Victorian villa from which the apartment is carved. On one side wall of the room a bunch of big speakers, their grilles removed, are visibly jumping with each thump of the bass coming from the expensive-looking hi-fi set-up, built into a tubular cabinet which looks custom-made standing beside the built-in cupboard which holds the speakers. Hung above them is a large, ceremonial samurai sword, put there as a kind of ironic statement on the crossed pistols or sabres you'd see in baronial homes in old black-and-white British movies. Cans of Red Stripe and Tennent's Super litter window ledges and a couple of Fender Twin amplifiers in the otherwise sparsely furnished room. Spread out on a small futon rammed against the staircase, three men and a cat are having a conversation, their voices raised enough to hear each other. The flat's owner, John Lydon, is barefoot, wearing striped, loose harem pants, a vest and, over it, an old silk dressing gown-cum-smoking jacket, tied loosely at the waist with a silk belt. Keith Levene is wearing an old Seditionaries T-shirt, Levi 501s and black crepe-soled brothel creepers. I'm in a Dread At The Controls T-shirt, straight-leg Levi jeans and desert boots, my locks held in place by my woollen crown. The cat looks bored.

'Satan... Satan... where's the grass?... Get the grass, Satan...'

'John, it's a fucking cat, you can't train a cat to do that shit.'

'Nah, Don, Satan's fucking smart, I tell you, he'll get it, I swear.'

The cat leisurely licks its arse. Keith Levene thinks it hilarious and slowly falls sideways. Sniggering, he rolls onto his face on the floor.

John snaps his finger at the cat. 'Satan, there's no fucking weed there, man, go get my grass...'

Satan stands and arches his back, his tail and ears quivering.

'What the fuck... what's that noise...?'

A loud banging and shouting is coming up the stairs from the front door, audible even over the booming bass. People have backed away from the sound, a couple of joints have been thrown out of the windows.

'Fuckers!' John leaps up, and grabbing the sword, makes for the stairs, shouting like a warrior. 'Heeeey-yah! Fuck off you cunts!'

He thinks it's either Teddy boys, skinheads or the press trying to crash his party and give his mates grief, and he's had enough of that lately. The party is being held because John's been virtually housebound since getting back from Jamaica, unable to walk the streets without being attacked or chased. Even some punks have taken to baiting him for having split the Pistols and conducting a very public spat with Malcolm and Vivienne, Paul and Steve. Our trip didn't help reduce public antipathy toward him. So, it's kind of understandable that he was ready to fight intruders into his home, the only safe space he had left in London.

As John makes the landing at the turn of the staircase, sword raised above his head like Toshiro Mifune, his dressing gown now looking more like a samurai kamishimo, he stops and half-shouts, 'Fuck off.' Then he turns back to everyone at the door to the flat above him, 'It's the rozzers.' Naturally that sparks a panic and people head to the toilet to flush away any incriminating evidence, or to the windows over the garden to throw bags and wraps as far as they can onto the neatly kept lawn below (the lower flat is still owned by someone else at this point). Since I'm no longer holding – the grass I brought is now in John's stash pot – I stand still, and prepare for the usual shit from the police, who are now backing John into the room. Two coppers shout at everybody, 'Stand still face the wall hands above your head'; a third is pulled into the party by a large Alsatian sniffer dog. At the sight of Satan, the dog leaps forward, and the cat almost idly jumps onto the top of the speaker closest to it. Luckily for everyone, on top of that particular speaker stands John's stash (tea)pot. The dog handler has to strenuously restrain the Alsatian from leaping at the speaker. 'Get the fucking dog out of here before he kills my cat!' shouts John and, amazingly, the handler does exactly that. John's cat and stash are safe, although the party's over – we're all searched, nothing found, but told to 'fuck off home' – and John is taken to the police station along with his sword, having been cautioned before being forced into the back of the Transit van, handcuffed and barefoot, in his pyjamas and dressing gown.

The rest of us melted away from the scene as smoothly and quietly as we could. A few returned half an hour later to search for the packages sent spinning into the night, but I made my way back to Forest Hill in my rusty old Morris Minor with Leo and a couple of others. No-one thought to go to the cop shop to see how John was, or how he was going to get back to Gunter Grove. By the time he was released it was early morning and the Fulham Road was just waking up, so a lot of shopkeepers and commuters saw a vaguely familiar apparition ghosting along one of the busiest roads in the city. Barefoot and freezing, John walked back to the flat, with only his anger keeping him moving. At least he didn't need any keys to get in – he didn't have any – because the front door was still hanging off its hinges.

That day he decided to move to another city in another country (New York).

John had recently formed a new band and called it, with typical contrariness, Public Image Ltd. Along with one-time Clash guitarist Keith Levene and an old Kingsway College mate John Wardle (he and Lydon were half of The Four Johns while at college) now better known as Jah Wobble on bass, he'd advertised in *Melody Maker* for a drummer and found Canadian Jim Walker. Together they fused dub and rock into a warped, paranoid and claustrophobic sound drawing on the stuff he'd been listening to ever since I'd known him. John told me that back in the Pistols days Paul and Steve hadn't wanted to travel on the tour bus with him because he continuously played my reggae compilation tapes along with avant-garde stuff like Can's *Tago Mago*, Curved Air and Tangerine Dream.

During our time in Jamaica we formed a kind of friendship that mostly excluded me from his fuckery when hanging out with the newly formed PiL, and for that I was grateful. John would fuck with everyone who turned up at his door if he could, turning his arguments on their head if it looked like there was any kind of agreement about to occur. It didn't take long for the Gunter Grove address to become known far and wide, and all kinds of people would turn up uninvited. Jeannette answered the door intercom one day for John and it was someone claiming to be Nico, the former model and Velvet Underground singer, who was asking to be let in, even though she'd never met him.

I'd introduced Jeannette to John, and she began spending a lot of time at Gunter Grove at a time when our relationship was ending (she eventually left me crying on the street). John – like Joe Strummer – respected what Jeannette had to say and listened to her in a way that he didn't with a lot of other people, and she was always welcome at Gunter Grove with or without me. It became more without me as 1979 began, and Jeannette then spent a lot of time with Keith Levene who moved into the basement of the house once John bought out the neighbours. Because Jeannette was smart, capable and trustworthy she essentially became the manager of PiL. John asked her to keep the books and help with the running of the band – getting Keith to rehearse, record and contribute was in itself a major task by the time they were on to their second album, but she could do it. However, her involvement was much more than just that. She helped to create the mystique around the band; that's her on the cover of their third studio album, *The Flowers Of Romance* (1981).

PiL's first recording session took place in July 1978, barely three months after we'd got back from Jamaica. When one of the music papers announced that John was recording, Virgin decided – without hearing it – that they'd release it in September. A few weeks later Virgin changed their mind and said that they'd hold back on releasing the single because, John later said, 'they weren't sure if the market was ready for it'. They were clearly worried about the new direction John was taking. That might have been when John decided that the single, 'Public Image', should have a video made to promote it. Either way, that was lucky for me because he insisted that I direct it and hired the company who'd provided the production elements of *The Punk Rock Movie* to put it all together. The shoot was booked for August 1978.

'Public Image' was my first music video and the first time that I had control of a crew with lights and camera operators, in a studio, which was actually a stage set up in Olympia. There was a budget, which wasn't enormous, but still way more than anything I'd had to make *The Punk Rock Movie*. This was a whole new ball game and I had no idea what I was supposed to do, not that I was going to let that get in the way. We decided that the video would be a 'live performance' shoot, with no frills or flattering effects. There was an element of old WWII propaganda films in the set, which was a shiny backdrop of industrial-strength rubbish bags, with one set of arc lights rigged high so they'd shine directly onto stage and performers, and another rigged low, so they'd shine up from beneath John, casting his face in shadow and giving it a slight horror-movie look. Maybe because it was being filmed, Wobble arrived for the shoot dressed like a cowboy, all in black with a wide-brimmed hat and a bass strap which looked like a gun belt, with a double row of metal studs. He wore tiny, round, wire-framed sunglasses and sat down throughout the shoot, taking the idea of the still, solid bassist to an illogical extreme. Jim Walker dressed in all black, T-shirt and trousers, and basically became a part of the drum kit – all you can see are his hands moving, sticks occasionally flying in the background. Keith and John both chose to wear glittery Teddy boy jackets (shocking pink for Keith, electric blue for John), but that was the only attempt at creating any kind of band uniform. Keith wore a home-made Public Image shirt and plain dark peg trousers, while John wore a stiff-collared white shirt and striped tie, with striped, baggy harem trousers. I directed the 16mm camera to remain fixed on John for the first couple of takes, the only movement being to track in close or pull back from his face and body. That turned out to be the best decision I made on the shoot because his performance, full of angry energy, is what carries the whole thing. Because it was John's band, I naively decided people just wanted to see him. His dynamics gave the video its substance; it was a very intense, dark performance but working with PiL was always tense because they were so volatile, even then. For subsequent takes the camera roved the stage, trying not to be reflected in Keith's mirror guitar, and occasionally pulling up to Wobble's immobile features. Both of them tried to ignore the camera completely, with Keith turning his back, walking across stage behind John while Wobble turned his head away from the lens. All of which was perfect and suited PiL's mood, being totally anti-celebrity.

Most video-makers at that time were using a narrative in their work but I thought that was kind of stupid and limiting. Everyone has their own idea of what a song is about, and I wanted to keep the 'meaning' of Public Image open to interpretation, which was John's aim, too. I think it worked. After making the PiL promo I began to believe in myself, to think that I really could learn and progress as a filmmaker.

The single was released in October and despite being a hit (it made number nine in the UK charts) Virgin were still hesitant about releasing the album *Public Image: First Issue*. Perhaps it was the screening of the video on *Top of the Pops* that changed their mind – it almost blew mine. I had to phone everyone I knew to ask if they'd seen it, including my mum – and Virgin put the album out on December 8. Traditionally, that's not a great time to release anything other than seasonal compilation albums or greatest hits collections, because it's hard to compete with Santa Claus unless you're Elton John. But it made it to number twenty-two on the UK album chart before Christmas.

Success didn't change much in the PiL camp, though, possibly because everyone was on a different drug. One person was up, one was down, one was coming in sideways, with the inevitable result that the initial sunny optimism that they had soon turned dark. They were all coming in on different wavelengths, and while out of that chaos came moments of brilliance in their music, personal relationships fell apart. Even Jeannette and I found it difficult to get on, especially after I'd been persuaded by Keith to take part in a side project with him and Wobble.

Needing some money, they'd taken up an offer of some left-over recording time in November 1978 to create a spin-off EP for Virgin Records, who'd clearly been reading too much into constant music press coverage of PiL and assumed that anything with Wobble and Levene's name on it, even without John's involvement, would sell. They asked me and an old mate of Wobble's to the studio to work on some vocals for what they would call 'The Steel Leg vs The Electric Dread' EP, even though I had never sung in my life, not even in a school or church choir. I didn't say no, though, figuring that I'd go with the punk spirit and give it a shot. I sat in the studio with a microphone trying to write some words, toasting along to the backing track. Eventually I said, 'OK guys, I'll go home and work out some lyrics,' not realising that there wouldn't be a tomorrow: they only had the day to do everything, and my experimental toasting was to be the final take. Barely two weeks later they released the recording with my demoed vocals as a 12-inch, which was annoying enough, but the worst part was that the cover of the single had a picture of someone wearing a kind of rubber gimp outfit, complete with a black bag covering their face, standing next to Wobble and Levene. I hadn't agreed to that – in fact I hadn't been asked about any of it and wouldn't be seen dead in an outfit like that. But naturally everyone thought the person on the sleeve was me. I was pissed off and, to add insult to injury, my unedited toasting caused a whole load of trouble with my brethren because I'd called it 'Haile Unlikely' and was messing around with the idea of being Black and not wanting to go back to Africa. Essentially, the lyrics questioned a return to Africa and the following of Selassie, and some dreads thought I shouldn't be writing lyrics like that. I don't think Levene and Wobble fully appreciated that I was going out on a limb writing stuff like that. A lot of the brethren were cussing, 'Don Letts, bloodclaat, you can't say dem t'ings!' To be honest, the whole of the EP is pretty dire, and while I'm not overjoyed that it's still out there on YouTube and Spotify, it is a part of my life and shows that I had the bollocks to pick up a microphone and call things as I saw them long before Big Audio Dynamite and Screaming Target.

However, my thinking at the time was slightly clouded by the amount of time I was spending at Gunter Grove, doing too many drugs – one escapade which involved everyone speeding on sulphate (a very much cheaper cocaine substitute at the time) left me with no facial hair for a couple of weeks. Bored and speeding I picked up a canister of lighter gas and sucked some of it in, having decided that I'd do a bit of fire breathing. When I tried to light a spurt of the fluid there was a BOOM, the whole room shook and all the hair on my face disappeared, eyebrows included. Everyone else thought it hilarious, of course, especially John. He usually found something to enjoy in other people's misadventures back then, and there was no shortage of people offering such enjoyment. Gunter Grove was the unofficial headquarters for the sector of ex-Roxy punks who were 'on John's side', as they saw it, and were tolerated by him – for a while, at least. Some were actively

At my Forest Hill home, 1978. (L–r) Me, John Lydon and Nora Forster.

encouraged to visit because John knew that he could fuck with them, and they soon learned that visiting meant undergoing a kind of trial by fire. If you had a weakness, John would find it and pick at it, poking fun, irritating you until you either left in a huff or submitted silently so that he'd become bored and pick on someone else. It was as if people were coming around for John's entertainment and would walk out of that place psychological wrecks. Only those who could take it would be let back in. He didn't pick on some people at all, though, especially those who were clearly suffering from problems that they were finding difficult to deal with. Poly Styrene from X-Ray Spex came around often, until one evening on a visit, after acting distractedly for a little while, she disappeared into the upstairs bathroom. Half an hour later she returned having cut all her hair off. John and I were freaked and trying to figure out what to do when there was a knock on the door. It was her manager Falcon Stuart and two guys in white coats who'd come to take her to hospital.

Me and the Forest Hill posse spent a lot of time at John's place in 1978 and '79. I even took Dr Alimantado around there one time, which was a major event for John, because the Doctor was one of his heroes and 'Born For A Purpose' something of a Lydon anthem. It had been written after a near-fatal accident on Boxing Day 1976, when he was struck down and nearly killed by a bus while walking up Orange Street in Kingston. The track, recorded during a free session at Channel One Studio, is an emotional and uplifting number, and tells the story of how the bus driver was intent on running him over for daring to wear his dreadlocks in the street. The lyrics resonated with the first generation of British-born Jamaicans and punks alike. John named it as one of his top ten tunes of all time when he played it on Capital Radio in 1977, and The Clash paid their respects to Alimantado on 'Rudie Can't Fail', written during the summer when Joe and Paul were going to a lot of reggae sh'beens and blues dances, partaking in herb and brew and generally being turned on by West Indian culture. Joe once told me that Paul Simonon played Dr Alimantado's 'Poison Flour' all the time, citing it as an example of how to sing about things that had an effect on daily lives.

I had the good fortune to strike up a relationship with Alimantado when we met in Daddy Kool, then London's premiere reggae shop, managed by Steve Barrow (the founder of the Blood and Fire record label), when he was delivering his tunes direct and personally to the handful of reggae shops in London from the boot of his Mini. Having got to know him, I directed the Doctor as he drove to Gunter Grove and an impromptu party with John and the various people who were there at the time. And there was always someone there; John was never alone, perhaps because he couldn't get out into the world without hassle and harassment, so he had the world brought to him.

A few weeks before the night of John's barefoot arrest, he decided to throw a party at Gunter Grove for Leo's birthday, at which the two tribes filled the room with Red Stripe, sensi and the heaviest dub reggae courtesy of the John Lydon Sound System. It was one of the best parties held at the place, and John wasn't in a contrary or fighting mood. He looked positively bemused watching Althea & Donna as they skanked the night away in his living room. The newly crowned first women of reggae had had an enormous international hit with 'Uptown Top Ranking' just a few months earlier, and here they were, a happy pair of natural young women (17 and 18 years old), having a great time in his home.

John could be a good friend when he wanted, and he agreed to help with a project I was working on at the time, which was to create a British reggae band who'd juxtapose the best parts of Jamaican reggae with the sound of the British Black experience. The band would consist of my Forest Hill housemates Leo Williams, J.R. Murray and Tony 'T' Thompson, and an old-style reggae singer named Winston Fergus. I thought that if they had some exposure then we'd begin to get somewhere, and John agreed. Probably the only good thing to come from the 'Electric Dread' EP experience was that I got Levene and Wobble to agree with John that Basement 5 (the name I'd come up with for the band) could appear at the first PiL gigs at the Rainbow in London on Christmas Day and Boxing Day 1978. After all, I reminded Levene and Wobble, they owed me something. And if they could get Virgin to put out such crap, I thought, then it must be easy to get something that's even halfway better released. I just had to figure out how.

Five Go to the Basement

Interior. A shabby nightclub, day, but lit solely by low electric light, the windows are blacked out. Around the edge of the room plastic-covered booths with small tables are occupied by people dressed for a warm summer's day. The small, square dancefloor is filled with people standing around talking, laughing and paying little attention to the poppy-sounding reggae playing in the background. Some of the crowd are holding drinks and cardboard plates of food, which they've served themselves from a long table set against the DJ booth. Set back in an alcove at the side of the booth is a door to the club's small professional kitchen, through which can be glimpsed a handful of dreadlocked Rastas preparing and setting out the food, all dressed in kitchen whites. The door is on a two-way hinge, and as one of the staff carries an empty serving plate back into the kitchen, a flash of something startlingly blue catches the eye for a split second. A half-beat later a dread pushes through the swing door into the room, dressed in an electric blue zoot suit with impossibly wide shoulders tapering to a cinched waist, from where peg trousers billow out over the knee before sharpening to sit just so, on top of pointy-toed black-and-white correspondent shoes. He stops briefly to speak to one of the guests, who looks surprised to see him, but points hesitantly to the centre booth on the back wall. With a few quick strides the zoot suit is standing in front of the booth, in which sit three men who look to be in their late thirties, all wearing denim shirts and jeans, chunky watches, their hair cut loosely and expensively long in the style of Mick Jagger, along with two much younger women. Everyone in the booth is white.

'Chris Blackwell? I'm Don Letts and I've got something I think you'd be interested in...'

I'd swear that the man I'm talking to has a twinkle in his eye. He leans back and takes in my suit, dreadlocks and dark glasses (I can't see much in the room, but it's important to make an impression, to not let him see the hesitation in my eyes). One of the other guys leans forward and opens his mouth, but Blackwell – the boss of Island Records who's paying for this event, including for my brethren to feed everyone (as assistants for his company chef, Lucky Gordon) – puts a hand on the other guy's forearm, shakes his head and then looks at me again. I'm now using my left hand to steady myself against the table.

'OK, what have you got for me?'

'Well, if you give me, say, £1,500, I can get you the best demo tape you've ever heard.'

'OK, and what will I hear?'

'Mr Blackwell, you'll hear some of the best damn reggae to come out of Babylon.'

He raises an eyebrow, smiles and says to the women next to him, 'May I?' before taking her paper napkin and writing something on it.

'Here, take this to that man over there...' He points to the booth three along at a younger, straighter-looking dude in a sports jacket and open-necked white shirt, and hands me the napkin.

'Uh...' I grunt. I can't read what's written on the napkin without removing my shades, but assume I'm getting the brush-off because everyone in the booth is smiling. Chris gives me a small wave toward the other guy. Not wanting to lose face, I straighten up and, clutching the piece of paper like it's a weapon, make for the other booth and hand it to sports jacket man. He pulls a pair of reading glasses from the inside pocket of his jacket, smoothes out the napkin and reads. Then he looks at me – I'm feigning disinterest, looking at the fine people on the dancefloor with their plates of plantain, rice and beans – and turns his head toward Chris Blackwell, who I see out of the corner of my eye hold up a hand, palm out, and nod.

'OK, er...?'

I turn back to him, 'Don Letts.'

'Mr Letts, Mr Blackwell has asked me to give you £1,500 so if you come to the office tomorrow, I'll get a cheque drawn up for you. OK?'

'Huh? I mean, sure, man.'

(I did it? It's that simple? Damn, I should have asked for £15,000!) 'But, where's the office, man?'

'Of course; it's at Island Records, you know where that is, don't you? Lucky can direct you to my office, ask him for the financial department. See you tomorrow.'

'Can I keep the napkin?'

'Sure, here. I'll have the cheque ready by 11am. See you then.'

With that I return to the kitchen, a broad smile on my face as I push the door open and find only Lucky there. He points a dangerous-looking knife toward the back door, which is slightly open. A puff of blue smoke floats by. I step out and find Leo, JR and Tony passing a joint around. They look at me with blank faces. I hold the now very crumpled napkin in the air and tell them, 'Boys, Basement 5 are on their way!'

Punk had changed everything in the music business by the time of the Pistols' demise; a huge number of diverse British bands had been 'discovered' and, because nothing ever really changes in the music business, signed by record companies desperate to get on the nearest bandwagon to high-street success. Despite the events of 1977, it seemed like every venue in the country were glad to put on punk and related gigs. The music press, having decided that new wave and post-punk were the 'new punk', got behind artists who played a wide range of different musical styles. At any other time, bands like The Models or The Vapors would have simply been considered pop bands and have to fight for any kind of record company attention after slogging around the country playing small clubs and pubs for at least two years. But as new wave acts they could play a showcase at a London venue like the Marquee, get a music journalist to write them up as the future of new wave, and they'd be signed and promoted in the following week's paper.

Partly because reggae had become a hip sound, that too now had the attention of all the major record companies. That first meeting with Chris Blackwell, Island Records' founder, was at an album launch party his company held for *Journey To Addis*, the third release by Third World for the label. It turned out that the first single from it, a cover of the O'Jays' 'Now That We Found Love', would become a worldwide hit, but prior to that Third World hadn't exactly changed the world with reggae. It was Blackwell's persistence and nous that made them a success (he put a specialist remix team on the O'Jays' number, speeding it up and making it a hit), and I dug the guy, which is why I wanted to meet him. I hoped that he'd be the person to help out with my band. I'd gained entrance to the party by way of the caterer, Lucky Gordon – the man at the centre of the Christine Keeler/Lord Profumo scandal of 1962 – a brother who'd become chef at Island Records after not making it as a jazz singer. Lucky used to employ Leo and Tony as commis chefs when he needed them and they needed the money, and the Third World

With my posse, Forest Hill, 1978. (L–r) JR, Leo (in front), T, Ariane, me.   RUDOLPH

launch party was such an occasion. I'd joined the team to get into the place wearing kitchen whites over my zoot suit until the time was right to get out and approach the big boss.

I thought my brethren – Leo Williams on bass, JR on guitar and T on drums – could be a great band. I came up with the name and we found Winston Fergus who'd left The Equators and signed to Lightning Records as a solo artist the year before but had no success with his only single so far, 'African Woman'. I was the 'manager' because I had management experience – at Acme and BOY – but mostly because I couldn't play anything and couldn't sing, either – which I proved to myself on 'Haile Unlikely'. Once I'd got the money from Island, I gave it to the dreads, who bought instruments.

I also arranged their first gig, of course, and Christmas Day 1978 was quite a night for Basement 5 to make their debut, being as it was also the first live appearance of John Lydon and Public Image Ltd. Naturally there was a lot of press attention – which could only be good for us, I thought. I DJed both nights and played pretty much what I had at the Roxy, which at least set the mood for the 5's performance (and that of Linton Kwesi Johnson, who read some of his work over a backing tape). Basement 5 weren't even bottom of the bill, either; they went on after a French all-female band called The Lou's, who'd clearly been inspired by The Slits and Raincoats and sounded not too dissimilar to both bands. Even though no-one was there specifically to see any of the support bands, they all got a decent response from the audience, which was surprisingly big given that there was no public transport on Christmas Day and only a Sunday service running the following night.

The gigs with PiL were a good test, which unfortunately Winston wasn't ready for. He sang at both Rainbow gigs and it was clear that his old-style lovers approach to the music wasn't what we were looking for. The following week it was agreed by all that he should leave. Lacking anyone else, someone suggested that I step in as toaster – I didn't want to, but at least I wouldn't have to 'sing'. Plus, it was a chance to show the dreads in London that I wasn't taking the piss after the debacle of 'Haile Unlikely', and that Basement 5 were a true roots reggae band (albeit with a different, slightly punky approach). Plus, we'd been offered gigs in Portugal early in 1979 and the brethren really wanted to go – it would mean them staying for a few months, and the chance of living, rehearsing and playing in a warm climate during what are always the coldest, most miserable months in London was too good to turn down.

Basement 5 went from Finsbury Park to Porto within a few weeks and I stayed in London, flying out to sing at a couple of gigs with them. Everything went pretty well out there – most of the time – and when everyone returned to London, I decided that I should take Basement 5 to Island Records and let Chris Blackwell see how his investment had turned out. For some reason the photographer Dennis Morris, who was working in the art department at Island, was appointed as my contact at the company, and he wasn't exactly enthusiastic about the band. I couldn't work out why until he mentioned that they really needed a 'proper' singer, to which I could only agree. I figured that he'd look for someone for the band, and I could return to being just the manager, not the singer too. As if to prove that the music business never really changes, it turned out that he had a singer in mind – himself – but that the singer didn't like the manager (i.e. me). I learned this when Leo, JR and Tony told me that they were signing for Island with Dennis as singer and manager.

I was sacked from my own band.

Naturally, I was fucked off, and hurt – who wouldn't be? It hurt that these were my brethren, my oldest friends, we'd shared a home and a whole lot of experience and they were willing to ditch me after years of doing stuff together. It took a little while, but eventually I came to realise that we were all growing up and apart, just like families do, and that doesn't mean it has to be the end of the relationship. (Leo and I were in Big Audio Dynamite with Mick Jones, of course, and more than forty years later we're still brethren.)

At the time of the split, though, feeling betrayed and angry, I looked around for the thing that would take me in my own direction, that would ease my pain. It didn't take long to find, and it turned out that it was just down by the river.

But I Have No Fear

Exterior. Late afternoon, grey sky and low daylight. Cadogan Pier on the north bank of the Thames opposite Battersea Park, London. To the right, Albert Bridge slouches across the river taking cars from bohemian, upmarket Chelsea to a prosaic Battersea still struggling to morph from working-class slum to gentrified middle-class ghetto.

Entrance onto the pier is set back from Chelsea Embankment, at the edge of a scrubby piece of green designated as Albert Bridge Gardens. A Ford Transit van is parked with two front wheels on the road, rear two on the green. Half a dozen men carry pieces of movie camera, boxes and cables from the van to a waiting pleasure boat. Another Transit is backed across the green, its back doors opened onto the pier entrance. A drum kit is being assembled on the pier as two other men put up lights.

'Does anyone know how to drive this fucking thing?'

I've lived in London my whole life and never actually been on the Thames. I've crossed it countless times on bridges, of course, in cars and occasionally on foot. But this is the first time I've been on a boat, and even while moored to the bank it's moving and rocking.

'The captain's inside, don't worry,' says someone with a snigger in their voice. It's clear that I'm uneasy, and since I can't swim, I've got a reason to be.

'Well can you get him to drive us out into the river, opposite the pier so I can get a...'

I've just looked at the pier, which is a few yards along the bank, and noticed that it seems to be on a different level to us, which is why I've stopped mid-sentence. A middle-aged man wearing a blazer that seems to have too many brass buttons on it appears from the cabin and asks, 'You in charge?'

He looks at me with his unbelieving head on one side. I nod and turn back to look at the pier again.

'We can cast off when you're ready,' he says.

'Right, er, what's your name?'

'Ron.'

'I'm Don. So, Ron, when we get out there,' I wave nervously toward the middle of the river, 'will the pier be on the same level as we are?'

Ron looks puzzled.

'Only, I need to film the band and it's not gonna look great if I'm pointing the camera up their noses.'

'Ah,' he leans back and puts his hands in the large square pockets of his double-breasted jacket. 'You'll have to wait 'til the tide comes back in, then.'

He turns on his deck-shoed heels and steps back into the cabin.

'But,' I shout after him, 'when the fuck will that be?'

Ron sticks his head out of the doorway and smiles. 'A few hours yet, chum.'

'Hang on!' I don't want blazer man thinking he's got me. Having never directed anything with a crew as big as this (ten) none of whom I know, I can't afford to let Ron take charge. That won't look good.

'We can still go out and find the best spot to shoot from though, right?'

'Welllll...' Ron smooths what's left of the hair over his right ear. 'We can try...'

Clearly there's a 'but' in there, but I'm not inclined to hear it.

'Alright then. Start your motor Ron, and let's get out there – everything on board, guys?'

The crew, who've been watching this exchange while ranged across the deck in a variety of poses, holding lights, boxes, plugs and the camera, all nod and murmur assent.

'Aye aye, cap'n,' says Ron. 'Unhook us from the bank, would you?'

I don't move, having no idea where to start with that. Ron points and the camera operator, who is nearest to where he's pointing, unwinds a rope from the bow. From somewhere beneath my feet a rumble begins, and smoke rises from the back of the boat. I feel myself being swung sideways as we point into the centre of the Thames.

When we get to a spot which looks to me as if it's perfect for a full-on wide shot of the 'stage' set up on the pier, I shout to Ron to park it. He leans out of the cabin and shouts to me, 'We can't park here,' as if he's a bus driver and there's a warden coming.

'But it's perfect, I want to set up a shot,' I yell back, and shrug to the camera op, in an attempt at establishing a sense of camaraderie. He turns his eye to the viewfinder like he's seen nothing.

'Listen,' says Ron, who's stepped out of the cabin and alongside me on deck (NO-ONE'S DRIVING THE BOAT! I scream in my head). 'I can't just stop the boat mid-stream.'

'Why not? Are there lanes you're blocking or something?' I think I'm being funny. Ron doesn't.

He speaks slowly. 'I can't sit still in this spot, because the river won't let me. There are currents which eddy and cross all along the Thames, which is never still. I have to navigate the streams using the engine to fight against head-on and following currents. If I cut the engine here, you'll soon be facing the power station and not the pier. Get it?'

Tides, currents – it'll be bloody whirlpools next, I think, but say, 'Got it. OK Ron, what do we do then?'

Ron relaxes (but the boat STILL HAS NO DRIVER! I am thinking) and says, 'I can try to ride the currents here and stay in roughly the same proximity to the pier, but your shot's going to change as the tide comes in anyway.'

Not only did I not think about this, but I had no idea I'd need to think about it. 'Right,' I said being assertive in a way that I imagine film directors are. 'Let's go back to land and finish setting up the band's stuff on the pier. They should be here soon.'

Looking self-satisfied, Ron goes back to the cabin, and I call after him, 'Thanks, Ron. Just let me know when the best time to head out again is, would you?'

Somehow during our brief trip to the middle of the Thames, most of what had been passing as daylight had become twilight, and it looks as if we're going to be filming at night. In order to spend as little time on the river as I can, I decide to shoot the band from the bank, too, and on the pier itself. Glad that we brought arc lights and thinking that as long as the band are wearing black suits and white shirts as I asked, we might get a nice, moody, noir-like film (I was shooting on 16mm stock), I begin to enjoy my first official, expensive (a budget of £10,000 felt like Hollywood money back then) job as director.

And then it rains.

'Fuck me, Don, couldn't you have filmed us somewhere warm and dry?' Paul Simonon wasn't smiling when I got back to dry land.

'Hey, Don, me drums are not gonna get wet, are they?' Topper chews a thumb and looks annoyed.

'You seen Mick yet?' asks Joe, shoulders hunched into the collar of his big black overcoat.

'Haven't seen anyone yet, I've been out there looking at how great the stage looks,' I reply. 'When Mick gets here, we can have a run-through, yeah?'

Johnny Green, the band's road manager who'd set the stage up with the drums, amps and mic stands about ten hours earlier and had been there ever since keeping guard of the gear, leans over Topper's shoulder and says matter-of-factly, 'When Mick gets here – Baker's fetching him – we'll just shoot the fucker, shall we?'

'Suits me,' Paul shrugs.

It was raining really hard by the time Mick arrived wearing his best three-piece gangster suit, homburg and overcoat. Being as it was a 'performance' video The Clash decided to actually play the song through on the 'stage' of the pier, and I filmed one performance from the boat, two from the pier. Along with the set-up shots of the band walking (in Topper's case running, removing his jacket as he did so) out to the end of the pier, I didn't use too many reels of film. The weather turned into a special effect, with bursts of rain coming and going as we rolled, adding a dramatic atmosphere in the close-up shots. Although completely unplanned, I'll admit that the rain really added something to the video, and also helped to keep the shoot short. After three takes I just wanted to get out of there. Johnny Green felt likewise and was so fed up with his day's work that he minimised the amount of clearing up he had to do by throwing the hired monitor wedges into the Thames – they were not the band's property after all, so why should he haul them about? The band thought it was hilarious to watch the speakers floating down the river. It didn't seem so funny when they got the bill for them, though.

I am now told that the 'London Calling' video is a classic, and I'd agree that it was a textbook punk classic in as much as I managed to turn what could have been massive problems into assets. I was still learning as I went along in my usual punk rock spirit at a time when videos and promos were starting to become effects-driven. I was looking back further in time for inspiration, to old James Brown footage I'd seen on television in the 1960s and early 70s, where the focus is concentrated on the stage with a couple of cameras locked on to capture the performance, which really appealed to me. James Brown's presence alone was enough to hold you, and I knew from experience that The Clash were at their absolute best when they were performing, that they held an audience's attention completely.

My relationship with The Clash has proven to be among the most long-lasting and significant in my professional, public and private life.

More than forty years after directing that and all subsequent Clash videos, not to mention that photo of me appearing on The Clash's mini-album *Black Market Clash*, people still relate to me as a part of The Clash set-up, and I'm not complaining. The Clash have been an intermittent presence in my life since we first met, in the summer of 1976 when Joe and Paul started turning up at Acme Attractions. From behind the counter at Acme, with Tappa Zukie's 'MPLA Dub' booming out of the speakers, burning spliffs and holding my corner, I'd noticed the same white faces coming down to the basement, checking me out as I checked them out – specifically, John Lydon, Paul Simonon and Joe Strummer. Initially we said nothing to each other and just observed. Jeannette got to know them first, which naturally pissed me off, as I didn't want anyone to steal my thunder or my girlfriend. I sometimes think that if it had not been for Jeannette, I would have stayed like that. Eventually everyone dropped their guard and we started talking about reggae and dub music while sharing a spliff in the basement. Through our mutual love of Jamaican music I quickly became friendly with Lydon (or Rotten, as he was then better known), Strummer and Simonon, because they were already into reggae and seriously interested in the stuff I was pumping out. They were familiar with tracks like 'Liquidator' and 'Return Of Django' but wanted to know more about things I was playing like King Tubby and Lee Perry's heavy dub, Keith Hudson's *Pick A Dub*, a set of records called *African Dub Chapters 1, 2* and *3*, the Big Youth album *Dreadlocks Dread* and Tappa Zukie's *Man Ah Warrior*. *King Tubbys Meets Rockers Uptown* with Augustus Pablo was virtually my theme tune. The Clash guys liked the music that I was playing in the shop and that we had a shared interest. They dug the bass lines and the fact that the music was saying something. They didn't mind the weed either and we became friends, which eventually led to a working relationship.

I now regard The Clash, the band and musical and cultural phenomenon, as something like an old flame – I have memories connected with them that are alternately fond, confused, happy and sad; we were almost family at times. We had some exciting, exhilarating and raucous times together, but we also had some infuriating, irritating and dull times, too. There were periods when we've drifted apart and I didn't see Joe, Paul or Mick for a while. Topper disappeared almost completely for the longest time. But I always knew that they were there and around, and we'd meet up for old times' sake if not for work reasons.

The Clash's legend has grown into the very thing that in the beginning only they and Bernie their manager believed it to be: 'the only band that mattered'. All of The Clash had definite ideas about which cultural anti-heroes they wanted to be. In the beginning Joe was the original protest-singing folk-rocker, one part Woody Guthrie to three parts Elvis, Dylan and Johnny Cash. Mick was the thin, glam, guitar-slinging poser along the lines of Mick Ronson, Faces-era Ronnie Wood or Johnny Thunders. Paul was a bohemian artist-rebel without a cause, a mix of James Dean, young Marlon Brando and Clint Eastwood with a Brixton sensibility. Topper was a Bruce Lee fan and true Funk Brother along the lines of Richard 'Pistol' Allen or Clyde Stubblefield, a rocksteady, groovy beat driver who said little but kept it all together musically. They'd all go on to become their own mythic musical and culturally cool legends, of course, but in the beginning, that's who they were and I identified with each of those individual cultural touchstones. I knew about all of that stuff and had been listening, watching and grooving along with it ever since I could walk. Simply, we spoke the same language and grew up with the same cultural references.

It's unsurprising that I got to know Paul Simonon first – partly because of our mutual love of reggae but also because of the fact that he was almost my age and had grown up roaming the same streets, at the same time. Joe was slightly older and had a completely different upbringing, having gone to a boarding school from the age of 10, which was sited way out on the very edges of south-west London, in a big country house on sixty acres of nature reserve. Mick, although the same age as us and living in South London in the 1960s, had a different kind of upbringing in Tulse Hill, and he wasn't as free to roam the streets as Paul and I had been as kids. Topper, having grown up in Bromley, was a soulboy through and through until he joined The Clash in 1977, and while he and I could communicate well enough, we didn't share much of the same background apart from sweaty nights on the dancefloors of Essex and London, and both being big Bruce Lee fans.

Mick and Joe mostly got their musical education from the radio, television and friends' record collections, and, while so had Paul and I, we had the added bonus of hearing the sounds of Brixton front rooms in summer when windows were thrown open and families partied. We also witnessed sound systems run by men like my father playing in church halls and street parties. As teenagers we must have gone to some of the same blues parties around Brixton, although we never met. Once we'd become mates, Paul and I didn't spend hours talking about life, the universe and everything; instead, we spoke volumes to each other through the mix-tapes we'd exchange at Acme Attractions. Reggae was an integral ingredient of The Clash's music from their beginning, having come from Paul's insistence on practising bass along to reggae. Joe was also into the sounds emerging from Jamaica, and his interest in the scene and culture of reggae only deepened over the years – aided by the reggae albums he stole from me, which was probably my own fault. Not long after it had begun in 1976, I got hold of tapes of Mikey Dread's late-night radio show in Jamaica called *Dread at the Controls*, and I lent them to Paul. People in Kingston thought that whenever Mikey's show was broadcast live on the Jamaican Broadcasting Corporation the crime rate went down, because it kept people off the streets, it was that popular – Mikey championing 'Uptown Top Ranking' by Althea & Donna on the show made it an international hit. His knowledge, approach and experience of making reggae music would prove to be invaluable to The Clash when they asked him to record with them as they made *Sandinista!*, but evidence of their respect for reggae was seen even before it was heard. The 'White Riot' single picture sleeve and Sebastian Conran's photo and design for the 'Complete Control' single sleeve draw on reggae symbolism, the latter being a speaker cabinet with mesh removed just like all the sound systems he'd ever seen. People make quite a big deal out of the punky/reggae connection, but what were The Beatles and The Rolling Stones listening to? It was Black music. It's just that to the uninitiated it was not that obvious, but with The Clash it was right up front. It was in their lyrics, in their bass lines and their subject matter. Not only did The Clash cover Willie Williams' 'Armagideon Time', Junior Murvin's 'Police And Thieves' and Toots & The Maytals 'Pressure Drop', they namechecked Prince Far I on 'Clash City Rockers', Dr Alimantado on 'Rudy Can't Fail', The Abyssinians' 'Satta Massagana' on 'Jimmy Jazz', and Dillinger, Leroy Smart, Ken Boothe and Delroy Wilson on '(White Man) In Hammersmith Palais'.

Unlike the British beat bands of the 1960s, The Clash weren't fascinated by exotic sounds from a place they'd never experienced; they were listening to music from their own neighbourhood brought there by Afro-Caribbeans in the 1950s. Like me, they were influenced by their surroundings, and the music we heard wasn't disguised or an interpretation – it was the original. The Clash recreated the sound of the Thames delta rather than that of the Mississippi delta.

It made me immensely proud that my culture was being represented by these guys and not just faked into a pale imitation. With The Clash it was not white reggae; it was punk and reggae. Their songs brought some of their culture to my culture and vice versa. They attempted to draw parallels between the life experience of Black youth and white from their first release. 'White Riot' had been inspired by the Notting Hill Carnival of August 1976, during which Joe and Paul found themselves caught up in what became a running street battle between the police and Black youth. It had kicked off when police tried to arrest a pickpocket close to Portobello Road and several Black youths went to help him. Things rapidly escalated and it became a riot within minutes, spreading into adjacent streets. Vans of reserve police were called into the area and the notorious Special Patrol Group (SPG) summoned. Back then there was no specialist riot gear issued to the police, who carried only truncheons and wore tall helmets held on by a chinstrap, so those caught up in the front line of the bricks, bottles and anything else to hand as it rained down on them grabbed dustbin lids to protect themselves. Before the SPG arrived – carrying truncheons which were designed to not break if used with force (unlike standard-issue ones), wearing motorcycle helmets, padded jackets and carrying round, clear, hard plastic shields – a police van was set alight and the coppers sitting in it only just managed to get out before it was engulfed in flames. Over a hundred police officers had to be taken to hospital after the riot, and while many were released after treatment, twenty were kept in for observation or further treatment. Sixty carnival-goers were also taken to hospital and at least another sixty were arrested. At one point during the ruckus, Joe and Paul were sheltering behind an overturned car under the Westway, throwing rocks at the police, when Joe noticed that the petrol cap had come off the car, so he decided that they should set fire to it. Thankfully he couldn't get a match to catch before they were chased away by advancing lines of police, but they were just two of the many white youth right in there protesting alongside the Black youth, including myself, all sick to death of the sus law, of the restraints enforced by an uncomprehending and rigid society that saw us not as people but as 'others', a threat to their way of life.

I spent hours wandering around with my Super-8mm camera that day, torn between getting the shot and throwing a brick. The following day's press reports of the riot made it out to be part of a racial war and drew on past history of racial riots in the area, particularly those of 1958 when Teddy boys spent six nights invading Notting Hill to attack members of the Black community with weapons that included guns and knives, to support their headlines. But to my mind it was not a Black or white thing, it was a wrong or right thing; it was more about working-class people of all racial backgrounds being harassed by the police. Which is also what Joe thought, judging by the lyrics of 'White Riot'. He was saying, 'Look, our Black brethren have had enough, and they have done something about it.' The band might have thought to give the song a different title perhaps, because it was misinterpreted by right-wing idiots as being a call to arms for Nazis and adopted by various racist gangs as a theme song, but that was preposterous. The skinheads who started turning up and giving straight-arm Sieg Heil salutes at Clash gigs in the months following the single's release in March 1977 were always promptly kicked out. They finally got the message when The Clash headlined the Rock Against Racism Carnival in Victoria Park in April 1978.

As early as the White Riot tour of 1977 I was impressed that they had reggae played over the PA between sets (DJed by me) to crowds in more insular and less cosmopolitan parts of the UK. The only reason that I didn't work with The Clash much after the White Riot tour until the 'London Calling' video was because Joe and I had a falling out over Jeannette. She and I were a couple and, although we had arguments and periods when we might not get on, we worked and practically lived together, too. That was until one night in November 1977 when she accepted an offer from Sebastian Conran to ride on the back of his motorbike to Cambridge for a Clash gig. There's no room on the back of a bike for two and I was doing something else anyway, but when she returned the day after the gig, having stayed in the same hotel as the band, I had a bad bout of jealousy, and when she told me that she'd spent most of the night staying up with Joe 'just talking' I didn't believe her. My suspicions about the relationship between Jeannette and Joe hardened over the next few months and culminated in her telling me she couldn't stand it any longer and walking off down the King's Road one wet and rainy afternoon, leaving me in tears. Convinced that Joe had 'nicked' my girlfriend – as if I owned her! – I shouted after her that I didn't want to see her or Joe again. I meant it too, and subsequently missed the Rock Against Racism Carnival because The Clash were headlining. It took some time for emotions to settle; we were young and not mature enough to handle complications like that in any kind of sensible manner. I'm glad that Jeannette and Joe found some comfort with one another, however briefly (and it was brief), and that we all regained our friendship. But for weeks after it happened, I didn't want to see or hear about either of them.

I watched the progress of The Clash from a distance as they went through the music press backlash unleashed when they hired an American rock producer named Sandy Pearlman to make their second album, *Give 'Em Enough Rope*. Best known for his work with Blue Öyster Cult, Pearlman was a long-haired, flared-jean-wearing, laidback New Yorker who was flavour of the month with CBS America because of the huge hit he'd created for Blue Öyster Cult in '(Don't Fear) The Reaper'. The Clash's first album hadn't been released in America because it was 'too British' – with the result that it became the biggest-selling import album over there in 1977 – and the American arm of the company, being bigger and more important, wanted something from the band which would sound more American, i.e. slicker. As such, Pearlman was the embodiment of everything that punks reviled about the music biz. There was a lot of 'told you so' among the 'zine writers who'd slagged The Clash for signing with a major instead of an independent like Small Wonder or Rough Trade. They'd accused The Clash of 'selling out' by taking CBS money, and the weekly music papers (*NME*, *Sounds* and *Melody Maker*) were just as dismissive of the pairing of band and producer, even before they'd heard anything. Ironically, the first release that Pearlman worked on was not at all what was expected. Instead of smooth heavy metal with lots of overdubs, '(White Man) In Hammersmith Palais', which came out in June 1978, had a rocksteady riff and typically hoarse Strummer vocals. It's since become one of the band's most loved singles, of course, and in 2003 Mick, Paul, Topper and Terry Chimes chose it as number one on British music magazine *Uncut*'s list of The Clash's 30 Best Songs. The song had been written by Joe almost a year earlier after I'd taken him to a roots rockers, ghetto kind of show featuring Dillinger, Delroy Wilson, Ken Boothe and Leroy Smart at the Palais on June 5, 1977. The night was something of a shock to Joe because he didn't understand that the brothers back home in JA were not revelling in a ghetto lifestyle. To anyone living there, the ghetto is something that you get out of, not into, but Joe had a romanticised idea of what ghetto life was about. So, what he describes in the song was something quite glam and glitzy, not political – a night of dance music not rebel sounds, which he thought was somehow wrong and almost the antithesis of 'White Riot'. Still, despite being a criticism of the entertainment on show, the inclusion of the headliners' names in the lyrics meant they'd expanded their reach among the punk audience.

By the time 'Palais' was released both Joe and I had made our first trips to Jamaica, although not together. He and Mick flew out before Christmas 1977 so that Joe could get over a bout of glandular fever and they could write some songs. Paul was pissed off about the fact that they went without him, since he had the biggest collection of reggae albums and had pushed them to play it as a band. Mick and Joe were only there for ten days and stayed at the hotel for most of the time, swimming while it rained, amazed that it was still hot. They tried and failed to get hold of Lee Scratch Perry, who'd 'produced' 'Complete Control' a couple of months earlier in London, unable to find his studio. They walked around the harbour dressed like London punks (Joe reckoned the locals thought they were sailors, or madmen) and went to the cinema a lot. They never got near to seeing the Kingston that they thought they knew from songs. All of which was very different to the time I'd spent in JA with John Lydon in February 1978, of course. Joe and Mick got one song out of their trip: 'Safe European Home'. It might not sound too much like 'White Man', but both songs describe how Joe felt about his JA experiences, which wasn't great, according to 'Safe European Home', because he sings about not wanting to go back there again. I asked him why he wrote that when I first heard it, and he didn't have a good reason. All he could say was that he didn't mean it. That was the thing with Joe, he liked to be 'enigmatic'. Or just plain bloody-minded – take your pick.

In 1980 The Clash criss-crossed England, appearing live at as many mid-sized venues as they could on the 16 Tons tour. They asked me to direct a new video for a forthcoming single (not on any album) titled 'Bankrobber' while they were touring. Which is how I came to be standing with my hands up, facing armed police in Lewisham on the afternoon of February 18. The band were due to play at the Lewisham Odeon in south-east London that night and, having come up with a bank heist storyline for the promo, I co-opted the band's road manager Johnny Green and Topper's drum roadie Baker to 'star' in it.

We filmed the video in the afternoon before the gig once the backline had been set up. While the band were soundchecking I'd scouted a bank on Lewisham High Street earlier for a shot of Johnny and Baker jumping 'out' of the bank and planned an 'escape' route which would take them, wearing scarves as masks and Harrington jackets with huge

Chilling as Joe records vocals at Wessex Studios, 1980.   PENNIE SMITH

Clash badges on them, to the Odeon, where they'd buy tickets for the gig. I described it as a sort of Ealing comedy to the band, who were happy enough about it, especially since they only had to play the gig as they would anyway. I also filmed Joe in the studio recording the master vocal and intercut that into the story with a bit of live footage as they performed the song onstage with Mikey Dread. Having never done this sort of thing before, I didn't ask anyone's permission to film on the street in broad daylight, and since we only used a single camera didn't think it'd be a problem. The reaction shots of shoppers on a busy high street on a Saturday afternoon as Johnny and Baker run past them at top speed add a touch of reality to the thing. Clearly no-one in Lewisham apart from a couple of Clash fans had any idea what was going on, which may account for what happened after we'd done a couple of takes of the 'robbers' emerging from the bank. We moved around the corner to the back of the Odeon, to film the 'robbers' buying tickets for the gig, and as Baker and Green ran to the back door of the Odeon for the third or fourth time, two police cars came screeching around the corner with their sirens blaring. Armed police jumped out and had Johnny, Baker and me pinned against the wall. It took him some time, but eventually Johnny persuaded them that we were art students working on a project. The ridiculous masks and bags of 'money', which were full of socks, helped I think. As it turned out, whoever had called the police did us a favour, because the story of our being held at gunpoint while making a pop video made all the music papers. CBS were delighted with the publicity, and the band had no trouble getting them to hire me to direct their next video that year, for 'The Call Up' (from *Sandinista!*).

Being an anti-war song about dodging the draft, we originally wanted to shoot the video in a cemetery, but having learned my lesson with 'Bankrobber', I applied for permission and the local council refused. Instead we ended up shooting at former sixties pop star Chris Farlowe's warehouse, which was full of military memorabilia and equipment, of which he was a renowned collector and dealer. Joe, Mick and Paul stood on various military vehicles of different types and ages, and we set Topper's drum kit up on a truck half-hidden behind a huge field gun. The band decided to wear various bits of old uniform that were also stored there, creating something of a bizarre sight – Topper became a Spitfire pilot, Paul wore a cowboy hat and parachute harness, Mick had a wide-brimmed cavalry hat, goggles and enormous leopard-skin poncho (I have no idea why). He and Joe both wore big pouch belts across their chest. I intercut the performance with a storyline in which Paul played a draft dodger, nailing up his letterbox (so the call-up telegram can't come through his door) and Topper escapes Military Police officers down a metal fire escape. Because everything in the warehouse was WWII-issue, the film was shot in grainy black and white, and I opened and closed it with 1940s-style film of air-raid sirens being sounded as if during the Blitz.

Making videos with The Clash was usually fairly painless because they knew what they wanted, but they'd also take suggestions on what might be added to their ideas. The first three videos we made together had worked out pretty well, so it seemed natural that I'd make more with them. Luckily for me, that would mean filming in another city, on another continent.

The City Knows

Exterior. Night. 42nd Street by Times Square, New York, New York. Imagine it as a 1940s black-and-white noir thriller, with Richard Widmark leading Linda Darnell toward Hell's Kitchen along rain-washed sidewalks, followed by a stranger, new to the city, peering left and right as he advances along the famous old street of dreams, toward the Great White Way. Every alley the stranger glances down looks like a set for a Weegee still photo of a crime scene. Towering buildings obstruct a moon eagerly playing hide-and-seek behind dark clouds blown by an ill wind. It's late, past midnight. Cut to a Martin Scorsese movie of the late 1970s. Yellow cabs trundle slowly past, axles wincing as they hit uneven manhole covers, subway vents and potholes. Drivers in shadow turn their heads slowly to watch all the animals who come out at night. Lit by theatre foyers and movie houses, closed stores with lights left on all night and pharmacies doing brisk business, couples and small groups of people stroll about as if it were midday. They're dressed for summer in billowing T-shirts, knee-length cargo pants, hi-top sneakers and baseball caps. A group of kids in Knicks vests, cigarettes glowing like tracer bullets, nod, dip and weave across the path of the stranger. One of the kids is carrying an enormous ghetto-blaster tape machine on his shoulder, blaring something that the stranger can't hear, because he's wearing a small set of metallic headphones over his dreadlocks, which are pulled back in a knot. He can hear booms, scratched breaks and a hip-hop style chanting over bass-heavy beats and tinny hi-hat, even with his own Walkman turned up loud.

'New York, just as I imagined it, skyscrapers and everything,'
I think.

Living For The City.

I've spent my life enamoured of Americana, and finally here I am
living it, breathing in the peculiar scent of subway, trash, petrol,
cigarettes and eight million stories in the naked city. I'm listening
to a brand-new sound on the Walkman cassette player tonight, one
of my first in New York. It's 'The Adventures Of Grandmaster Flash
On The Wheels Of Steel' and I can't help but think it the perfect
soundtrack to my late-night strolls around Manhattan. The mixture
of excitement and danger, Hispanics and Blacks, movie theatres
showing kung fu, porn and horror triple bills, yellow cabs, hos and
dealers all fighting for space can be heard in the jangling, bubbling
samples as they smack into the Grandmaster's beats. Times Square
is populated with drug pushers, prostitutes, muggers and break-
dancers 24/7, all looking like they're extras in a Scorsese movie –
which they were, of course, because the director used them and the
area as backdrops to the action in *Mean Streets*, *Taxi Driver* and
The King of Comedy. In the future, Times Square, all cleaned up and
family-friendly, will be even more sterile than London's Piccadilly
Circus. The two tourist traps will share a lot of the same stores and
kinds of visitors, all buying souvenirs made in Thailand, umbrellas
made in China and mobile phone cases made in South Korea. But on
this night in May 1981, in Times Square, you can buy H, pills, grass,
pleasure and pain twenty-four hours a day, none of it advertised on
billboards.

I was in New York with The Clash, who'd taken me along to document on
film their 'taking' of New York. In December 1980 they'd released the
triple album priced as a single, *Sandinista!* Months were spent writing
and recording the album in London, Manchester, Kingston Jamaica,
and New York, and the range of styles and sounds on the album show
the influences of their surroundings, from Mikey Dread in JA, to Futura
2000 and Fab Five Freddy in NY. Every member of the band had their
own romance going on with the Big Apple, and that played out in the
music. Mick loved the sounds coming out of the Bronx or Harlem and

added a lot of hip-hop, dance rhythms and breaks to his new songs, while Joe and Topper loved the city for its constant edge, sounds and experiences on offer all hours of the day. Because *London Calling* had been reviewed well in America, they were ambitious to conquer New York and make it there because, to paraphrase the song (coincidentally written, recorded and released at the same time as 'London Calling'), then they could make it anywhere.

Originally booked to play seven shows at an old ballroom on Times Square called Bonds Casino, plans had to change on the first night when it became clear that the owners had oversold tickets, and the city fire and safety officers shut the place down. The band could either cancel the shows and refund everyone or add extra appearances to cover demand. Naturally they went for the second option, and ended up playing seventeen shows back to back, sometimes twice a day. The demand for tickets had grown long before The Clash arrived in New York because their 'Magnificent Dance' single, a remix of 'Magnificent Seven' inspired by the first rap 12-inch to crossover commercially, The Sugarhill Gang's 'Rapper's Delight', had been played constantly on the Black radio station WBLS. Preceding Blondie's 'Rapture' hit by several months and Grandmaster Flash's 'The Message' by two years, Frankie Crocker from WBLS mixed a version of 'Magnificent Dance' and overdubbed bits of dialogue from the movie *Dirty Harry* with lines from Bugs Bunny cartoons. The station played the remix constantly for the first half of the year, gaining a new audience of B-Boy Clash fans and high demand for tickets for the Bonds shows.

The shows promised to be the usual Clash mix of cultures and musical genres because they liked to do things differently to most guitar bands. Suicide, Bo Diddley and Joe Ely had been support acts on UK and European tours, and for Bonds they asked a bunch of different acts to play support on different nights, among them Grandmaster Flash, The Treacherous Three, Sugarhill Gang, Mikey Dread, Lee Perry, Bad Brains, Dead Kennedys, The Fall and even Allen Ginsberg reading his poetry (which Paul was not too mad about). Whatever they might say, the band had benefited from the influence of Bernard Rhodes. He was not the puppet master that he might want people to think, but his knowledge of underground cultures that went before definitely gave The Clash more depth to their music and shows than other punk bands.

They could see the tradition they were following and made music as a way of communicating ideas and protest, rather than just wanting to sell records. The Clash's audience in New York was mostly made up of white rock fans, though, and many of them weren't ready for a musical education, even if it was being presented by their heroes. The white rock fan experience of Black music in America at that time came from mainstream acts like The Commodores and Earth, Wind & Fire or from disco music, because that was the only kind which got airplay. While The Clash were hoping to turn downtown New York on to something that was going on in their own backyard, the audience simply weren't interested. On one night at Bonds, Grandmaster Flash was bottled off the stage, which enraged Mick so much that he went out and shouted at the crowd, 'How dare you? Not only are you disrespecting our guests, you're fucking disrespecting us too!'

Mick's love for the New York hip-hop sound meant The Clash took to it in the same way they had reggae, and a lot of Sugarhill Records' output found its way into both Strummer's and Jones' record collections within weeks of release. It's little wonder that 'This Is Radio Clash' got onto both the Club Play and Mainstream Rock *Billboard* charts when released at the end of 1981, because not only was it recorded in New York, but it sounded just like New York.

Since The Clash knew (or thought they knew) New York from paying close attention to the movies made there, the idea of making a movie of their trip seemed an entirely natural one. The title was agreed before we left London: *Clash on Broadway* – so-called because Bonds was on the Broadway corner of Times Square and because it paid homage to the song 'On Broadway', as well as referencing all the musicals of the thirties, forties and fifties in which Broadway played a part (I reckon *42nd Street* is probably the pick of them).

The Clash intended to finance the film from the proceeds of the New York shows, and they wanted it to be as much about the city as about them. It was a kind of redistribution of funds, taking from the fans and putting them into a film, which might tell them something about their own city that they didn't already know. In 1981 the graffiti and hip-hop scene was still largely underground (except when the subway trains ran overground, of course... sorry), but The Clash wanted to explore the hard, dirty, stinking underbelly of New York. Which is why, during the day and after the Bonds shows, we filmed all around New York, and not just Manhattan.

I filmed Joe talking to a scat singer on a street corner, Mick engrossed by the whole hip-hop thing watching B-Boys breakdancing and the sun coming up over Coney Island. There was other footage of Nuyoricans street singing, Futura 2000 shoplifting paint and creating his art, Paul getting tattooed, protesters shouting at police, members of the NYPD with guns on rooftops, locals hanging out of windows and walking the streets, graffitied trains running through projects, the band skanking round town with skyscrapers in the background, and hanging out under Brooklyn Bridge at night, chewing the fat. I wanted to capture each band member's relationship with New York, but it wasn't easy – at the time Topper had certain needs that New York (and the Bowery in particular) proved spectacularly easy to satisfy. One night I asked to follow him and managed to film a candid conversation in the back of a cab on the way. I wasn't going to put a camera in the places Topper was heading for, and that taxi ride was the only way to get him to talk. I can only assume that the people he copped from knew who he was, because it was almost impossible not to know about The Clash in New York that month. They were constantly on the local news network and all the rock and dance radio stations. The near riot which occurred when police on horseback had to control the crowds in Times Square who were blocking traffic made the front page of the *New York Daily News*. After that, The Clash had the metaphorical keys to the city and could get into any club for free.

The full film has never been seen by anyone, though, because it was never properly finished. Bernard Rhodes put the negatives into a lab in NYC but didn't pay the bill, so after a few years the lab destroyed them. Luckily, years later I found a rough cutting copy of *Clash on Broadway* tucked away in a cupboard and managed to include some of it in the *Westway to the World* DVD.

The 'Radio Clash' video was supposed to be a kind of trailer for the *Broadway* film, which is as much about New York as it is about the band. The Clash loved *Mean Streets* and *Taxi Driver* and when director Martin Scorsese and Robert De Niro came to Bonds on a couple of occasions, naturally they were welcomed backstage to meet everyone. They were in the city making *King of Comedy* with Jerry Lewis and invited everyone to visit the set on 5th Avenue. Seeing the band there the following day, Scorsese had the bright idea of including them in a scene for which they're credited as 'street scum'. I'd love to say that I'm also in *King of Comedy*, but despite my name being on the credits (albeit as *Dom* Letts) I was not. The band's Black bodyguard Ray Jordan is in there and he's mistakenly identified as me – or rather a brother named Dom. Backstage at Bonds was the closest I'd been to Scorsese since 1977, when Jeannette and I shared an otherwise empty viewing theatre in Soho with him. He'd been in town and asked for a private viewing of *The Punk Rock Movie*, which I was so fired up about that I managed to garble about three words to him.

Not all great directors had that effect on me, though. A few years later one paid me a real big compliment, of sorts. At dinner during a film festival in Milan where the video for 'Radio Clash' was shown, I was introduced to the great Federico Fellini. When told who I was he smiled and said, 'Hai la visione di un terrorista.' Not understanding what he'd said, I smiled and walked off to find someone who could translate for

With the great Federico Fellini in Milan.

me. A waiter obliged: 'You have the vision of a terrorist.' For which I can only say, 'Grazie, Federico.'

While I was still in New York and editing *Clash on Broadway* before Bernie lost the film, I met Charlie Ahearn who was working on *Wild Style*, the first and best movie about graffiti and hip-hop, in the editing suite next door. I went to see the final scenes of his film being shot at the Coney Island Amphitheater (now demolished and replaced with a covered one) and it reminded me of Walter Hill's *The Warriors* (1979), only with a better soundtrack and everyone was a genuine B-Boy or graffito, not a paid extra. *Wild Style* showed off the language, style, moves, art, culture and attitude of hip-hop and it struck me how similar it was to punk, in offering an alternative to AOR and FM-friendly pop which dominated American airwaves and said nothing to people who lived among inner-city ruins in places like the Bronx. As with punk, kids from the Bronx who had nothing were coming up with the most interesting ideas despite their economic and social situations, out of necessity.

In the final years of the 1970s the Bronx had looked like a European city of 1945. Slum clearance decimated streets and left them looking like bomb sites, undeveloped because the city entered bankruptcy in 1975 and cut staff and services so harshly that no-one could service building, social care or community projects. Smack shooting galleries were set up in semi-derelict buildings along part-empty streets dotted with burned-out cars where once families and communities thrived. Smoke continually drifted from various parts of the borough as landlords burned out residents who had nowhere to go and couldn't afford the rent – the buildings' owners invariably sold the ruins to project housing constructors who put up shoddy, dangerous units, many of which lasted barely a decade. The rot had started with the building of the Bronx Expressway, which began in 1959 and opened ten years later. To build it the city cleared away some nice-looking, large brownstone houses and wide streets, local businesses and stores, and scattered the middle-class community of largely African-Americans who'd settled there in the wake of WWII. Now, with the area open to any and all criminal activities (the NYPD had unofficially declared the South Bronx a no-go area), gangs had taken on the 'running' of the area, and one – calling themselves the Ghetto Brothers – took a lead from the Black Panthers in Oakland, California, by setting up community outreach programmes and giving drug dealers a hard time. The average family in the Bronx had only $5,200 to live on per year if they were lucky, and cases of malnutrition and infant mortality were seriously high. Despite, or perhaps because of, all of that, hip-hop emerged from the Bronx and similarly suffering Harlem, before moving downtown via New York trendies and The Clash.

When Strummer, Jones, Simonon and Headon left New York, I decided to stick around and experience what was happening for as long as I could afford it. There was a 'punky hip-hop' thing going on, with like-minded people getting it on and making rebel sounds just as they had in London, 1977. The hip-hop scene had roots in Jamaica, inspired by the rapping style of Jamaican toasters, which was ironic since the Jamaican DJs had originally been inspired by American jocks broadcasting out of Miami in the late fifties. The Bronx pioneer Kool Herc, credited as being the father of hip-hop and coming up with the B-Boy tag, was born in Jamaica in 1955 and moved to New York in 1967. Having seen enough JA sound systems to know how to build one, Herc worked twin decks powered from lamp posts and put on block parties in the projects where he lived. Surprisingly, the cops turned a blind eye to him stealing NYC power, but that was probably because they knew where everyone would be when one was on. Herc's parties inspired countless rappers and DJs, including Grandmaster Flash, who worked cuts and spin-backs into his DJing after watching Herc in action, Grand Wizzard Theodore, who developed scratching and 'needle pick-up' skills with his own sound system, and Afrika Bambaataa. Herc's contribution was cultural, creative and hugely inspirational.

I found lodgings downtown on Orchard Street between the Lower East Side and Chinatown, sharing with a guy called Peter Dougherty, an American who I'd met in Acme Attractions in 1975. He was into exploring dub reggae and we traded tapes, his being made up of Patti Smith, Ramones and Television tracks. When he got back to New York, Peter sent me tapes by the Harlem World Crew and from the Disco Fever club in the South Bronx. When I got there, he introduced me around his scene, which I thought wasn't too dissimilar to the one back in London. When Mick came back to New York toward the end of 1981 we started hanging out at a guy called Gerb's apartment on St Mark's

Place. That was where all the graffiti artists would meet up in the kind of cultural exchange I'd created in Forest Hill after Roxy gigs. Gerb put a lot of people together who went on to enjoy long-lasting friendships and working relationships that produced some great work, like Fab Five Freddy and Debbie Harry. Freddy took Debbie to hip-hop events in New York at the end of the seventies, much in the same way that I had taken Ari, Lydon and Strummer to reggae sessions in London. Subsequently, Blondie's 'Rapture' became probably the first 'rap' mainstream music fans heard on release in January 1981. Malcolm McLaren's 'Buffalo Gals' video – inspired by his visit to a Bambaataa block party – introduced the world to the look, moves and style of the NY scene in 1982. Malcolm claimed that Bambaataa was wearing a Never Mind The Bollocks T-shirt when he first saw him, and it's certainly true that Bambaataa had the idea of merging punk and hip-hop. Of course, the Black youth thought Bambaataa was crazy in the beginning, which I understood because that was what my Rasta brethren thought about me playing reggae and dub at the Roxy, but he did it when John Lydon worked with him on Time Zone's 'World Destruction' single in 1984.

By the end of the seventies the hip-hop scene was well established in the Bronx and Harlem at Disco Fever and Harlem World, but during my stay in New York it migrated downtown, eventually finding its way to the Roxy in Chelsea, via Club Negril on 2nd Avenue, between 11th and 12th Streets. Negril had one of the best sound systems in New York, which frequently belted out cutting-edge underground reggae and dub (Bob Marley used to visit whenever he was in New York), but late in 1981 it became the hippest place downtown when it started playing hip-hop. Negril's hip-hop success was in no small part due to the work of an Englishwoman named Ruza Blue, who had originally planned on visiting New York for a two-week holiday but, after meeting someone who worked for Malcolm and Vivienne, ended up managing and representing their fashion empire in New York (out of their Worlds End 2 store on Prince Street). After a few visits to Negril, Ruza persuaded the owner to let her put on a club night that she'd run, and which would be new and different to the usual dub and reggae nights the club was known for. Having met and been hugely impressed by Bambaataa and the Rock Steady Crew when they supported Malcolm's Bow Wow Wow at the Ritz in September 1981, Ruza asked if they'd DJ and perform at her club night. They agreed and, knowing that it wasn't going to be easy to get a crowd for Bambaataa and co. downtown, she put out flyers stating that The Clash were going to be guest DJs for the opening night on January 7, 1982. They were in the city at the time recording but none of the band were at the club; instead, it was Kosmo Vinyl, Clash road manager and sidekick, and DJ Scratchy Sounds (Barry Myers) who worked as warm-up DJ for the band when they toured after I'd stopped doing it. The crowds poured in, saw Bambaataa and the crew in action and went home buzzing. After a brief write-up in *The New York Times* on February 26, 1982 ('Thursday night is the best night for Negril... organised by a young Englishwoman who calls herself Blue, the Rock Steady Crew or the Funky Four Plus One from the South Bronx come down to perform a type of dancing called breaking'), Negril drew white folk unlikely to travel into any of the Black areas of New York for a night out. They'd get to groove with members of what later became the Beastie Boys and Public Enemy, and see kids spraying, breaking and popping on the dancefloor.

Every time I visited (once or twice with Jeannette and Lydon who were also living in New York at the time, once early on with Mick Jones) the energy was electric, and as the word spread via the *Times* people from every borough started to turn up, engendering a cultural diversity that had been missing on the scene up to that point. Rick Rubin met Russell Simmons there and not long after decided to take hip-hop to the masses with their Def Jam label.

Negril was a fairly small basement club and easily filled to bursting, so in May 1982 Ruza moved her Wheels of Steel club night to Danceteria, which had just expanded from four floors to six (she took over one of them). A month later she moved again, to a former roller-disco joint called the Roxy at 515 West 18th Street which she didn't need to share with other club promoters, and from there the scene really grew. The place was enormous but after a slow start it was filled on nights when talent supplied by Rock Steady's manager Michael Holman – the man who'd initially introduced Malcolm around the NY scene – spun the decks. The first few events featured mixed media in an attempt to get people in and *The Great Rock 'n' Roll Swindle* (1980) was screened before DJ sets by Jazzy Jay one night, while Soulsonic Force, Run DMC and Kurtis Blow all made appearances. Jon Baker, the founder of Gee Street Records, worked the door and on any given night graffiti artists would paint big canvasses while DJs spun tunes on the stage in the middle of the dancefloor as B-Boys did their thing all around it. Posses who loved the culture on display from the Bronx, Queens and Harlem were all in the house. It became the de facto headquarters of the complete subculture of New York hip-hop, with its own dress code, filmmakers, artists and photographers. The graffiti artists who performed at the Roxy gained enough notoriety that soon East Village walls became giant canvases displaying writers' tags. Naturally that attracted the attention of the mainstream press (in the form of the *New York Post*), and following on from that came 'name' stars who loved a bit of notoriety – with Studio 54 now considered passé, where else could Jagger and Madonna mix on the dancefloor with 'real' folks?

With the Roxy's success and expansion through graffiti into midtown streets, it didn't take long for war to be declared on street art by NYC Mayor Ed Koch. Harsh punishments were promised to anyone caught graffitiing any public or private property. But when Patti Astor (who had a lead part in Charlie Ahearn's *Wild Style*) opened the Fun Gallery in 1981 at a tiny space at 229 East 11th Street, she exhibited graffiti artists alongside emerging 'fine' artists like Keith Haring and the great Jean-Michel Basquiat.

I first met Basquiat at the Fun Gallery, and we gave each other the look that brothers on the mostly white scene used to show mutual respect. We met a few times after that and one time he visited me in London. I really wanted to buy one of his works but didn't have the $5,000 he quoted me (and that was a mate's rate, believe me), which is one of my lasting regrets. After his death I was kind of stunned to discover that he'd put my name in the centre of one of his works, and that my name and phone number are in one of his notebooks. I only wish we'd had time to become better friends, but he died of an overdose in 1988, aged 27.

When Astor put the graffiti artists in her gallery the scene quickly attracted serious collectors and upmarket art dealers, giving them status and credibility. Fun Gallery put on shows by old- and new-school writers like Phase 2, Lee Quiñones, Iz the Wiz and Lady Pink alongside sculptors that the graffiti writers dug, like Obdewl X (aka Kiely Jenkins).

There were also installations by Dondi White and Kenny Scharf – it was a cool place.

That same summer of 1981, hip-hop reached one of the prime spots for New York's dancing elite, when the Lincoln Center at West 65th and Columbus Avenue staged a breakdance competition between the Rock Steady Crew and the Dynamic Rockers, with graffiti writer Rammellzee as compère. I went along and it seemed like the whole of the Bronx had invaded Manhattan. Thousands of Black and Hispanic B-Boys and fly-girls, dressed to impress, crowded the area. We're talking fat laces, Adidas shell-toe trainers, Kangols and those funny Italian glasses without the lenses. Symbols of cultural and social identities were manifest in articles of clothing and accessories. Some of the B-Boys stuffed their Kangol hats with plastic bags to get the same puffy aesthetic as dreads got with their headgear, others wore their jeans low on the hips, trainers unlaced in an attempt to look as if they'd just come out of prison. If you were unlucky enough to end up in jail at Rikers Island, laces and belts were removed as a matter of course (reason being that they could be used for suicide or attacks on inmates and guards). The clothing styles of outlaw gangs, mobsters, pimps, sports celebrities, actors and martial artists were also thrown into the equation as the B-Boys and B-Girls customised their sneakers to give them their own identity. For most of those kids, funds were tight, and they had no choice but to mix and match and create their own unique style of dress – which was much the same DIY ethic as punk.

The atmosphere at the Lincoln Center that day was tense. The competition was chaotic with the judges unable to see the dance action because of the circle of youths taunting whoever was doing their thing on the floor. All I could see were sneakers spinning in the air. The judges eventually gave up and the Rock Steady Crew won by decree of crowd noise. After the show there were some smashed windows in the surrounding (Upper West Side) vicinity and a few hot dog stands pushed over, but it wasn't exactly a riot, and it'd been amazing to witness such an event. That day, hip-hop and B-Boy culture really made its presence felt in Manhattan, and fittingly the event was reviewed by *National Geographic* magazine – proof if needed that hip-hop was of major anthropological importance.

Toward the end of 1981, The Clash returned to New York to work on what would become their fifth album, *Combat Rock*, at Electric Lady Studios in Greenwich Village. I was living in Spanish Harlem on the Upper East Side with a statuesque Viennese blonde named Constantine at the time. We had a lot of fun together until her father discovered that she was sharing an apartment with a Black man. Then he flew over and dragged her back to Austria.

The Clash stayed at their favourite midtown hotel, the Iroquois, a renowned rock 'n' roll hotel best known for being the place where James Dean used to stay when in the city, and within easy walking distance of Times Square. I spent a fair bit of time with Mick and Joe in the bar before going to clubs and places we'd got to know well. They were determined to get back to London for Christmas, though, and when they returned to the UK, I went with them.

I stayed in London in January 1982 when The Clash flew out for a five-week tour of Australia, New Zealand, Japan and Thailand – where Pennie Smith took the photo of the band on railway tracks which would become the cover image for *Combat Rock*. That tour was apparently a stressful slog, and at some point during it Topper was given an ultimatum to clean up his act and quit smack or quit the band. He didn't leave then and helped to finish the album with the band back in the UK, but before its release in May 1982 Topper was sacked. That same month the band set off on a seven-month tour of America and Europe with the original Clash drummer Terry Chimes in place of Topper. They started in Amarillo, Texas, in May and by June 8 were in Austin, Texas, where I joined them to make a video for the second single from *Combat Rock*, 'Rock The Casbah' – which ironically had been largely written by Topper. Maybe because of the internal troubles or the gruelling touring schedule they'd been on, there hadn't been a video for the album's first single 'Know Your Rights' (released in April), and it hadn't charted anywhere. That must have been seen by CBS as proof of the ever-growing influence that MTV was exerting over buyers, and why a video was needed for 'Casbah'.

I'd heard the song of course and read the lyrics and along with the band decided to create a story in which Jews and Arabs got along. I thought that was a brave move for The Clash, considering what could be shown on MTV and what couldn't. For the narrative I hired actors to play an Arab in traditional dress and a secular Jew with hat and peyot, and put them together in a white open-top Cadillac with cattle horns on the front fender. I filmed them breaking all kinds of taboos besides them just getting along: drinking alcohol, eating hot dogs, buying gas and dancing together by a swimming pool. I also decided to film an armadillo (officially the state animal of Texas) running around, because I'd never seen one and wanted to. I was told by the keeper that in order to get the creature to move I had to crawl along backwards, blowing on its face, pretending to be the wind (I was also told not to turn them on their back or they'll piss on you). I filmed the armadillo running along a line of fans waiting outside the Coliseum in Austin where the band were due to play and discovered that most Texans have never seen an armadillo either, or at least not a live one. They're usually only spotted as roadkill or turned into ashtrays, apparently. The sight of me, the Arab, the Jew and armadillo driving around in the cattle-horned Cadillac was the most talked about news items for a week in Austin. The rest of the video featured the band 'playing' in front of an oil derrick. While we were setting up a simple one-camera direct-to-band set, I was amazed to see Mick walk toward me wearing red long johns and black DM boots. Apparently he was pissed off about something that day, so I had to pull him to one side and say, 'Look Mick, you look like a matchstick, and don't forget film lasts forever, so if you look like a cunt today, you'll look like one forever.' He thought briefly before returning to the trailer dressing room to put on some combat gear. However, he was determined to keep his face fully covered with a camouflage net attached to a baseball cap as a protest (which Joe forcibly pulled off in the video). The performance shoot was great, just as it always was with them. They were like four sticks of dynamite. On the cue of 'ACTION' they went off, and it looks as if they're playing in front of thousands, not just a camera, a skeleton film crew and an armadillo. Despite the irreverence of the video it got enough airplay on MTV to lift the single into the Top 10 in America later that month. Its success had an unfortunate consequence, though, when eight years later and despite the intention of the song's lyrics to encourage inter-faith cooperation, 'Rock The Casbah' was used by the US military in the first Gulf War as a rallying cry for troops going into battle. An ironic and arguably more insulting use of the number came in 1993, when the FBI played it at full volume throughout the night during a stand-off with the religious sect Branch Davidians in Waco, Texas. Both prime examples of left-wing political statements being hijacked, distorted and completely misunderstood by governing authorities.

After a two-day shoot for 'Casbah', I returned to London, but I wasn't finished working with the band that year and was with them again in New York in October 1982. I was there to film them playing at the largest venue they'd appeared in yet, Shea Stadium. The Clash were supporting The Who on a few American dates, and the home of the New York Mets baseball team was the most prestigious. Being a huge Beatles fan I leapt at the chance to film at the same place that the Fab Four had made famous around the world when they played there in 1965 – I'd never heard of Shea until then, and I'm sure most people outside of North America hadn't either. I had permission from the promoter and headliners to shoot what would be the video for the next Clash single release, 'Should I Stay Or Should I Go', at the gig, although that didn't mean everything would go smoothly. For a start, whenever The Who came out of their dressing room everyone had

Kung fu and cake with Andy Warhol, backstage at Shea Stadium, 1982. BOB GRUEN

strict instructions to back off about thirty yards or something, which was fucking ridiculous when you're in charge of a film crew who're not interested in them anyway. They also wouldn't let The Clash have as much sound volume onstage as them when playing, which was a typical headline act's way of letting the support act know who's boss. Not that the people who'd travelled all the way out to Flushing Meadows to see the support act noticed. As can be seen from my video, plenty of Clash fans had a wild time during their performance. I had a great time, too – I got to film from a helicopter for the first time, and managed a two-car tracking sequence with me filming as we drove alongside the drop-top Cadillac with The Clash perched on the back seat looking chilly while we travelled through Queens to the gig. Later backstage, I jokingly told Andy Warhol that there was LSD in a cake, which I'd spotted him eating. Bob Gruen took a photo of us from that night with Andy looking terrified as I mug for the camera, which must have been about the time I'd told him about the acid-laced cake. He flipped, left early, and I felt really bad about that, until I thought about it more. Warhol was a trickster, possibly the most famous art world trickster there was, and I'd tricked him. In a short space of time I'd gone from being a rube constantly looking up at skyscrapers as I wandered through Manhattan, to freaking out the man who virtually invented pop art and made New York the coolest place to be in the 1960s and 70s. I'd been living for the city just like Stevie sang.

Adventures in Music Television

Interior. Day. New York. A small, grey, nondescript room with an empty desk in front of which are two slightly wobbly typist chairs, their arms at different levels, a castor missing from one. The door is set into a glass wall covered by dusty, closed blinds; the other three walls are bare but for a *National Geographic* calendar showing the month of June 1982 beneath a colour photo of an ostrich with its head in the ground. A large, grey push-button dial telephone with a dozen lights unlit beneath the handset is positioned at the outer edge of the desk, which takes up almost the whole of the wall opposite the thin, dark veneered door. Behind the desk a small rectangular window looks out at the rooftops and blank corporate office buildings lining Broadway and Times Square beyond. Enter the room a short, white male, balding, about 28 years old, wearing a large-shouldered, light blue seersucker sports coat with the sleeves rolled back. He's wearing a white T-shirt under the jacket, tucked into the elastic waistband of stonewashed denim jeans, rolled up to show off a pair of that year's most expensive sneakers, Nike Air Force 1s in bright white and dark blue. They look box-fresh. He's wearing a badge pinned to his left lapel that says in bright red letters, 'MTV'. Mr MTV holds the door open and sweeps his arm in to the room ahead of [enter] a Black male wearing dark glasses, loose dreadlocks, a well-worn black leather Schott Perfecto jacket, Levi 501 jeans, white T-shirt and biker boots, carrying a badge on which is printed 'MTV – visitor'.

'So, Don, er... take a seat... maybe not that one...'

I sit on the least-damaged-looking chair and feel like I know where this is going. Mr MTV sits on the edge of the desk and pulls his jean leg up better to show off his Nikes. He's embarrassed, so I decide to fuck with him a bit.

'Nice shoes, man, what they cost you?' I reach out as if to touch them and he instinctively pulls his leg away and laughs in an embarrassed way.

'About ninety bucks. They're new, can you tell? I reckon they'll be everywhere soon, but these are early issue.'

'I bet they are, and I bet you get all the cool stuff first, right, and a lot of freebies?'

Mr MTV shifts uneasily on the edge of the desk, not sure if I'm fucking with him. 'Well, working here, which is kinda like the music business, you know, we get lots of free stuff – but I bought these.'

'Cool, I get you,' I smile. 'Hey, I'm heading over to the Bronx later to meet with some brothers and Kool Herc, I bet he'd love a pair of those. You wanna come, maybe?'

His eyes widen, his mouth goes all tight-lipped and his body stiffens. 'Uh, yeah, maybe, look, the reason we asked you here was because as you know we all love your work – that Psychedelic Furs' one, "Sister Europe", and the Public Image were fantastic, but The Clash "London Calling" and "Call Up" were classic film nwah!' (I think he means noir.)

I interrupt with a friendly smile. 'Cool, so when are we doing the interview?'

Mr MTV sits perfectly still, his mouth slightly open. He's frowning, eyes now fixed on the bright white of his foot. He speaks quietly. 'Look, Don, I don't know how to tell you this, but we didn't know you were Black.' He glances up at me as I whip off my dark glasses and hold them in my left hand, which is extended out in front of me.

'Yep, always was, always will be!'

I knew this was coming, I'd known it ever since I'd entered the reception and announced my name to the starch-stiff, highly hair-sprayed woman on the desk. She'd actually loosened her high-necked Laura Ashley flower-print dress as she spoke into the phone, eyes averted. When Mr MTV came into reception and first saw me, his smile wavered, his step faltered and he didn't know whether to shake my hand or lay some skin on me. It was classic white middle-class unease at my being Black. I should have known: I'd lived in New York long enough to know what was what by this point. Still, I'd expected a bit better than to be hustled quickly into a side room at the back of the building and be told that I was Black.

'So,' I ask Mr MTV, who at least had the decency to look sheepish, 'no on-camera live interview?'

'Damn, I'm really sorry Don, but MTV plays rock music, adult-oriented rock music which is nearly all white as I'm sure you know, and we can't play videos which show Black people even if the music is by white folks. Listen, you've seen "Wordy Rappinghood" by Tom Tom Club, used to be in Talking Heads?'

'Yeah, looks like it was drawn by kids.'

'Exactly! The video is all cartoon, but the song sounds Black and the guys upstairs won't show it because of that. If it was up to me, of course...' His shoulders rose toward his ears as he spoke, his palms up in a 'What can I do?' gesture.

'Yeah, I get it,' I put my shades back on and rise to go. Mr MTV puts his right palm out to me as he slips off the desk. 'Really sorry man, but come the revolution and I get to be the boss, MTV will play all kinds of videos by all kinds of people, you know what I mean?'

Ignoring his hand, I exit with a shrug and walk to the elevator with a wave to Laura Ashley who's turned bright pink and look forward to getting some fresh air on Broadway.

The irony of that meeting with MTV was that after the PiL, Furs and Clash videos I'd become one of the growing number of music video directors to be offered regular work. Chris Blackwell hired me in 1982 to go to Jamaica and film live performances by Black Uhuru and Toots & The Maytals. As well as the live footage, I took a camera along on a visit to see Michael, Duckie and Puma of Black Uhuru in their yard, and got some great film of them reasoning with me and licking the chalice, throwing up clouds of smoke. That is the only footage of the original line-up 'at home'. I filmed Toots (Frederick Hibbert) on the same trip as we drove across the island at 100 mph (or so it seemed to my lurching stomach) to visit the Coptic Church where he worshipped. Getting such rare and personal footage helped me and my movie-making partner Rick Elgood to persuade Blackwell that we should start a reggae film archive and record the last living reggae artists of Jamaica.

Blackwell agreed and got Daddy Kool's Steve Barrow to work with us so we spent three weeks filming about a hundred interviews with reggae legends, many of whom have now passed. We hired Carl Bradshaw to make initial introductions in JA, which was a big buzz for me because he'd played José in *The Harder They Come* (he was still called that name by people as we travelled around). I've worked with Carl on every project filmed in Jamaica since then, some of which probably wouldn't have happened without his involvement, and he really does epitomise the spirit of the island. We got rare film of Prince Buster, John Holt, Tappa Zukie, Yabby-U, Derrick Morgan, I-Roy, Ken Boothe, Jah Stitch, Bunny Lee, Prince Jammy, Delroy Wilson, King Stitt and Count Machucki talking about their roots and careers. We also went to Black Ark, Lee 'Scratch' Perry's studio which he burned down in 1978, and caught Lee on camera wandering around the shell of the building, bending down to say hello to a banana plant and talking to various trees. That footage is still in the Island archives as far as I know, and not much of it has been seen, for whatever reason. But it gave me (and Rick) invaluable experience in making documentaries, which we later put to good use.

Even with all my experience, though, I didn't get a union card to 'legally' direct until a well-known female producer offered to help me with the union and made a few calls. Not that collecting it was an easy matter. She lived off the Marylebone Road, in a smart square near Mayfair, and the day she called to tell me to come and collect it, I drove over and parked in the street some distance from her house. Because I'd never been there before I spent a few minutes walking along looking for door numbers – for some reason not many of them seemed to have any. I searched for her place by going in and out of front paths up to big, black doors to peer at plaques and doorbells. Not long after beginning my search I could hear police sirens wailing in the near distance but being so close to the West End that wasn't unusual at any time of day or night, and this was midday so I thought nothing of it, even as the wails grew closer. That was until exiting a front garden (which wasn't the one I wanted) I saw a squad car parked diagonally across the road and three coppers running toward me. One shouts, 'Stand still, do not move!' so I do what I usually do in such situations and make a star shape with arms out, legs spread, face to the railings. Another cop car squealed to a halt from the opposite direction and there's more shouting, all directed at me. Luckily the woman I was trying to find had been expecting me and looking out of her window into the street. Hearing a commotion just up from her place, she ran up the street to get between me and the nearest policeman. 'Excuse me,' she shouted indignantly in a posh voice, 'this is a friend of mine!' Sizing up my friend's expensive dress, jewellery and cut-glass accent, the coppers went quiet and, looking disappointed, returned to their cars except the one closest to us, who got an earful of threats ('I know the commissioner and will be talking to him as soon as I return to my house. What is your number, officer?').

After she'd handed me my union card and finished apologising for the way I'd been treated, I could only smile and say, 'It's OK, that was just another reminder not to forget who I am.'

Making music videos gave me my first experience of regular well-paid work – relatively well-paid, that is – and the beginnings of a career. I made a name for myself just as the genre was expanding and record companies were taking promo videos seriously, and the rapid growth of MTV helped in that. As the only Black music video director around for quite some time in the UK and America I was first choice when it came to the few that were commissioned for Black artists. Of course, being for Black artists the budgets were tiny compared to those for white ones, and MTV's refusal to show Black videos played a big part in that, too. MTV's attitude in the first two years of their existence (1981–82) was not only racist, it made no real sense. Not least because their head of talent and acquisition at the time was Carolyn B. Baker, a Black woman, but also because there was an ever-growing market for all types of Black music across America (MTV Europe didn't launch until 1987), led by Michael Jackson, Donna Summer and Tina Turner in the pop charts. Still, in the early 1980s most Black artist videos were made at little cost, which suited my punk can-do attitude. Whoever it was that said necessity is the mother of invention knew a thing or two. I specialised in creating videos out of little but necessity. I had to work with whatever I could find, wherever I could find it. Even a few years into my career, one day while hanging out at Island Records, I looked in on Black Uhuru during a photo session for an album cover (*Anthem*, 1984) for which they'd created a post-apocalyptic set. The band were there along with Sly & Robbie and I thought, 'That's a lot of money on a set for just some stills,' so I jogged up to Blackwell's office and said, 'Give me a grand so I can get some film and a camera.' Bemused, he asked, 'What for?' and I told him that I'd make a video there and then for whatever the first single was going to be from the album – which turned out to be 'Solidarity'. He said OK, called through to accounts and I organised for the equipment to be delivered. After lunch we shot the video, which turned out to be the only one of Black Uhuru with Sly & Robbie. I did the same thing a few weeks later for Linton Kwesi Johnson's 'Di Great Insohreckshan'. While walking around Island Records offices and studios I found a fucking great big ghetto-blaster prop, standing about eight feet high. It had been used in a photo shoot for Madness, apparently, but I thought if I put a black cloth over the centre of the blaster it'd look like two speakers in a sound system. I called through to Chris Blackwell again and said, 'Give me £1,500 and I'll make a video,' which he did. I got Linton and the band (including the great Dennis Bovell on bass) to perform in front of the speakers, intercut the performance with news footage of the Brixton riots of 1981, and created what turned out to be the only promo video for Linton. What I didn't realise was that the money men at Island must have been laughing because they'd basically spent the equivalent of their lunch expenses for a week on that video.

The first video I shot for a Black artist that became a big success was not done for Island but was initially shot on the very cheap. It was for Musical Youth's version of The Mighty Diamonds' 'Pass The Kutchie', which had been retitled 'Pass The Dutchie' because a kutchie was a Jamaican herb pipe and little Brummie kids couldn't be singing songs about weed, so they used 'dutchie' – a Jamaican cooking pot – instead because it rhymed, even though it made the rest of the lyrics nonsensical. I was asked to make a video for the song before the band were signed, with a budget of about £200. Then they were signed to MCA and allocated a budget of £10,000 for a new video, which was a massive amount back then (it'd be recouped from the band later, of course). We filmed during a sunny day in the shadow of Lambeth Bridge, looking across the Thames at the Houses of Parliament and Big Ben. The video may have shared a similar location with 'London Calling', but everything else was completely different, from being shot in bright colour at mid-afternoon, to the storyline for which I ignored the lyrics and came up with a scenario about the kids bunking off school and being taken to court by a truant officer. The most important part of the video for me was the location, right opposite the Houses of Parliament. I imagined the video would be shown around the world, and by placing these Black British kids at such an iconic location I'd mess with the audience's preconceptions about what London was like. At the start of the song one of the kids sings about ruling the nation 'with version' and you then see them playing, full of energy and cheeky attitude – they could really play their instruments, by the way.

Imagine how delighted I was when the video became the first featuring a Black artist to be played on rotation on daytime MTV in October 1982, beating Michael Jackson by several months – although Herbie Hancock's 'Rockit' video had been shown on MTV by then, and while it was predominantly animated the directors Kevin Godley and Lol Creme (once of 10cc) included Herbie on screen, but only in short, small bursts. I guess because the band were cute little kids MTV felt that their audience wouldn't feel threatened by their presence on TV, or maybe it was the beginning of a change in attitude of the bosses at MTV. Not long after, 'Pass The Dutchie' reached number one in eighteen countries including the UK and the Top 10 in America, eventually selling five million copies. The video won five awards at the first annual MTV Video Music Awards show in 1984, by which time the threat by CBS records to withdraw all their artists' videos from MTV unless they played the video for Michael Jackson's 'Billie Jean' on rotation had forced a change in programming. After 'Billie Jean', videos by Prince,

Tina Turner, Eddy Grant and Donna Summer soon became staples of the station.

In 1987 MTV Europe began to air *Yo! MTV Raps*, created by Ted Demme with Peter Dougherty and presented by Fab Five Freddy. A year later it went out on MTV America and became one of the channel's most successful shows. It was the beginning of the domination of Black music on MTV that continues to the present day.

Not that things were changing rapidly back in the early 1980s. In 1983 I was asked to direct a couple more Musical Youth videos, for 'Never Gonna Give You Up' and 'Heartbreaker'. It's clear from watching any of my videos that I like to film in foreign locations, to immerse myself in foreign culture and include locals as much as possible in each one. When I was growing up I didn't get the chance to leave Britain and explore faraway lands, so when I was asked to make the new Musical Youth videos, I thought the kids would like to see the land of their ancestors – Jamaica. Naturally, it was a major culture shock for them, even though they were treated with the utmost respect and treated as heroes or returning sons of the island. Life in Jamaica is hard; people might think it's all sun, sea and sand, but there's also a lot of poverty, corruption and decay all on prominent display. The shoot for 'Never Gonna Give You Up' went off smoothly because I'd chosen a local girls' school as the location, with the pupils as extras. But filming 'Heartbreaker' was a fucking nightmare. The idea was to have them playing on top of a bus in the middle of Kingston, with a cameo appearance from a local reggae star. We started filming outside a record shop where the bus was parked. After a few minutes of shooting the owner of the store came out and demanded that we pay him $4,000 to film there and use his power supply. No way could we afford that, so we struck a better deal with Randy's Record shop further down the road and rolled along.

We set up again, but as we did so a massive crowd gathered around the bus, and each and every member of that crowd demanded that we pay them for being in the video, even though they were desperate to pose for the camera. Arriving late, our cameo star then stepped up and demanded $3,000 for his appearance. My producer haggled with him until it became impossible to reach a deal and I kept the cameras rolling to get what footage I could. The kids seemed to have fun up on top of the bus, the crowd clearly liked them and all the milling around was so typical of JA that it felt more like the making of a social documentary than a music video.

In an echo of what I'd experienced before in the country, Jamaicans on the street didn't know what to make of me. However, once they'd realised that an English dread was in charge of a film crew of ten white honkies, people kept coming up to me demanding, 'Don give me a job, Don give me some money.' It got to the point where I had to walk around with the pockets of my shorts hanging out to show that I had no money.

The following day we moved to the beach for another scene and one of the MCA execs arrived on set as we began shooting. In a break for a set-up change he came over to where I was standing in the shade of a tree scoping the scene, smiled widely and said, unbelievably, 'Hey, Don, I hope there's not going to be too many Black people in this video!' I flipped and pinned the guy to a tree, pointing out to him that not only were the fucking band Black, but also that we were in Jamaica, so who did he think was going to be in the video!

He didn't stick around too long after that, and I never heard from him again. Back in the UK, and even though the video and single of 'Never Gonna Give You Up' were Top 10 hits, MCA let me know that they didn't like the direction I was taking and wanted a 'cleaner' image for Musical Youth, because I'd made them 'anti-establishment'. I had other film work at the time, so wasn't too bothered, but I did feel sorry for the kids. Their next video (for 'Tell Me Why') had them dressed in clean white shirts and trousers (one wore a panama hat) miming on a shiny, sparkly disco set. The single failed to chart and ironically the next video MCA commissioned (for 'Unconditional Love') had the kids at school. Even though it was a collaboration with Donna Summer, that also flopped.

I'd been getting video directing work through people I knew until 'Pass The Dutchie' became a big hit, after which I joined the books of Limelight, a London-based video production company who'd recently joined forces with an Englishman living in Los Angeles named Simon Fields. When they told me that there was a lot of work on offer out there, it was hard to refuse the opportunity of taking an extended trip – it was Hollywood! I agreed to spend six months in LA, and for the first few months lived at the Sunset Marquis. While there I began to understand why Hollywood was often spelled Hollyweird; I was introduced to a lot of different people – one night out ended with my sharing a pizza at Jack Nicholson's place, another day I had lunch with Brooke Shields, while an evening spent with Lauren Hutton ended with me politely leaving her at the bar in Spago's, because I was too freaked out by the situation (and her eyes!).

Professionally, I was still making stuff up as I went along and adjusting to my surroundings as best I could. I may have become the best-known Black British video director in the UK, but it was never planned that way, and in truth, even in LA, the 'Black' bit was always foremost in white folks' minds. It was still the case in 1983 that I could be driving through the streets of London and be pulled by the police with a shout of 'Oi, you Black bastard' simply because I'm a dread out at night. In Los Angeles, at any social or professional event I was inevitably asked how I made videos, the unspoken part of the question being 'because you're Black'. One night I went to visit the agent and producer Shep Gordon in Beverly Hills but didn't know exactly where the house was, and – just as it had been in London – I can't see any house numbers so I'm driving slowly through the neighbourhood, when suddenly from nowhere eight squad cars surround me and force me out of my car at gunpoint. As has often been the case, when the odds were stacked against me my finest English accent and total politeness to the police helped me to get back in the car and continue to my destination – this time escorted by the police to show me the way (and check with Shep that I was legit).

After a few weeks I moved into an apartment on La Jolla with Simon Fields and got to work on a range of videos, some of which might not have been my first choice, but all of which were interesting (and decently paid). One of the best shoots took place on the beach at Santa Monica, which I'd assumed couldn't be any more trouble than filming in Jamaica. But I hadn't reckoned on The Gap Band being a little too relaxed to do many takes for 'Party Train'. I designed a tracking shot for them to walk about fifty yards along the beach – they managed it twice and then clambered back into their stretch limo and left. For the rest of the video I worked with the crowd of extras, who were – as was often the case – much easier and more fun to deal with than the 'talent'. The editing of the video was more instructive than the shoot, though. After I sent in my first cut it was returned with instructions to cut the final scene altogether, because they couldn't have the Black lead singer disappearing into the sea with a white woman in a bikini.

Determined to go with wherever Limelight sent me, I made the video for Stephanie Mills' 'Pilot Error' at LAX airport (of course!) and tried to

Filming in Salt Lake City, 1983.

work a cast of comedic extras and incidents into the narrative – among them a chimpanzee as the pilot and a Japanese WWII kamikaze officer as the co-pilot. What was I thinking? Hey, it was Hollyweird, baby...

Another time, Limelight arranged for me to go to Utah and make a video with the former Gentle Giant and Mandrake (both prog rock bands) guitarist Martin Briley, who'd just had a big MTV hit with 'The Salt In My Tears'. The new song, 'Put Your Hands On The Screen', was a critique of television evangelist preachers, and I wrote what I thought was a great script for it. As with 'Pilot Error' I had a cast of dozens, plus sets and special effects to work with. It was shot in Salt Lake City, Utah, the capital of the Mormon faith, at a studio belonging to The Osmonds, who were looking to attract more productions to their facility. So I was flown there in The Osmonds' private jet, with 'Crazy Horses' ringing in my ears.

I tried to keep 'Love Me For A Reason' going around in my head as I worked, though, because I was constantly aware of being under strict observation. There were no other Black men on set wearing sunglasses and dreadlocks, after all – hell, there were probably none in the whole of Salt Lake City. The single flopped, the video was hardly seen, and even now it has hardly any views on YouTube.

Following the Utah trip, I escaped to Jamaica to work with Jimmy Cliff on 'Reggae Nights', which was a big deal for me, of course – I was working with Ivan from *The Harder They Come*! Naturally, I wanted to shoot on the beach, but it was full of tourists and because it was still easier and cheaper to work without the authorities, there was no-one around to clear the area for us. So, thinking on my feet I grabbed a megaphone from the assistant director and shouted, 'You'll have to leave the water, there is a shark in the area!' Panic ensued and everyone ran out of the sea, screaming and shouting, falling over in their rush to leave the beach. Once they'd seen what was happening, the staff of the hotel on whose patch we wanted to film came out and threatened to beat me up – I understood why, the tourists left and didn't return for a week. Clearly, they didn't know that there are no sharks in Jamaica – not in the sea, anyway. It took all of Jimmy's fame and charm to calm things down enough that we could get the video shot.

I got to work with another musical legend in Jamaica, when Eddy Grant – co-founder of The Equals – asked me to direct 'War Party'.

Deciding to get out of Kingston and inspired by *Countryman* (1982), we trekked inland and made for the Rio Grande to make my second music video on a river. Filming from the bank and on board a hand-made bamboo raft as it cruised in fast-flowing water, I had the cameraman on the raft focus on Eddy's fierce face and bright yellow tracksuit. I stayed on dry land, directing from the riverbank and the bridge under which Eddy floated at the end of the video, cheered on by the scores of locals who'd gathered there unasked (and unpaid). Some of the shots of the locals going about their business on the banks really looks documentary-like, and that's because most of the 'extras' in those shots were fishermen and women who lived that life; they had no idea nor cared what we were doing filming a dread in a gold tracksuit sailing down the river.

Back in LA, Limelight kept coming up with distinctly obscure acts to work with (well, they were to me) and had me direct a video for bass player Tyrone Brunson's single 'Fresh'. Up to that point in his career Brunson had been the bass player for Family and Osiris before becoming a solo act. 'Fresh' was the follow-up single to a minor hit ('Sticky Situation') and the title track of his second solo album. Mercury Records had decided to spend some money on the promo, for which I built a sci-fi-style set with lots of TV monitors and extras. What story there was had an actor – an up-and-coming youngster known to you as Ice-T – wearing a futuristic outfit and 'scratching' some discs in search of the perfect number to play on his TV show. Naturally Brunson's demo is the chosen one. The video got some airplay and the single made the R&B Top 30 in the States, so it was something of a hit. It was nothing like as successful as the oddest job I was asked to do in LA, though.

The great soul and R&B label Atlantic Records hired Limelight to make a video for one of their newest acts, and I got the call. They were not at all the kind of band I'd associate with Atlantic, though. Ratt were what became known as a 'hair metal' act who not only looked like Spinal Tap, they actually outdid Spinal Tap at times. As you can imagine, we had little in common, but making people feel at ease so that they can relate to you is part and parcel of being a good director. When I met them, they were dressed in glittery spandex and had long hair teased out, above and around their made-up faces. I managed to connect with the dudes, though, and we pulled off a really good video which did so well on MTV that while they were then on tour supporting Mötley Crüe, the promoter had to swap the billing on the rest of the dates and make Ratt the headliners. Have to admit that I'd only said yes to the job because Milton Berle had already been cast to play his 'Uncle Miltie' character in it. An old-school Hollywood star of radio, film and TV, he was related to one of the band members. I'd watched and loved him in many a movie on black-and-white television when a kid. An extra bonus for me on that shoot was that Mel Brooks was in the studio next to us working on his *History of the World Part 1* movie. Being such a fan I couldn't resist the opportunity of getting a photo, which I still have – Mel dressed as Adolf Hitler standing next to me, a dread. That was the pinnacle of my brief Hollywood 'career', though. After six months of living and working in LA I could create videos with a storyline and a cast of dozens, commission props, build sets and spend a lot of money, but only as long as the artist I was working with was white. One of the last videos I made in LA, though, was a slight exception, being as it cost a small fortune and was for Andy Fraser, the former bass player of Free whose father had been of Barbadian-Guyanese descent. He'd never had a hit single but this cover of 'Do You Love Me', written by Berry Gordy Jr, had been a hit in 1962 for The Contours, an early Motown all-male vocal group, and Island Records thought it had potential. I worked some cool Black pop culture into it – body-popping sisters and vintage tap-dancing brothers, for instance – in the hope that MTV would play it. They didn't, it flopped, and it'd be another three years before *Yo! MTV Raps* would take over the station. Before then, though, I'd be appearing on MTV, not just making product for it.

Sudden Impact!

Exterior. Night. Two men wearing large woolly hats stand in the basement well of a three-storey, flat-fronted mid-Victorian house in what is clearly an up-and-coming area of London. Steps leading to the raised ground floor shelter the men from a light rain that is falling, droplets refracting the sodium light from a streetlamp across the road. They're arguing in low voices and standing in front of a sturdy-looking door into the basement flat. A bay window next to them is showing a flickering light through white muslin curtains that picks out the bars fixed firmly in the render surround, providing security for the occupants of the building. Every house along the road has high-security grilles and doors; a few also have alarms fitted on their wall at first-floor level. The basement flat where the men are standing has well-spaced metal railings at pavement level, and a slender, six-step stairway down to the well, in which stand two corrugated metal rubbish bins, only one of which has a black rubber lid, which looks as if chunks have been torn from it. One of the men moves away from the door, as if to leave.

'Don, wait man, I'm telling you, you'll love this woman, come on.'

'Tony, we've been banging on the door for five minutes and she's clearly not in, let's go.'

'Tch, it's been about half a minute, and you can hear the sounds of the music in there, we gotta knock harder.'

Tony slams his fist against the door three times in rapid succession. 'Come on, I promise it'll be worth it, if only to get in from the rain.'

As I'm about to sprint for the car, the door jerks open inwards, lighting Tony's face, which breaks into a huge smile. 'Audrey baby, how you doin'?'

There's an inaudible female murmur.

Tony takes half a step inside the flat, and asks, 'OK if me and my brethren Don come in from the rain for a smoke?'

The response must have been positive, because Tony continues on through the door and I decide to follow, although uninvited, along a short corridor and turn right. The flat is warm – there's a big fire burning in the living room, making the shadows in the bay window – and the lighting is low. I catch a glimpse of a slim female figure walking in front of Tony dressed in soft white trousers and a loose cardigan. She's barefoot, her hair held back with a colourful scarf.

'Come in, come in both,' she waves us forward without turning around, and flops onto a big leather sofa next to the fire. I peel my wet leather jacket from my shoulders and pull off my hat, shaking my dreads as I do.

'Hey, honey, I'm Audrey.'

I lift my head and stare into a pair of beautiful brown, cat-like eyes which I swear spark as she looks me up and down. Audrey. She smiles widely and shows off finely sculpted cheekbones, a ripe bottom lip and rounded chin which looks almost dimpled in this light.

Fuck, I almost say out loud, you're gorgeous.

'What, cat got your tongue, Don?' She laughs and turns to Tony, who's just sat on the sofa with her. 'Where you been, Tony, haven't seen you for weeks.'

Feeling dismissed, I stand in the doorway and stare as Audrey and Tony have some mundane conversation. I can't hear what they're saying because my mind is working away at trying to find something to say, anything, which might make her look at me again, to speak to me.

I step forward onto a kilim rug that separates the sofa from a single, matching leather armchair across from them. 'Alright if I...'

Without looking Audrey waves assent and carries on talking to Tony.

I sit and wait.

And wait.

The pattern that night was repeated over the next couple of weeks. I'd visit Audrey alone, but there'd always be someone else dropping by, or already there each time, and they'd talk while I stared, smoked and occasionally managed to get a sentence out. Still, I did get to talk with her more each time and we got to know each other well enough that by the end of week two I was sleeping over – but on the sofa, not in her bed. That would take a couple more weeks.

Audrey made jewellery, which she sold from a stall on the Bayswater Road by Hyde Park every Sunday. She had a lot of male admirers, but there didn't appear to be any one special male friend around at the time, and she'd recently ended a serious relationship with a guy who'd moved out of the flat in Maida Vale a few months before. She was slightly older than me, and a bit of a hippy, laid-back and chilled most of the time. Yet she had her own flat and seemed to be settled somehow, there was a permanence about her life that had been lacking in my own ever since leaving my parents' house. I wasn't totally aware of it, but it's not too much of a stretch of the imagination to say that I was looking for stability after ten years of constant moving about, and a relationship with Audrey offered the chance of that.

After being evicted from the flat in Forest Hill for non-payment of rent, along with Leo, JR and Tony, I spent a few weeks living in Kennington at Joe from the Roxy's two-bed flat. That needed a lot of organisation because there were six of us 'living' there, so we had to book a night in a bed well in advance. Luckily, just as I was getting to the end of my patience in Black Prince Road, I discovered that my name had risen to the top of Lambeth Council's housing list (put there after the compulsory purchase of Mostyn Road). It took a couple of visits to the Housing Office to get the keys for a one-bedroom flat in

Sherborne House on Bolney Street, SW8. I didn't argue with the council, or ask for any other options; I took the place happily.

Ironically, I became a council tenant just as I was offered directing work which meant a lot of travel, so spent only a few weeks living in Sherborne before flying to New York. While I was gone, I let first Tessa from The Slits stay at the flat, and then my brother Desmond – who got himself arrested and banged up while out and about in London with my keys one night, which meant that I had to get a locksmith to let me in to my own home when I returned to London. I got into the habit of letting other friends who needed a bed stay there while I was away, which wasn't actually a great idea, as it turned out. Too often I'd get in after an overnight flight feeling gritty, tired and jetlagged to find my flat looking as if it had been burgled, records had gone missing, the sink full of dirty dishes, the bed in a right state. It didn't exactly feel like a welcoming 'home', and I was beginning to feel down about it when, not long after getting back from a work trip to America, I was sitting at a bar with Chris Blackwell and moaning about my life. He asked, 'What do you need?' I said it was doing my head in, flying around the world and coming back to a tiny council flat which was always full of people who I'd let stay there while I was away. So, I told him, I need a bigger place, but I didn't have a deposit for the mortgage. For the second time in my life Chris wrote something on a napkin and told me to take it to Tom Hayes (the Island Records accountant) and he'd take care of it. He gave me £15,000, which I used for a deposit on a one-bedroom flat in Bassett Road, W10. I wasn't asking for it, but Chris gave it to me and never mentioned it again, ever.

So, at the time that Audrey and I met I was living in West London proper, had made something of a name for myself as a music video director, and was looking at another career as part of Big Audio Dynamite with Leo, Mick, Greg Roberts and Dan Donovan. After my pursuit of Audrey had succeeded, and we became a couple, I moved some stuff into her flat, she left some at mine, and we began to live as man and wife, although we were never married (I was still technically married to Marilyn until the mid-1990s).

Audrey became the still centre of my world for a while, and we'd spend days hunkered down, away from everyone else, not taking calls, just chilling. Our relationship became kind of low-key, and self-contained – there was a definite separation of my work and home life. That sometimes led to arguments between us, with Audrey either not wanting to go somewhere with me or feeling left out while I was away. And I was away for long stretches, even during her pregnancy, either recording, touring or making videos. Once our son Jet was born in May 1985 the work trips didn't stop and there was no such thing as 'paternity leave', so no-one was paying me to be home. I told Audrey that I felt responsible for her and Jet, and she understood my need to earn money and keep our new family in food and clothes, to pay the bills, mortgage and all. Which was just as well, because I have to own up here – even if I didn't there and then – that I'd found another reason to be on tour or at video shoots away from home.

Audrey, mother of Jet and Amber, at the Bassett Road flat, mid-1980s.

Who's B.A.D.?

Interior. Night. A mid-1980s nightclub. Pan to show walls covered with floor-to-ceiling mirrors and heavy swag curtains tied back to allow customers to see themselves. Velvet low-level sofas squat awkwardly around a carpeted area, arranged so as to leave a route through to a small, underlit dancefloor with different-coloured squares, just like the one in *Saturday Night Fever*. Pan back around to show a small, velvet-fronted balcony above the entrance to the club, accessible via red-carpeted curving staircases on either side, a red rope hanging across each to block unauthorised entry. Focus on a small white card on one of the ropes with 'VIP Area' printed in gold ink. People mill about wearing wide-shouldered suits and dresses, the women have high hair, most of the (white) men have exaggerated 1950s-era Elvis quiffs. Pan up and zoom to the back of the balcony and along a small, sparsely populated bar to focus on an almost invisible door, which is thrown open, outwards. Three men walk through the doorway. At the front is a thin white man dressed in a knee-length white duster coat and a red baseball cap. Either side of him are two dreads, both in wide-shouldered leather jackets, slim-cut trousers, light shirts and dark glasses. They stop and look around the club, each in a different direction. The frontman turns his head to each side, taking in the tableau they're making – every eye in the balcony bar has turned their way.

'We look like a band!' says Mick in his slow West London burr, a crooked smile creasing his long face.

'Ain't we?' Leo laughs and pushes my left shoulder, so I swipe his hand away.

'Get off man, you two are in a band, I'm a video director.'

Mick turns to look at us both.

'Nah, really – look at how fucking cool we are man, this is a great idea. Join the band, Don!'

'Tcha, what am I gonna do?' I think he's joking. 'I ain't no Chas Smash, Mick.'

'Y'can't dance like that, Don,' Leo laughs. 'S'true!'

'You don't need to.' Mick is leaning in and not smiling as widely any more. I think, he's getting serious. 'We got synths and samplers and you can be the keyboard player.'

'Fuck off, Mick, I can't play any keyboards. I can't play any instrument!' I walk around him to the bar and climb onto a stool. Mick slumps against another stool; Leo takes up a position just over his left shoulder, arms folded, trying not to laugh.

'Don, remember,' Mick says, taking his cigarettes out of a coat pocket, 'Paul couldn't play a fucking note when I asked him to be in London SS, and he had stickers on his bass for the first year in The Clash showing where the notes were. I had to shout them out to him when we played!'

'Leo's the bassist, Mick,' I say reasonably enough, I think. But I know what he means. I'm playing for time, trying to sort out in my head if I want to do this, because I know when Mick gets an idea like this, he goes with it.

'Course he is.' Mick makes a 'what a dick' face to Leo, nodding to let him know it's me he means. 'Topper's gonna play drums but we ain't got a keyboard player, and me being flanked by two cool dudes like you is gonna make us look great.'

'Topper's back?' I am genuinely surprised, because I know he's still chasing the dragon most of the time.

'Yeah, says he's getting clean, man,' says Leo.

'C'mon, Don,' Mick smiles again, lighting his fag. 'Join Top Risk Action Company and you can do what the fuck you want in the band, I'll show you how, put stickers on the keys so you know what's where.'

'Mick, that's a fucking terrible name.'

He giggles. 'It can be shortened to TRAC, right?'

I can't help laughing. 'Let's have a drink and a smoke, chill for a bit and if you can come up with a better name maybe I'll come down to the studio and see what you're up to.'

'Yesss.' Mick blows smoke over my head and waves to the bartender.

While I'd been making music videos in Los Angeles, The Clash had been busy falling apart. The gig I filmed at Shea was a tense affair for lots of reasons. Not least because, just as it had been before Topper joined, no-one else really seemed to engage with Terry and small camps had been set up within the larger Clash one. Joe and Paul were always tight, but Mick seemed to be on the edge of things at Shea. He'd never been exactly punctual in the past, but by the end of 1982 everyone was calling him 'the late Mick Jones', as if he was long gone, and it was no surprise to me when he was sacked from his own band. Their last performance had been a mini-disaster at the US Festival, a three-day televised event set up by Apple co-founder Steve Wozniak at a park in a place called Devore, California, near San Bernardino. There'd been arguments all day about how much the headline acts were being paid, which was $1.5 million for Van Halen and $1 million for David Bowie; Joe told the organisers they should donate some of that money to charity, which he also repeated when they were onstage. In response they put up a photo of a cheque made out to The Clash showing their fee of $500,000 on a screen behind them as they performed. Pissed off, the band refused to play an encore and much debate was had among themselves about what they were doing and how Mick was 'behaving like a prima donna rock star most of the time these days'.

Mick's sacking was inevitable and exactly the way it was meant to be, as far as I was concerned. I subscribe to a long-held theory that bands have a creative lifespan of roughly seven years, which is about as long as musicians can stand working together before they feel the need to move on and grow as individuals. It was exactly that with The Clash, and The Beatles before them. The Rolling Stones had major personnel changes every seven years that refreshed the creative and social mix, and three separate periods of real creativity, from 1962 to '69 with Brian Jones and from 1969 to '75 with Mick Taylor, before Ron Wood joined. They haven't made a decent album since 1983's *Undercover*, but nor have they had any major creative changes in the line-up during that time. (With that in mind, I kind of expected to be a member of Big Audio Dynamite until 1991 at the outside. Which was close.)

When Mick left The Clash he went straight into General Public with Ranking Roger and Dave Wakeling, who'd just left The Beat. They were joined by The Specials' Horace Panter and a couple of blokes from Dexy's Midnight Runners and were ironically called a 'supergroup' by the music press (at least I think it was ironic). Maybe it was too soon, but Mick made it to halfway through the recording of the GP album *All The Rage* before bailing. It wasn't long before he got together with Leo and John Boy and then had that fateful night out with me.

Not knowing what to expect, I went along to rehearsals with Mick and Leo and we talked about what I could add to the mix for the band, which by then had changed names to become Real Westway. Thankfully he wasn't so attached to the name that he couldn't take someone else's suggestion of using Big Audio Dynamite instead. And for that we have to thank Yana YaYa who was adding sound effects to Tony James's Sigue Sigue Sputnik demos, which Mick helped to create. Topper didn't last until the name change from Real Westway, by the way – he disappeared when a fat royalty cheque from The Clash's accountants arrived. We got in Greg Roberts to drum when he answered an ad we'd put in the *NME*.

Having had a crash course on what samplers could do and talking through ideas for songs with Mick, I decided that the best thing I could do was be myself and add samples of speech and sound effects from our favourite movies to the music, which I did using a Harmonix sampler Mick gave me. My sampling was only ever the seasoning in our mix, though, and while it made tracks sound unlike anyone else at that time, it was Mick's unbelievably good tunes and his skills as producer which made B.A.D. a real success. I saw him throw away ideas that other people could make albums out of when we were writing. Having learned to triple-track his voice across the stereo range he even managed to make my vocals sound passable. I found it quite daunting working with the band at first, because all these guys could play instruments. I was desperately trying to find my own space, so I also threw myself into writing lyrics, which I approached the same way as writing a treatment for a music video. With Mick's guidance, that evolved into my co-writing nearly half the songs.

Mick once described the B.A.D. sound as being 'dance rhythms with a rock 'n' roll guitar', but it was more than that. The B.A.D. philosophy was to utilise all the elements of the media to create a fuller sound – and it wasn't just about making music, it was about ideas. I'd sit watching films endlessly in the studio finding the right snatches of sounds for each song. None of us had any interest in making mega-budget rock 'n' roll like U2; instead we had a wide-screen approach to it all. The only example of someone doing it before us that I can think of is Brian Eno and David Byrne on their *My Life In The Bush Of Ghosts* (1981) album.

At our first UK gig, at Sheffield's Leadmill in July 1984, we showcased rough songs that were still being worked on like 'Strike', 'Nation' and 'Interaction' and an early version of what would be our first single, 'The Bottom Line'. It was difficult to tell how the audience took to the mix of New York beats, Jamaican bass lines, English rock 'n' roll and sampled dialogue from movies, but it went well enough that we decided to carry on, and a couple more gigs were booked for October, in France. Because they happened to be support slots with U2 we decided to get some PR photos done for posters and flyers. Mick asked a friend of his from West London called Tricia Ronane if she knew anyone who could take the photos. Trish was a model and is a tough, smart South Londoner who takes no shit from anyone. She knew a kid named Dan Donovan, she told Mick, whose dad was the great sixties photographer Terence Donovan, and Dan was also handy with a camera. Mick took Trish's advice, and carried on doing so for some years after that, because although we were 'managed' by a New Yorker named Gary Kurfirst, a big-hitter who also managed Ramones, Blondie and Talking Heads,

Trish ran things for us day to day in London (she'd later successfully manage affairs for The Clash, after the final split).

As it turned out, Dan Donovan wasn't just a snapper, he also played keyboards. He didn't immediately join the group, but we got on well and he started to hang out with us and came up with artwork for what would be our first album. By the time we got to recording it properly, though, we still had no keyboard player, so Mick asked Dan to come down to the studio to play some parts. Dan, who'd studied classical piano for ten years, basically winged it. Having been written almost a year before he got there, the music was locked down and once Mick had explained what to play and where, it took Dan very little time to get it on tape (and it was still tape in those days). When it was done, we were sitting around listening to playbacks and Dan showed us a photo he'd taken of the band, which Mick had asked to see with the idea of

The cover for our first LP, *This Is Big Audio Dynamite*, 1985. THECOVERVERSION/ALAMY

using it as the cover for the first single sleeve. Pointing at it while Dan held it up, Mick said, 'There's a space for you, there.'

The album, *This Is Big Audio Dynamite*, was released in October 1985, a year after our first gigs, and five months after the birth of my son, Jet. While Mick was busy mixing and overdubbing the album tracks, I took on work as a director. Not on a pop video, but as second unit director on a feature film which Chris Blackwell had asked me to do. It would mean being away from London while Audrey was in the late stages of her pregnancy, but it was well paid, and I got to film the prime movers on a new music scene developing out of Washington DC called Go-Go.

Good To Go (1986) was supposed to take Go-Go global, in the same way that *The Harder They Come* had reggae. Unfortunately, Go-Go did not translate well to film, which is not a put-down of the music or the scene – if anything it's praise because there is something about it that is intangible. It was almost too hot for vinyl and definitely too hot for celluloid.

I'd originally been asked to direct the whole of *Good To Go*, but because of Audrey's pregnancy and B.A.D. building into something I really wanted to be a part of, I didn't have the time to direct the whole film. So instead I directed live performances of Trouble Funk, Chuck Brown & The Soul Searchers and Redds & The Boys among others on the scene. The movie's story involved a Washington street gang called The Wrecking Crew who kill a woman when they are turned away from a Go-Go club. The police put pressure on a burned-out reporter named Blass (played by Art Garfunkel) to give Go-Go a bad name after he witnesses the brutal murder.

Chuck Brown had been the catalyst for the DC scene and considered the godfather of Go-Go (check out 'We Need Some Money'). His band, Chuck Brown & The Soul Searchers, had made a few locally successful records during the seventies – their beat on Ashley's 'Roach Clip' was later sampled by Eric B. & Rakim and Soul II Soul – but it was his use of extended live jams which really made their reputation. In the early 1980s Brown noticed that clubs in DC were booking more DJs than bands because DJs could mix one track into another without breaking the beat. So, he figured, to get work bands would have to play whole sets without stopping, with each number segueing into the next. George Clinton and Isaac Hayes had stretched songs out to ten or fifteen minutes, but Brown managed to keep his groove going for two hours and the crowds loved it. Go-Go, a precursor of swing beat, sacrificed structure and slick production to create a loose sound that oozed a community vibe. Clubs like Washington Coliseum and the DC Armoury had thousands moving and grooving to the Go-Go beat, sweat dripping, driven by a distinctive call-and-response vocal style – the dancers would fire lines back and forth with the groups onstage. Most of the Go-Go bands had ten or more members including horn sections, many of whom had begun in school marching bands that gave poor kids access to expensive instruments and a musical education.

When Go-Go emerged, DC had become America's murder capital, and the part of Washington the sound came from was as violent and deprived as the Bronx or Harlem. So it was natural that the NY hip-hop and DC Go-Go scenes would come together – Kurtis Blow collaborated with EU, Grandmaster Flash & The Furious Five covered 'Pump Me Up' by Trouble Funk, and the sound spread. In the mid-eighties Rick Rubin produced DC's Junk Yard Band's 'Sardines', Spike Lee featured EU's 'Da Butt' in *School Daze* (1988) and Grace Jones used EU on 'Slave To The Rhythm' at the end of 1985.

With the Go-Go scene came Angel Dust, though, and that created a few problems on the fringes which had people demonising Go-Go, saying it was all about drugs – but that was never the case. Perhaps because it was the ultimate Black tribal rebel sound in Washington, home of the White House and the capital of America, Go-Go never managed to completely break out of its environment beyond the mid-eighties and the *Good To Go* movie didn't help much with that. The shoot turned into a nightmare, with directors coming and going, the whole thing took far longer than it should have and, while I loved the Go-Go scene and bands I filmed, I couldn't help but be anxious about becoming a father. I was only too glad to fly back to the UK and be at Jet's birth. I was also happy to be at 'home' now that I had my own place, and with the birth of a son I was entering a new phase of life.

In truth, Audrey and I hadn't exactly planned to become parents, and we'd had some ups and downs in the year before Jet's birth, which is why we had two separate places to live (I kept the Bassett Road flat while Audrey and Jet nested at her place). I barely had time for any paternal bonding with Jet before I had to work the launch of Big Audio Dynamite the band, and then make an album. We were at the cutting edge of the London music scene, and hosted a regular club called Planet B.A.D. on Kensington High Street. Naturally, that meant late nights, which new babies and tired mothers don't appreciate. Running the club and prepping for the release of our first single, 'The Bottom Line', and album created a close-knit unit of band members and assorted crew (including Island's in-house studio engineer Paul 'Groucho' Smykle, Mick's guitar tech Adam 'Flea' Newman and Greg's drum roadie Adele Hocking). We became a self-contained and self-assured team and simply handed the record company (CBS) the finished album with completed artwork when we were ready. That was undoubtedly because Mick had a lot of clout with CBS, who were expecting great things of his new musical venture.

'The Bottom Line' had originally been written while he was still in The Clash (when it was titled 'Trans Cash Free Pay One'), and if it had been the follow-up single to 'Straight To Hell' it wouldn't have surprised anyone. Clearly CBS liked what they heard when Mick played them the first mix because we were given a decent budget for a video to 'The Bottom Line', which we chose to shoot in Trafalgar Square. Obviously, there were loads of people there when we set up, but what I hadn't reckoned on was there being even more than usual because of a political protest going on. The organisers of which came over to tell us that we were messing up their protest, to which I replied, 'Fuck off, we're making a video.' I didn't listen to what they were protesting against, I'm sorry to say. Turns out it was an anti-apartheid rally. (We kind of made amends the following year when we closed out a Free Nelson Mandela gig on Clapham Common, even though the police closed us down before we'd finished after people reported hearing gunshots at the gig – which were actually my samples...)

Because of our contacts and Mick's Clash connection, the word about B.A.D. spread quickly in the business and we were approached by Rick Rubin, who had Def Jam up and running with Russell Simmons by then, asking if he could hear something. He'd always wanted to work with Mick, and he liked 'The Bottom Line' enough to remix it and put it out on Def Jam. Pretty soon the Beastie Boys and Chuck D were talking about us too, and so a buzz built on both sides of the Atlantic.

While Big Audio Dynamite were being written about in mostly favourable terms even before we'd finished making the first album, Mick's old outfit were getting some dodgy press. Joe and Paul had recruited a drummer after Terry left and two guitarists to replace Mick. They went on a British tour in May 1985 and busked outside venues, in town centres, and a couple of times outside gigs by The Alarm, which made me laugh. The music press really took the piss out of them, though. Tribute bands were not really a thing at the time, but if they had been then The Clash who recorded the *Cut The Crap* album (which came out a month after ours) would have been slammed as being a not very good one. The only good thing on *Cut The Crap* is 'This Is England', which is not exactly an original opinion I know, but it's definitely the best thing Joe ever wrote without Mick. We'd heard that Joe didn't have a good time making the album and that Bernard Rhodes had declared himself Joe's co-writer and producer. We figured that since they'd finished it in March, but release wasn't planned until November, there must be trouble in The Clash camp.

When Joe turned up unannounced at Mick's house toward the end of that summer saying he wanted to talk, there wasn't enough time to find out what about, because when Mick opened his door he expected to see a taxi driver; he and his family were on their way to the airport to catch a flight to Nassau. Which is what Mick told Joe, and then the taxi arrived, so they said goodbye. There was no hint from Joe that he intended to follow them, but he did, arriving on a rented motorbike a few days later at Chris Blackwell's house where they were staying. Joe was carrying a bag of locally sourced weed and after a smoke he told Mick that he'd made a mistake and that he wanted him to return to The Clash. In reply, Mick played a tape of the B.A.D. album, explaining that this was what he wanted to do. Maybe Joe realised how much better it was than *Cut The Crap* and felt jealous or something, but he told Mick that it was no good, and that he – Mick – needed Joe to make great music.

Mick didn't agree.

This Is Big Audio Dynamite earned pretty good reviews and some people suggested that it was the album that The Clash should have followed *Combat Rock* with. The themes of the songs are certainly Clash-like, with 'A Party' being about apartheid and 'Stone Thames' about Aids (its title being a play on 'Rock Hudson'), but there are obvious differences, too – particularly the movie samples I chose to use on songs. For 'E=MC^2' I sampled dialogue from Nic Roeg's *Performance*, *Walkabout*, *The Man Who Fell to Earth*, *Eureka* and *Bad Timing*, and we got Nic Roeg's son Luc to direct the video for the single, which incorporated clips from his dad's films. When it was released in March 1986 it became a chart hit and we appeared on the BBC's *Top of the Pops*, which was Mick's first time because The Clash refused to go on the show. I, however, had appeared on the show before, as 'keyboard player' with PiL as they mimed to 'Rise'.

Comparisons with The Clash were always going to be made, which worried me a bit. While there was no way I could ever measure up to Joe as a songwriter (and I always felt in his shadow when working with Mick), I think Joe appreciated what I did with Mick and B.A.D., and by the time of the release of the second single from the album in June 1986, he was well into it. For 'Medicine Show', which is about media manipulation and our part in it, I sampled dialogue from *A Fistful of Dollars*, *The Treasure of the Sierra Madre*, *A Fistful of Dynamite* (aka *Duck, You Sucker!*) and of course *The Good, the Bad and the Ugly*. The advertising campaign for the single borrowed Eli Wallach's killer line from *The Good, the Bad and the Ugly*: 'One bastard goes in, another bastard comes out.' If you're wondering how we got away with using all those samples, it was because it was all so new that no musical precedents had been set and there were no rules about it. That'd soon change, of course – as De La Soul and The Verve found out.

The 'Medicine Show' video (which I co-directed with Kevin Hewitt) includes cameo appearances from Joe, Paul Simonon and John Lydon and was the first time all three founder members of The Clash had worked on anything together in a very long time and helped heal old wounds. It was also the first time I'd seen Joe and Paul since a telephone call the previous year when Paul told me, 'We can't be friends if you're with Mick.' I thought he was joking, but it turned out he (and Joe) were serious. The video ends with Joe and Paul playing cops who've just locked B.A.D. in a jail cell in the foreground, with Mick slowly edging toward them, smiling. Almost the final frame has all three looking at the camera as if The Clash had never ended... Mind you, it hadn't been an easy or trouble-free shoot. For some reason Lydon decided to drink a case of beer, after which he got into a fight with a journalist on set

Together at last! (L–r) Joe Strummer, me, John Lydon and Paul Simonon at the shoot for the B.A.D. 'Medicine Show' video, 1985.　　ADRIAN BOOT/URBANIMAGE.TV

about something he'd written a few years previously, and then he 'shot' the still photographer on set with a blank-firing machine-gun at close range, which deafened him briefly. We hired a DeLorean car for the shoot and had great plans for it until the owner told us it would cost extra to drive it (he's driving at the beginning of the video), so we had to push it into shot with us out of frame when what we really wanted was for it to screech in with rubber burning. Still, it's great fun to watch and includes a lot of our friends as extras, including Neneh Cherry, Andi Oliver, Tricia Ronane and Audrey.

By that time B.A.D. had played a few 'proper' gigs, including two in America, and I worked out how and what to play at them using stickers on the keyboards. Turned out that it was the way to go for a non-musician like me, although unlike Paul I never got rid of mine. The fans at those early gigs quickly realised that this was not a Clash Mark II and were definitely up for the ride with us. I'll never forget watching one guy being ushered toward an exit in New York by the crowd around him for constantly shouting for 'London Calling'.

That American trip turned out to be one of the most significant in my life, but not for musical reasons. While in New York I met someone, and we made a connection that was instant, and proved to be lifelong.

There Are Some Places in the Universe You Don't Go Alone

Interior. Day. A cinema, summer 1986. A line of laughing, jostling men and women file messily through the foyer from Times Square, New York to the screen entrance. The rest of the foyer is quiet and as the doors slowly shut out the car horns, shouts and sirens from the Square as they close, the shouts, giggles and slap of feet on the shiny floor bounce off popcorn displays and glossy posters showing Jack Nicholson and Meryl Streep in close-up profile suffering *Heartburn*, of Tom Hulce and Susan Dey grinning against an impossibly blue sky in *Echo Park* and of Dom DeLuise, Gene Wilder and Gilda Radner hamming it up for their *Haunted Honeymoon*. We follow the group of leather- and denim-clad men and women through black swing doors and into a dimly lit auditorium. They arrange themselves noisily in a row near the back. There are shouts and squeals, groans and hisses as they switch seats in order to be next to someone in particular. At the dead centre of the minor squall of noise and movement, a couple settle easily and quietly alongside each other. She has a peroxide-blonde haircut like a marine sergeant, which ironically makes her look incredibly feminine. She wears several earrings. Her impossibly long neck elegantly rises from the collar of a beaten-up motorcycle jacket. He's wearing a cotton Hawaiian shirt, off-white chinos and Florsheim playboy shoes. His chest-length dreadlocks hang loose. The lights go down

217

in the cinema, the curtain parts to reveal the screen, and from the darkness comes the sound of wind, building slowly as if from far away. The screen shows black and then, in bold white letters, 'A BRANDYWINE PRODUCTION' flows out of the blackness, fades to black and under the sound of the wind a metallic hum builds as the next title glows into shape.

'A JAMES CAMERON FILM' fades and the hum grows louder.

'SIGOURNEY WEAVER' in larger, bolder type appears out of the blackness at the top of the screen.

The blonde woman's head turns toward the dreadlocked man. She speaks, easily, softly.

'It's going to be my birthday soon.'

From the blackness, hazy electric blue lines appear mid-screen as the words 'MICHAEL BIEHN' appear beneath.

I turn my head to her, and reply, 'I know.'

Her beautiful, bright blue eyes reflect a pulsing glow from the screen.

She pulls her head back slightly, wrinkles her brow and says, 'How do you know that?'

'Because,' I find myself saying, 'I love you.'

Shocked, we stare at each other as the screen gets lighter. When I turn back to it, the electric blue lines have formed the word 'ALIENS' and are moving toward us.

The screen becomes a blinding white light as the sound of a scream reaches top volume above the electronic hum that has become a roar.

I brace for impact.

A galaxy of stars fade in from the light.

I'm there.

Grace is with me.

We first met in December 1985, when B.A.D. were in New York to play a gig and meet the American record company. Grace was brought to the after-show party by a friend of a friend, and as soon as I saw her, I felt something more than just physical attraction. I really couldn't take my eyes off her, and as she moved easily around the room, smiling, joking and pushing away anyone who was trying to be too familiar, I thought she was the most beautiful woman I'd ever seen. More than that, I wanted to break through the crowd and defend her against the backstage hangers-on who were hassling her. But I didn't move, I had to wait to see if she'd come to me. After what felt like hours, I found her standing in front of me, smiling. After introducing myself we talked long into the night and into the next day. I knew that I couldn't, and shouldn't, but felt an immediate connection to Grace which wasn't just lust, it was far more. We'd had no meaningful physical contact up to the day we went to see *Aliens*, nor did we until long after that. From the off we spoke about everything and anything and connected emotionally. We were friends long before we became lovers. I told Grace about my relationship with Audrey and that we had a son, and for months that was an immovable object in the way of our becoming lovers. But the heart wants what the heart wants, and not long after Jet's first birthday, I was completely in love with Grace. As contradictory as it might seem, I also loved Audrey and Jet, and felt a huge responsibility for them both. Grace and Audrey were like chalk and cheese, but when I met Grace, her appetite for life spoke volumes to me. She felt insecure about herself, being so young and hanging out with 'rock stars' and women like Tricia Ronane – who was Paul Simonon's partner by then – and the other models who were around. But Grace had the same kind of curiosity and sense of adventure for life that Jeannette had when we'd first met – plus, Grace and I had very similar tastes in music, film, fashion, and life in general.

She also fitted beautifully into my life as part of Big Audio Dynamite.

Being a 'pop star' meant that I had to spend months on the road or in a recording studio, always away from home (wherever that might be). B.A.D. was the reason I was in the cinema in the middle of the afternoon that summer. We were in New York to mix our second album, *No. 10, Upping St.*, most of which had been recorded in London at Trident Studios in Soho. There'd barely been two weeks between our first major tour and the start of the recording in the summer, but Mick had plenty of song ideas, and we settled into the making of the album and then found a new co-producer and songwriter for him. Or rather, an old one: Joe Strummer.

I was on my way to Trident one day in June, walking through Soho, when I was grabbed from behind and a familiar voice yelled loudly, 'Look! It's Don Letts!' Joe spun me around and pointed to a poster for our latest single 'Medicine Show' pasted on a wall, and then at me again. He looked and smelled as if he'd been drinking, his hair had grown out of the mohawk he'd had when he announced the end of The Clash seven months earlier, and he looked slightly mad. 'You going my way?' he asked. 'I wanna see Mick, it's his birthday, right?' I had forgotten that it was, so took him along to Trident as a kind of birthday gift and from the moment he got into the control room, he and Mick were reunited as a musical team. Joe's infectious energy and enthusiasm gave us all a lift, and it was great to see him and Mick at work and seeming to be happy for the first time in an age. Just as I'd watched him do at Electric Lady Studios in New York, Joe set up a songwriting bunker under the studio piano – with coats for a bed, notebooks and food – and got to work. They co-wrote 'Beyond The Pale', 'Limbo The Law' (which was a rewrite of a track I'd written called 'The World Is Yours'), 'V Thirteen' and 'Sightsee MC!', the second single from the album. Joe got his mate Jim Jarmusch to direct the black-and-white video for 'Sightsee', and we filmed it underneath the Westway where the gypsy encampment used to be. I wrote 'C'mon Every Beatbox' with Mick as an anti-racism chant which sampled dialogue from *The Cotton Club* (Francis Ford Coppola, 1984), *Batman* (1966) and a sample from Rammellzee. At the time we were listening to a lot of Def Jam, especially the Beastie Boys and Public Enemy, and a lot of Prince, too – we used to close our shows with a version of '1999'. I also co-wrote a track called 'Sambadrome' for the album, about a Robin Hood-type drug dealer who lived in the favelas in Rio de Janeiro. Brazilians loved that song, even if the powers that be didn't. Mind you, when a Brazilian newspaper published a picture of the police chief flushing our record down the toilet it was great publicity.

Joe suggested the album's title, which was supposed to be a take on 'No. 10 Downing Street' but nobody got it. It didn't exactly fit with the cover either, which was an homage to the Brian De Palma film *Scarface*

(1984), but by the time Joe came up with *No. 10, Upping St.* we'd lost all our other ideas for a title because we'd written them on Post-it notes and plastered them all over the studio walls and a cleaner had thrown them away. Joe came to New York with us for the mixing, which turned into a kind of rock 'n' roll party, with Iggy Pop, some of the Red Hot Chili Peppers, Jim Jarmusch, Matt Dillon and Laurence Fishburne turning up at different times. Joe got Matt and Laurence to do a bit on one of the tracks, 'Dial A Hitman', and they acted out a scene in the studio. A constant visitor to the studio who I was always happy to see was Grace, who came in almost every day along with her friend Jessica. That was when we became really close, and I wasn't looking forward to the sessions ending, because when they did, I wouldn't be able to see Grace every day.

When they did end, we previewed *Upping St.* in the penthouse suite of Morgans Hotel in New York. The event turned into a highly debauched affair, as was usually the way at that time. The party had all the extremes, excesses and drugs of the period you'd expect. Not that we ever went too crazy – we knew when to stop and the drugs threatened to get out of control. Well, most of us did. It was already a cliché, but drugs were a commonplace of the rock star life, and if our first and third albums were ganja-fuelled, *Upping St.* was a cocaine album (*Megatop Phoenix* would be an ecstasy album). I admit to being as much into rock star recreational activities as anyone else, and occasionally it'd catch me out – I had to make a red-faced, sweaty exit in the middle of the conference in front of a couple of hundred press people in Brazil in 1987 because I'd partaken of too much local product. I could hear Mick's guffawing laugh as the door swung shut behind me.

But my one massive, illicit indulgence during those weeks in New York, which shaped the beginning of a new (and lasting) addiction, was Grace. When I returned to the UK with the band to rehearse for the tour to promote the album release, set for November, I had to face withdrawal from her. And I had to do it knowing that it couldn't show on my face or in my mood when I was around Audrey and Jet.

I'm not sure how I managed, but I got through the weeks between returning to London and going out on tour again without Audrey sensing that anything was different or wrong about us. Maybe it was having to care for Jet, who was as much of a distraction as any small child can be. He demanded her full attention and deflected any real scrutiny of me, for which I was grateful. He also gave me something else to think about and direct my love toward other than Grace, until I left them again.

Touring was a long and steep learning curve for a non-musician like me. In the early days I had to sample the parts for every upcoming song while we were onstage, using the most basic sampler ever invented, which had very little storage space. Eventually I got an Akai sampler, which was also covered with coloured stickers, because despite Dan Donovan spending five years trying to show me where Middle C was, I never found it. At least the Akai was programmable with the whole set, so long pauses between numbers were avoided.

When we'd finished the tour of the UK promoting *No. 10, Upping St.*, during which I spent a lot of money on transatlantic phone calls to Grace, I didn't have much time at home with Audrey and Jet before taking them off on a holiday. Along with Mick and his family we headed for a well-earned break in Jamaica, at Goldeneye, Ian Fleming's old house, now owned by Chris Blackwell. We were coming down from the year's hard slog recording and performing, so naturally Mick and I spent a fair bit of time relaxing in the only way we knew how – smoking herb and occasionally tripping. One day, while we were on the Goldeneye beach tripping, an exotic figure emerged in the distance, walking along the shoreline. As he got closer it looked to me like a ghost of an eighteenth-century barefoot pirate, with a hoop earring, bandana, cut-off shorts, and what looked like a cutlass in his waistband. I pointed toward him, and gurgled, trying to get Mick's attention. When the pirate ghost got within three feet of us, though, I realised that it was Keith Richards with a huge bowie knife in his shorts. We struck up a conversation that must have been friendly despite my incapacity because he invited Mick and I back to his place, which was Tommy Steele's old house in Ocho Rios. Over the next few weeks we spent many evenings there and met the Wingless Angels, a band of Rastas who looked after the place for Keith while he was away. It wasn't wholly relaxing being there, though, because it was overrun by massive bugs, which the Angels used to hit with hammers, making them squeak. Still, it made for a lasting memory. I'd sit watching Mick Jones and Keith

Richards jamming on guitars, with a Jack Daniels bottle between them, while some of the Angels beat their drums. It was the occasional sound effects supplied by the brethren mashing bugs that made the nights surreally memorable, I think. The visits to Keith's house were made without our families, so I didn't spend as much time with Audrey and Jet while there as I might have done. That was becoming normal and something that Audrey seemed to be getting used to. In late January 1987 I returned to New York and Grace for a tour which kept me away from London for four months, pretty much.

The 1987 B.A.D. tour set the template which kept us almost permanently broke. Just as it had been with The Clash, we took along lots of artists that our audience might not have known about before as support – among them LL Cool J, Paul Simonon's Havana 3am, The London Posse, Adamski and Schoolly D, whose beatbox was so big that once we had to buy it a seat on a plane. There was also the B.A.D. crew: Raymond Jordan (security), Flea (Mick's guitar tech), Josh Cheuse (art department), Adele Hocking (Greg's drum roadie), Guy Gillam (merchandise) and my brother Desmond (road manager). It made for one hell of a ride.

We were booked for a shedload of American dates because US college radio stations were really into us. Gigs came thick and fast and while we'd play three nights at the Brixton Academy in London, we were booked for eleven nights at the Irving Plaza in New York and seven nights at the Roxy in LA. We loved residencies at one venue because it gave us time to get to know whatever city we were in and could make the most of our time there. We earned a reputation as a band to see live on that tour and grew in confidence, especially when we began to attract other musicians to our gigs. One night we came offstage at the Plaza and when we got to the dressing room a stage manager stopped us and said, 'Bowie wants to meet you.'

'Yeah, right,' I snorted. 'Where is he then?'

The guy pointed to a door in the corner of the dressing room that looked like a broom cupboard and said, 'In there.' Bowie sat in that tiny space waiting for us to get dressed before emerging, smiling broadly. That same night I looked around the dressing room to see Peter Frampton, Dave Stewart, Jimmy Cliff, Mick Jagger, the Beastie Boys, and Paul Simonon as well as Bowie milling about, drinking, smoking and chatting. Not that we were ever that impressed by famous visitors, or calls from superstars, come to think of it – while we were on tour Mick got a message from Bob Dylan's office asking if he'd fly out to LA to work on a song with him for a new album just for the day. Mick said, 'Tell him that ain't long enough to have a cup of tea!' I'd previously turned down an invite from Dylan to direct a video after witnessing the kind of heavy-handed security he used. Backstage before one of his gigs that I'd flown to France especially to see, a team of bouncers came barrelling past with the head guy shouting 'Get out of the way' and pushing people clear of Bob's path. One of them crossed the line when he pushed me and I said, 'Dude, what the fuck are you pushing me for?' He just yelled in my face, 'Get outta the way, don't argue with me!' So, I left a message at the production office saying, 'Tell Mr Dylan thanks, but no thanks,' and got out of there before the gig started.

That night backstage in New York, though, the only face I really wanted to see was Grace's. That was when I first asked her to come on the road and she did, which made often tedious journeys between gigs

The B.A.D. all-star after-show party line-up. (L–r) Greg Roberts, Dave Stewart, me, David Bowie, Jimmy Cliff, Mick Jones, Peter Frampton, Paul Simonon; (front) Leo Williams, Dan Donovan, 1987. BOB GRUEN

much more fun and interesting. We had to hide our relationship from the record company people and the tour promoters in case Audrey contacted them for whatever reason. Desmond always arranged for me to have a room to myself when we stayed at hotels, and a couple of times pretended that Grace was with him at record company events – which neither she or I were exactly happy about, Desmond being a little too eager to persuade people that they were a couple. But all the B.A.D. people on the bus understood that what happened on the road stayed on the road, for which we were very grateful (even if we didn't say so back then).

In the summer we went out as a warm-up act for U2, which meant we got to play in front of a new crowd. We went down really well and initially it was a buzz for me as we were playing in front of 100,000 people at times, so I'd run around onstage and sometimes, in the middle of a performance and moved by the spirit, I'd hold up my keyboard, complete with stickers to show the crowd. It was my way of saying to the audience that with a punk attitude they could do this, too. By the end of the tour I was a bit blasé about it all, but I guess supporting U2 was more of a trip for Mick and must have been a reminder of what he could have had with The Clash. One night we were sitting at the back of some huge stadium watching U2 plough through 'Bullet The Blue Sky' when we looked at each other and didn't have to say a word. We were thinking the same thing: that could and should have been The Clash.

I suspect U2 were paying attention to what we were doing on those early gigs, because long before they staged their Zoo TV tour (in 1992) we were performing in front of numerous TV sets, or sometimes a single screen showing a visual collage of cut-ups I'd created – mostly images I'd nicked off the telly. Apparently that stage set didn't work for everyone, because one punter was so enraged about what he'd seen that he wrote to the *NME* to complain about it. I don't know what exactly had upset him, possibly the iconic shot of a razor slashing an eyeball from *Un Chien Andalou* (1929), but whatever it was he swore to never buy another B.A.D. record again.

So that was one less sale of the next album, which we needed to get out quickly because *Upping St.* had cost so much to make, most of the advance having been spent on mixing the damn thing in New York City (Mick said it was the most expensive record he ever made).

As soon as we got back to London in August 1987, we started putting ideas together for the new record at Mick's studio in his basement and began the recording of what was to become *Tighten Up Vol. 88* (the title a play on Trojan's groundbreaking compilations of the late 1960s) at Beethoven Street Studios, a small place in West London that had the huge attraction of being cheap. We were back to it being just the band in the studio. Joe Strummer was out on tour with The Pogues at the time, as a replacement guitarist for Phil Chevron who'd developed a stomach ulcer. Joe had acted in and recorded an excellent soundtrack for Alex Cox's *Walker* (1987) earlier in the year, and we hadn't seen much of him since finishing *Upping St*. He was getting his own band together and had a tour planned for the end of the year when he'd finished with The Pogues. We did have one Clash connection on the album, though, because Paul Simonon supplied the cover art. We also had a future famous teaboy named Seal, who lived in a squat up the road and hung around the studio all day.

Paul's painting of people of different races and tribes partying in front of West London tower blocks summed up the multicultural vibe of London and B.A.D. If there is an overall theme on *Tighten Up,* it's race, which arguably is best demonstrated on 'Funny Names', for which I used samples from Indian movies and old ska albums. 'The Battle Of All Saints Road' looks at the impact of gentrification in London and uses samples of 'The Battle Of New Orleans' (by Johnny Horton) combined with some ragga-style toasting courtesy of yours truly. 'Esquerita' is an ode to American rhythm and blues singer Eskew Reeder (aka S. Q. Reeder) who Mick hipped me to. For 'Just Play Music!' I sampled sixties pop quiz *Jukebox Jury* and the voice of sixties pop promoter Larry Parnes, while 'Other 99' featured the sampled voice of Richard Attenborough in *Brighton Rock* (1948).

Released in the summer of 1988, *Tighten Up* was our least successful album, but the tour to promote it was as successful as ever, with its fair share of strange happenings. When we were in Ireland in July, Leo and I were attacked by drunk locals at a shitty hotel we were staying at in Tralee. To check in we had to walk through the bar and when we stepped inside it was like the pub scene in *American Werewolf in London* (1981). The room became silent and everyone stared at us, giving off evil vibes. Later that night some drunk guys came out of their room, saw Leo and me in the corridor and totally freaked out. They started attacking us, in an extremely drunken way. Leo grabbed a fire extinguisher and sprayed them to dampen their spirit, and they eventually stumbled off cursing. Maybe seeing two dreadlocked Black men for the first time had freaked them out. That had become a common problem we'd faced when on the road, especially as we travelled further abroad. Whenever we went through customs it was always Leo and I to be given a hard time, so the others used to make sure that we went ahead first, in order that the whole band wouldn't get turned over.

Because we'd blown so much money on the previous album and tour, we had a smaller crew for the *Tighten Up* gigs, and my brother Des had been sacked at the end of the previous tour. He has his version of events, which involve a lot of stuff that I simply wasn't aware of, because for most of the 1987 tour Grace and I were wrapped up in our cocoon of coexistence, which was punctured only by my having to soundcheck and play the gig. Because Mick hated touring the US by bus, he flew pretty much everywhere and that meant that Grace and I could have the 'master bedroom' at the back of the luxury coach and we didn't know about the nefarious activities going on up front. Because I was with Grace, I had no need for the usual on-tour boredom relievers, but apparently they were plentiful and Des did his job as general all-round fixer perfectly. Ultimately, we had to make cuts for the *Tighten Up* tour (pun unintended), and since it was mostly of the UK and Ireland, we had no need for a full-time road manager.

Come mid-tour, though, we needed a doctor for Mick. He'd contracted chickenpox from his daughter, and it led to pneumonia. Luckily, we were in London when things got really bad and he was rushed to St Mary's hospital in Paddington where he was put in intensive care. That was a scary time, and it was touch and go as to whether he'd make it out of there. Visitors were restricted to short periods of time and in pairs at the most. He looked terrible, and it was heartbreaking to see him lying so still, all wired up and looking frail.

For a few weeks the rest of Big Audio Dynamite didn't know what we should do. For the first time in three years we didn't have a schedule – there was no recording or rehearsal time booked, no promotion, touring or video shoots to do. It meant we could rest, of course – at least as much as was possible with Mick being so ill – but it also meant an extended period at home. Which was something of a strain for me because after spending so much time with Grace I now had to make do with snatched phone calls made where and when I could. Audrey and I had started arguing loudly and often, at least we were when I was talking to her. I'd become quiet and distant, scared that I'd use the wrong name when talking to Audrey and call her Grace. Yet I still couldn't bring myself to break up our relationship. I refused to become that cliché of an absent Black father with a growing son.

When Mick was out of intensive care, I got the band together to demo new songs for the next album and told him that we'd do what we could until he could get out and sprinkle his magic over it. As I mentioned earlier, *Megatop Phoenix* (a reference to Mick's 'rebirth') was far more psychedelic than the previous album and sounds like a trip because I was tripping while we worked on it. The second 'Summer of Love' of 1987 had a huge influence on us, and acid house had a massive impact on youth culture in general. Because B.A.D. had such an open brief we could accommodate whatever we chose within our sound. Mick and Dan had been into the rave scene (much more so than me) and they brought influences from that to *Megatop*. By the time Mick was well enough to get back to work, we'd laid down tracks and asked Bill Price to come in to engineer and co-produce the recording, which was done at Konk Studios in Hornsey, just down the road from Muswell Hill. The studio was owned by Ray Davies of The Kinks, and the first meeting of the band and studio owner was the only time I ever saw Mick in awe of someone. Ray Davies and The Kinks had been such a huge influence on him (and me), and Mick was incredibly embarrassed when we accidentally locked Ray in the toilet for an hour one evening. We tried to make up for it by putting nice things about him and The Kinks in the album sleeve notes.

I spent a lot of time working on samples for the album, and they're packed with stuff that mean a lot to me and Mick. The first single from *Megatop*, 'James Brown', featured sampled bits of dialogue from the Godfather of Soul, while the second single, 'Contact', sampled The Who (remixed by Judge Jules). 'The Green Lady' was inspired by the Vladimir Tretchikoff print that Mick's nan, Stella, had on the wall when they were living in Wilmcote House, a council tower block in West London. Nan also figures in 'Everybody Needs A Holiday'.

When we finished the album, we took a trip to Amsterdam for the opening of MTV Europe. Of course, before we got to the studio we had to check out some of the local produce. We began with spliffs, followed by space cakes and washed down with space yoghurt. By the time we climbed onstage we could just about stand up and look at each other. Needless to say, that TV appearance was never broadcast.

As much as we tried, though, things were never quite the same after Mick got out of hospital, and the band started to implode shortly after *Megatop Phoenix* was released in September 1989. Each of our singles had performed worse than the previous one since 'Medicine Show', and although *Megatop* reached the highest chart position in the UK of all our albums, it was short-lived and disappeared from the Top 40 after three weeks.

The tour in September '89 wasn't a happy one, and we had all the usual creative and financial arguments that most bands go through after being together for so long. We hadn't quite made my seven-year band lifespan, but by the time we'd recorded 'Free' for the film *Flashback* (1990), starring Dennis Hopper and Kiefer Sutherland, it was clear to me that it'd be the last recording I made with B.A.D. It had been an honour to be in a band with Mick Jones, and to have written great songs with him, but even at the end I still felt in Joe Strummer's shadow. Plus there were topics that, as a Black man, I wanted to address in songs and I couldn't really expect Mick to sing about, and that made my mind up.

I couldn't leave Audrey and Jet, but I had to leave Mick and Big Audio Dynamite.

Independence Day

Exterior. Day. Fade into bright contrast a bare, flat, arid landscape. The earth is sun-scorched white and dotted with patches of scrubby brown bush and small, solid, dark mounds. Pan 180 degrees; the sky is bleached blue with not a cloud in sight. Two or three spindly trees offer a stark contrast with the emptiness of the land. There are no birds, no visible animals, just something slithering haphazardly and slowly across the ground in the middle distance. Camera discovers a speck of green-and-brown camouflage in the far distance. Slow zoom into a shape that slowly reveals as a large Land Rover, with cab doors open, the back covered by metal hoops but no canvas to shade the two rows of bench seats beneath them. Slumped with their backs to the Land Rover, four men try to avoid the sun, but the vehicle offers little shade, even under it. The sun and stifling heat permeate every inch of the land, air and sky. On the bench seats are some large canvas bags and a film camera. The men who sit, squat and lean against the car are arranged in a line. There are two white men wearing white safari shirts with large patch pockets, cargo shorts which end mid-calf, and Timberland work boots. One of the two Black men is dressed in dark green, military-looking long trousers and shirt with epaulettes; he has a red beret on his head and army-style boots on his feet. The other Black man has dreads halfway down his back, dark glasses, and is wearing a voluminous white T-shirt, khaki cargo shorts and light Timberland work boots.

'How the fuck did we run out of petrol, Ken?' I can't believe this. We're in the middle of fucking nowhere with nothing and no-one around, and nobody knows where we are or when we're due back in Windhoek.

Ken, our driver, minder and useless map-reader dressed in ex-army uniform shrugs his shoulders. 'Sorry, man.' At least he's not smiling.

'It doesn't matter, does it?' says my cameraman, sweat pouring down his wind- and sunburned face. 'We're kinda fucked if no-one comes along in the next couple of days, because we'll have run out of food and water.'

'S'OK,' says my producer. 'People like us don't die in the Namibian bush.' He looks at Ken. 'Do they?'

Ken looks the other way and says nothing.

'Hang on.' I suddenly remember. 'Ken. Those two guys we passed a couple of hours back, where were they going d'you think?'

'They're OvaHimba, they live out here.'

'Huh? Where? There's nothing here man, we drove away from civilisation all day yesterday and didn't see anything except bush, and we didn't get to anywhere either, so where the fuck can they live?'

Ken shrugs. 'Nomads. They set up camp with cattle wherever there's water and shelter from the wind, there's no one place they live.'

'Why would anyone do that in this desert?' the cameraman asks.

Ken laughs. 'This is not a desert, and they're beautiful people, man. They have a lot of things sorted – like the men can have two wives if they want.'

Shit, I think, I'm not sure that's 'sorted'.

The producer perks up, 'So those two we saw might be part of a tribe, and they'd have food and water, which might be around here somewhere?'

'Nah man, you'd never find them.' Ken punctures that bubble of hope.

Everyone sits and thinks, saying nothing.

Fuck it, I think, we should have registered our travel plans and let people know where we were going. But that would have taken too much time and I wanted to get this done as quickly as possible, because I hate camping. My 'crew' kipped down in the dirt in their sleeping bags last night, but there's no way I was gonna risk waking up with a snake or spider in my bed, so I sat in the truck – not sleeping, just admiring the enormous, star-filled sky until dawn. Now, in the suffocating heat of the midday sun, I keep coming back to the recurring thought I had as I twisted and turned, trying to get comfy on those bench seats last night – we are completely cut off from civilisation and I am totally unequipped for this shit. If it were down to Black people, events like Glastonbury wouldn't exist. We've spent our lives trying to get off the ground and into a comfortable bed, why the fuck would we want to get down in the dirt again?

Sitting there in the heat I get to thinking about the irony of the dread going back to Africa, dying in the bush, and the whole back to Africa thing. It's not just a Rastafarian idea, although in Jamaica the movement had been first promoted by Marcus Garvey, who is usually considered the 'founder' of Rastafarianism. Born in 1887 in Jamaica, Garvey launched the Universal Negro Improvement Association in 1914 with the intention to give Black people a government and voice of their own. He strongly believed that if you were Black, then you should be proud of it and saw no way of achieving Black suffrage in a white-run society. In the 1920s Garvey said, 'Look to Africa, when a Black king shall be crowned,' and a decade later a king (Haile Selassie) was indeed crowned, which many people saw as a fulfilment of Garvey's 'prophesy'. The Rastafarian religion quotes Garvey liberally, which is why reggae artists like Burning Spear and Big Youth namechecked him forty years later. But I wonder as I sit in the African dust, why did none of the reggae singers who sang about going back to Africa ever actually go? Their dream of going 'back to Zion' might have been tempered if they'd seen the reality of the place. Now that I was in Africa it struck me that I might be Black, but there's no sense in my pretending to be African, because I'm not. Being in Namibia has made me realise that.

'What's that?' The cameraman interrupts my thoughts, and climbing to his feet and shielding his eyes from the sun, he points into the distance.

'A fucking mirage probably,' I grumble, deciding not to stand because it'll only make my head swim and feel faint. Ken jumps up, though, to look in the same direction.

'Dust trail. Must be a jeep.' He climbs into the cab and starts rummaging through the glove compartment.

'Here 'tis!' he shouts excitedly and turns toward us, waving what looks like a fat handgun.

'Fuck,' I think, 'Are we about to be attacked?' I stand up so quickly that I have to hold onto the car to stop myself falling over again.

Ken points the gun straight up in the air at arm's length and pulls the trigger.

There's a bang, a whoosh and a long string of orange light, white smoke and sparks fly up and loop back down to earth somewhere in the distance.

It's a flare gun. 'Ah, smart,' I think.

About ten minutes later a safari truck filled with plump, pink Germans arrives at the scene of our near disaster. I've never been so glad to see white people in my life. Being much smarter than us, they're carrying a huge can of extra fuel with them, which they give us. We then follow them back to their base, from where we eventually find our way back to the capital.

I was in Namibia working as a second unit director on a film commissioned to record the country's official day of independence (March 21, 1990). I'd taken the job because B.A.D. were done, for me at least, and I'd always wanted to see Africa. But when I got there, I was shocked to discover how far removed I was from the Black African experience. I realised that I was the lost tribe, and with all my so-called civilisation, I was totally out of my depth among a nation of Black people. My first reaction on landing was that it was the greatest culture shock I'd experienced so far.

After a few days I saw how African Blackness is different to Jamaican Blackness. I'd always been aware of a certain prejudice that Jamaicans felt for Africans and vice versa in the early days – actually, it didn't subside until relatively recently, to be honest – and being in a country where everyone is Black and everything is run by Black people made me wonder why. I had grown up thinking of Africans as different to me, to Jamaicans. Being the only 'Jamaican' among Africans made me the odd one out, as something strange and other. My dreadlocks were a source of amazement and humour for kids who followed me around the city while we were filming – there's footage of me being in the middle of a scrum of them, all trying to touch my dreadlocks, and I look annoyed, amazed and delighted all at the same time, which pretty much sums up my experience of being in Africa. The locals' reaction to my hair was nothing compared to the suspicion I created because I was ordering around a white film crew. Often it seemed that Namibians related to the white guys better than they could to me, and as it so often had been in Jamaica, the Black, English-speaking man with locks directing white people was confusing for everyone. They had never seen people who looked like me in any position of power over a white man, and definitely not in perfectly executed Queen's English.

Putting the oddness of my position aside, I was aware that I was filming people after they'd travelled a long, hard and violent road to independence for their country – SWAPO guerrillas had started fighting for freedom from South African rule in 1966, and they'd been under white control since 1918 – and that was a humbling experience. Clearly independence was a big deal for not just the country, but the continent.

On the day of the ceremony I joined thousands of people filing past Nelson Mandela to shake hands, while my unit filmed proceedings. At the touch of his hand I thought how, despite the weight of the people's hopes and dreams being on his shoulders, this was the only man for the job. When the South African flag came down and the Namibian flag replaced it, a tear came to my eye. It was deeply moving and left a big impression on me.

I returned to the continent in 1992 to make a video for Baaba Maal in Senegal (for 'Yela'), and it almost killed me. We filmed in a one-bar, one-shop and one-donkey town where Baaba owned the only car, which was wrecked in a collision with a donkey while we were there. I nearly died after being poisoned by ice cubes in a drink – I only drank bottled water but didn't even think about the ice being put in my drinks. Africa left a different, physical impression on me that time. But when I returned to London following Namibian independence, I felt energised but undirected, if that makes sense. Back home I needed distraction and direction and got together with Leo and Greg to decide on a name for the band we'd agreed to form after calling it a day with B.A.D. We chose Screaming Target after the Big Youth album and with a couple of female singers, Chezere (real name Lynette Braithwaite) and Mary Cridell, plus Dan Donovan and Greg's brother Steve Roberts, started writing and rehearsing. I think now that I did it because I wanted to know if I could – although there's no getting away from the fact that it was also an ego trip – and because I thought we might get to tour and so I could be with Grace. As is often the way with such things, I failed with Screaming Target because I wouldn't listen to good advice – Chris Blackwell signed us to Island Records and said we should get a singer.

I didn't.

He was right.

The album we released in 1991 – *Hometown Hi-Fi* – had more of a reggae and world sound than B.A.D., but it lacked the magic of Mick Jones. Despite Chrissie Hynde featuring on 'This Town' and Pete Wylie on 'Bedazzled' helping to get us a few blinding reviews, after a while I realised that being in a band wasn't really what I wanted after all. It's a difficult existence at the best of times, and especially when you're trying to do something different. We were not naive 16-year-olds; we were grown men and it was hard to put up with a lot of the shit we'd avoided when in B.A.D. because we never had to play the 'scampi circuit' with Mick Jones as band leader. We hadn't had to travel around in Transit vans, sharing hotel rooms and trying to get our money out of promoters after gigs. We were old mates but being in a band on tour means that you can't have an argument and not see each other for a while. Screaming Target lasted for about a year before I lost interest and it was getting to be quite hard work. Leo, Greg, Steve and Dan decided that they wanted to play more dub dance-oriented stuff and formed a new band which I named Dreadzone.

I loved Dreadzone from the get-go, still do, and sporadically write lyrics for them to this day. With not much regret I decided it was time to give up the pop star thing. I'd never felt happy or comfortable being one, really. Flattery played to my ego as it does with most people, and because Mick Jones wanted me in his band, I was ready to be persuaded. Likewise, when I was asked to be in a movie called *Midnight Breaks* (1990) with Toyah, Robbie Coltrane and Edward Tudor-Pole during the period when Mick was in hospital, I said yes. The production company (Intercontinental Releasing Corporation) even made me the movie's poster boy and gave me lead billing along with Dawn Hope, above the proper actors. I didn't pay enough attention to the script to realise that the film would be so terrible, and the fact that no-one's ever heard of it is proof of how bad it is. It was interesting to see the process from in front of the camera, though, and it made me determined to make films rather than be in them.

I'd enjoyed the Namibian trip, and the music video industry had continued to grow while I'd been in B.A.D. I needed to make a living – B.A.D. created no new millionaires, believe me – and I still had connections in the industry, so I returned to making videos. One of the great things about directing music videos was the opportunity they offered for foreign travel because, when budgets allowed, I'd always write a treatment that required plane tickets. Not just because it meant that I could fly around the world at someone else's expense (although that was part of it), but mainly because it meant that Grace and I could spend time together again. When I could no longer tour with B.A.D. I had no reason to be in America or anywhere else in the world that work didn't send me so couldn't be with her. We somehow managed to keep our relationship alive over the telephone, but it wasn't easy, and by the time I'd decided to return to video-making full time it had been a year since we'd been together. Over that time a lot of our long phone conversations ended badly, in arguments. But still we couldn't leave each other.

When I started making videos again, I hired Grace as a crew member as often as I could and flew her out to be with me. We carried on our love affair in Paris, Amsterdam, America, Jamaica... and India.

Because my mother's family had travelled to Jamaica from India it was a big deal for me to visit Mumbai, just as it was for Apache Indian, a British-Indian hip-hop artist I was there to film on our first visit to the subcontinent. His material, a combination of Asian and Jamaican culture, came out of his upbringing in Steel Pulse territory, Handsworth, Birmingham. He started out with reggae sound systems but, by the end of the eighties, Apache was best known as a dancehall rapper. After releasing a couple of indie singles which sold well, he'd just signed to Island Records when I persuaded the MD there, Mark Moreau, to let me make a longform video of Apache visiting the land of his parents for the first time. My price was low enough that Mark thought it worthwhile and, more importantly, that I could take Grace, and so Apache and I flew out to find ourselves – or at least some ancestry.

Of course, once there we got a skewed idea of the place, because we were staying in expensive hotels in a major city (Mumbai) when the majority of the population live in dire poverty. We didn't have time for

Dread in Mumbai, 1991.

any real exploration of the country, nor for reflection on what it was to be Indian, because I had promised to return with something the record company could use for promotion – *Apache Over India*. That meant working long days, and my nights were occupied with Grace, who flew in separately, from New York, for the two-week shoot.

When I first arrived in India, I took a walk through the streets of Mumbai and was immediately surrounded by gangs of kids and beggars, all asking for stuff – and I gave everything I had on me to them. By the time Grace arrived a couple of days later, I just had to shout, 'Fuck off, I don't have anything left!', and most would scatter. Some of the kids pulled my dreadlocks hard to see if they were real, and then begged for money as my eyes watered. But because of my locks I also discovered that, seen from behind, I could be mistaken for a mad sadhu and all I had to do to get rid of them was spin around snarling, then they'd run away screaming.

India was a mystery to me before I arrived, and it wasn't ever successfully solved. My parents were not interested in their past history. There were a couple of photos in our old albums at home of my mother wearing a sari, but she never, ever talked about being Indian nor her heritage. I think her parents had also been born in Jamaica, and that the Indian roots go back several generations, but I didn't know for certain. What I did know was that I was overwhelmed by the heat, the smell and the poverty of the country. Still, I turned in a satisfying piece of work and the execs at Island loved *Apache Over India* because it became a 'news' item and was broadcast on TV in the UK, which got them far more publicity for their act than a pop video alone could ever have done ('That was the best £1,500 I ever spent!' Mark Moreau told me later). Which had kind of been the intention with *Slits Pictures* more than ten years earlier – we'd just been too ahead of our time. As a result of *Apache Over India*'s success, Island sent me back to the subcontinent to direct Apache videos for 'Chok There' and the international hit 'Boom Shak-A-Lak'. I also took him to Jamaica in 1995 to make a video for 'Ragamuffin Girl', a duet with Frankie Paul. He was cool with Jamaica, unlike Boogie Down Productions had been a few years earlier when they were there with Sly & Robbie to make a promo for 'Dance Hall'. They'd only previously been as far from New York as Miami for holidays and coming to Jamaica was a big shock for them –

during the shoot they were standing on the beach in their big leather puffa jackets, complaining about getting sand in their sneakers and needing a piss, so I told them to go and find a bush. They looked aghast and wanted to find a toilet. Even my white film crew pissed behind bushes and ate the food in Jamaica, while the Black Americans wanted to find a McDonald's. BDP never 'got' Jamaica; their vibe was too stuck in New York.

As the music promo business became more corporate in the 1990s, I preferred working with artists who were considered 'difficult' by record companies and managers, people like Shane MacGowan, for instance. When I directed The Pogues' video for 'Summer In Siam' I wrote two scripts. One for if Shane appeared at the studio for the shoot, and the other in case he didn't. I'd known him from the days of the Roxy, of course, so there was a bit of mutual respect and Shane did turn up. We propped him up on a tea chest, did about two takes and he was off. It turned out to be a great-looking video.

Another 'character' who was famously unpredictable and had a bad rep was Shaun Ryder. He'd split with Happy Mondays in 1992 and then formed Black Grape. They had the same management as Big Audio Dynamite, which is partly why I got the call to direct their first video, for 'Reverend Black Grape' in 1995. Made in Manchester, I wrote a script in which Shaun played two parts, one as the Reverend and the other as a TV show host. While we were shooting a scene with him as the TV host dancing with two Bunny Girls, he waved his arms at us and said, 'Wait a minute!' We stopped, he leaned over and threw up – he'd just done some smack round the back of the set. Then he wiped the spew off his face, gave us the signal to start rolling again and ended the song without stopping.

For the next Black Grape video – 'Reverend Black Grape' having been a Top 10 hit – MCA allowed me to take them to Jamaica to make the promo for 'In The Name Of The Father'. On the way there the plane was nearly diverted when Shaun got into a fight with one of the air hostesses, but they landed in Jamaica, and I went to the airport to collect them. Where I soon discovered that even before they'd got out of the airport they'd managed to score drugs. Back at the hotel everyone retired to their rooms to have a rest, but within a few minutes there was a knock at my door. It was Shaun.

'Don't tell the others,' he said, pushing his way into my room, 'because we made a pact that we were not going to do crack any more. Can I borrow your bathroom?'

'Sure, Shaun,' I said, as the door closed and his lighter sparked.

It didn't take long, and after he left there was another knock on my door.

'Shhh,' said Kermit stepping inside my room. 'We've made a pact that we wouldn't do crack...'

'Sure,' I shrugged, 'go and use my bathroom.'

That carried on for about four or five days. One day Shaun was feeling hyper on the set, and I had some Valium with me (I hate flying), so I gave him the four pills that I had and he chucked the whole lot down his neck. It has to be said that he performed very well after that. Experience has shown me that a lot of people are better on these things than off them. When they're off or trying to find them, they're a fucking nightmare. Give them the shit and they can get on with the work – that promo ended up being great, as did the promo for 'Kelly's Heroes' in which Shaun played Jesus and Bez was Batman. As fucked up as some of Black Grape seemed to be, there was also an admirable quality to them. They didn't give a fuck about how their behaviour, or videos, would affect record sales and naturally their debut album went straight into the charts at number one. It always seemed to me that Jamaica changed the artists I took there to make videos, but with Black Grape it was the other way around. Jamaica was never the same after experiencing Black Grape.

Between Black Grape videos I directed another one starring Shaun, for The Heads, which were Chris Frantz and Tina Weymouth of the Talking Heads. 'Don't Take My Kindness For Weakness' featured Shaun on vocals and I shot it in a New York transvestite bar. Shaun was so out of it that he couldn't remember his lines – you can see that in the video from his half-closed eyes – so we had to hold up a prompt board with the lyrics behind the camera. You'll notice that he's not on camera for too long when seated at the table, singing to camera. I also filmed him walking through dirty, wet New York streets, lit by neon sex show marquees, car headlights and streetlamps. While the grimy, sleazy backdrop suited him, I thought then that there were fewer and fewer people who I could fit into such a scene.

That period of my life was the last time I was truly busy making pop videos (I've made about 400 in all) because I grew tired with the process and the lack of characters in bands who were inspiring and self-directed. In the early days, video directors were in control but by the 1990s it was video-making by committee. As the old saying goes, 'what is a camel but a horse designed by a committee', and pop videos went camel-shaped when record companies brought in stylists and choreographers to tell bands what they should look like, how they should perform. If a stylist has to tell a band what to look like, then they are not a proper band as far as I'm concerned. As a director I prefer to direct and not follow orders and making music videos wasn't much fun any more, so I stepped back from it. I wanted to direct films, which were more challenging and satisfying to make. Luckily for me my timing was perfect, because Chris Blackwell hadn't given up on the idea of producing movies.

Walk and Live

Exterior. Night. Wide shot of a cinema marquee with the words
'DANCEHALL QUEEN WORLD PREMIERE' on two decks beneath
Kingston Caribe Cinema. Under the marquee a huge crowd of
people are shouting, waving, laughing. They're dressed in bright
colours, all gold, green, electric blue, vivid yellow and shocking pink.
Hairstyles are high, long, braided, beaded, some with pieces of what
looks like tinsel woven in. A few clearly fake 'Cleopatra' wigs in
bright red and purple Tina Turner shock wigs bob among the crowd
on women wearing tiny shorts cut to reveal butts and tops only big
enough to barely cover nipples. Men wear large-shouldered jackets in
rainbow colours with no shirt, cut-off jeans and what might be Gucci
loafers. Spangles of light reflect from diamanté brooches, earrings
and sunglasses. Loose, oversized Rolex knock-off watches are waved
around as greetings are made. The atmosphere is happy, light and
expectant but there's an edge of barely suppressed competition
running through the mass of heaving bodies.

Standing across from the Caribe, two men watch the gathering
hordes in amazement.

'Fuck, Don, I didn't expect this.'

'Me neither, Rick. Must be half of Kingston here.'

'Yeah. Looks like it could be a scene from the film, doesn't it?'

'I hope they like it, 'cos if they don't the place is likely to be torn apart, and us with it. There are some real bad bwoys among that lot, and I bet there are more than a couple of guns.'

'Relax man, they're gonna love it!'

They did, too, all of them. No-one knew exactly how many people turned up at the premiere of *Dancehall Queen* in Jamaica, but they were sharing seats in pairs or threes, and the aisles were full, even in the balcony. The audience laughed, yelled, cried and danced along with the action on the screen. That might have been the proudest night of my life. A movie that I'd co-written with Suzanne Fenn and directed with my old mate Rick Elgood was premiered at the same cinema where *The Harder They Come* was first shown, and it had gone down a storm. It continued to sell out for weeks after, and the cinema had to take off *Men in Black* (1997) starring Will Smith in another auditorium so that they could play my movie on both screens at once. *Dancehall Queen* was a major turning point in my life for many reasons, not all of them professional, but this was my feature film directorial debut.

Chris Blackwell commissioned, produced and distributed it through his recently created Palm Pictures. Although I always figured my first movie would be made in London, Chris said he wanted to make a Jamaican movie that would do for the island and its music now what *The Harder They Come* had done twenty-five years earlier. That was fine with me, and the script I spent three months rewriting was essentially *Harder* with a major, important difference – it was told from a female perspective (hey, as Bernardo Bertolucci once said, we all only have one good idea and we spend the rest of our lives reinterpreting it).

It is about a girl called Marcia (played by the excellent Audrey Reid), a humble street vendor who plots a way out of her poverty-stricken, violent and sexually abusive situation for herself and two daughters through the world of dancehall. Call it Cinderella without Prince Charming coming to the rescue, because Marcia does it all on her own. Just like *Harder*, I wanted to show the social and cultural state of Jamaica through an imaginary story, but instead of focusing on the macho would-be gangster world of the men of the island, I wanted to show how it was women who were making all the real and best social changes. All the guys in the movie wanted to be Ivan from *Harder* but

Marcia has ambition and a real need and drive to achieve something more. At the time it was becoming more common for Jamaican women to carve out careers in academia and politics, from where they could help rebuild the infrastructure of the country. Proof of that came in the form of Portia Simpson-Miller, who served two terms as Jamaica's prime minister for the People's National Party after *Dancehall Queen* was made (in 2006–7 and 2012–16).

Making a movie in the middle of Kingston was like filming at the Notting Hill Carnival if it was being held in a war zone, but it was important to me that we capture the full flavour of the city, with all its traffic, street life, poverty and spontaneity. We never had any idea what people might do when they saw us filming; some demanded money to film on 'their' patch, others insisted that we give them a job. Dogs, goats and chickens were always getting under our feet and it still amazes me that we managed to pull it off. We worked with what was then 'new' tech, using mini-DV cameras, which was something of a major feat in those days, and without realising it made the kind of movie which Lars von Trier's Dogme 95 manifesto of 1995 described. He'd written about wanting to 'purify' film by not using any special effects (we couldn't afford any), or post-production effects (ditto). Dogme 95 states that the film has to be shot on location (we did), the camera must be hand-held (as the mini-DV cameras were) and not contain any superficial action – all our action was very real (Paul Campbell, who played the arch villain Priest in the movie, was particularly convincing). And Lars didn't get around to releasing a movie made according to his own manifesto until a year after *Dancehall Queen*.

I wasn't trying to make a movie according to Dogme 95 'rules' – hell, I didn't even know they existed – it was just that the hand-held digital mini-DV cameras are so tiny no-one took them seriously, and because of that the actors (many of them not professionals) would open up, they didn't feel intimidated by the camera. That was really useful for working with non-professionals and we employed quite a few, although not as many as I'd planned, because after giving out scripts to guys during rehearsals they'd disappeared and didn't come back. It took a while to work out what was going on until I realised that they couldn't read. After that I tried not to expect little things I took for granted being the norm, and attempted to make the process as unthreatening as possible. Small cameras got us through a lot of doors, both literally and figuratively. We could move around the streets quickly and shoot scenes before passers-by fully realised what we were doing. Plus, of course, generally it's true that the bigger the camera, the bigger the bill because you need more operators and crew. Here I have to say that big respect is due to Louis Mulvey, the cameraman I worked with on most of my films, who made things run smoothly even when they were difficult, which was often. Some things we could do little about, though, like every night shoot for *Dancehall Queen* taking place against a backdrop of dogs barking all over town. If one started, they all joined in. When I asked 'fixer' Carl Bradshaw (aka José) what we could do about them he said, 'There is two options: either feed dem or shoot dem.' So, we made sure to take a bag of scraps out with us at night and hoped we could keep the local dogs quiet long enough to film.

Working with people like Beenie Man ('King of the Dancehall') was also a bit of a test. When those guys turned up on set something that should have taken half an hour instead took half the night. He'd be distracted by his entourage, or by Carleen, the real Dancehall Queen, not to mention 'nuff herbs. But, despite that, his undeniable charisma brought something extra to the whole story. Lady Saw also featured in the film, and she was like a Jamaican Millie Jackson, using her sexuality to get her point across. She scared the shit out of me, and her contributions to the movie were essential for that reason.

When I first saw *The Harder They Come*, some of the lines of dialogue struck a chord, like 'Who's a bad man? One bad man come out an' draw,' and they became 'samples' in our culture, thrown around in everyday discussions among people who knew where they were from and used in countless remixes over the years. Hoping I could do the same with *Dancehall Queen* I wrote lines that might become everyday phrases among the audience – cultural samples, like Priest's warning to people who witnessed him killing Sonny: 'Walk and live – talk and bomboclaat dead.' It's great hearing young Jamaicans repeat that line to me whenever I mention the movie, even to this day. Amazingly, it was the most successful home-grown movie in Jamaica for decades, beating even *Harder* in ticket sales in JA. That it was a wholly Jamaican-made movie was really down to Chris Blackwell, because he insisted that we use only Jamaican actors and no American or English stars. That was a brave decision because it ultimately limited sales around the world – Americans and plenty of Brits need subtitles to get everything that's going on in *Dancehall Queen* because the dialogue is genuine Jamaican, not Anglicised. Pretty much every movie made in Jamaica between *Harder* and *Dancehall* were romanticised or watered-down versions of life on the island, and Chris didn't want that, for which I'm grateful.

Of course, Chris had other motives for making the movie truly Jamaican, one of which was that he wanted to create a Jamaican film industry. When *Dancehall* was successful enough he commissioned another film, called *Third World Cop* (1999). Directed by Chris Browne, the script was written by Chris Salewicz and Suzanne Fenn and it starred Paul Campbell playing an anti-hero cop called Capone. It was the opposite of *Dancehall* in that it was all about macho men, guns and gangsters, and it was hoped that it'd crack the US market. It didn't. Sadly, Jamaican movies didn't get made in huge numbers after that, although in 2003 Rick and I were approached to make one called *One Love*, which was described to me as being a 'feel good' kind of film, sort of *Romeo and Juliet*, only without the gangs and guns. Written by Trevor D. Rhone, who co-wrote *The Harder They Come* (that movie runs through Jamaican culture like Kingston would through a stick of rock), it starred Ky-Mani Marley and Cherine Anderson, who was cast for *One Love* because of her riveting performance (her first) in *Dancehall Queen*. I remembered that she used to sing when waiting for her takes on set, and she had a really good voice, which this script called for. I thought the storyline was dated but it looks fantastic, which is all down to Rick Elgood. It is really Rick's film, just as *Dancehall Queen* is mine. My job on *One Love* was to get the best out of the cast, being a mixture of first-timers and pros just as it had been with *Dancehall Queen*.

Although it was only six or seven years since we'd made *Dancehall*, it seemed to me that Kingston and Jamaican society in general had changed, and a lot of that was down to the emergence of coke, which replaced ganja as the drug of choice for many in the yards and dancehalls. The music culture had moved on too, from analogue to digital, with most artists toasting over studio-created riddims. While the idea of 'Dancehall' had existed since the fifties, over the years the meaning of the word shifted several times and became associated with a specific incarnation of reggae. That's always been the way: the cultural climate and changes in technology influenced the changes in reggae. When independent producer Henry 'Junjo' Lawes used the Roots Radics as a backing group for sessions at Channel One to create Barrington Levy's *Bounty Hunter* album, engineered by the Scientist, it took reggae in a new direction in 1979. Wayne Smith's hit 'Under Mi Sleng Teng' marked another big change in 1985, one I liked because it kept the organic feel of a reggae bass line. But in the 1990s the musical emphasis moved to the kick drum rather than the bass line. Advances in music technology brought cheapish keyboards with built-in sounds to the scene – all you had to do was hit a pre-set button and boom, the tune was there – or not, as I knew from experience. In a weird way, although technology freed up plenty of people around the world, it seems to me that it almost fucked Jamaican music. There is a downside to affordable technology and that's mediocrity, especially when it's used by people who have no learning or grounding in the culture into which it's been inserted. I always thought a combination of the organic and the technological made things more interesting culturally, but in many ways ragga was a backlash against those who'd reaped the rewards of reggae's international success, carried out by those who had no such reach. Kingston's drug trade forged strong connections with New York, Miami and Washington in the 1990s, and that brought about a shift in Jamaican culture that can be heard in the music. Most of the lyrics in ragga are bragging and violent, with all political themes lost.

I learned a lot about my heritage directly through reggae music at a time when it spoke of change for the better, of political revolution, not just guns, drugs, misogyny and homophobia. Ragga music, as it was then known, seemed to be made for the moment, not longevity, and best heard only in the environment of the dancehall. With Bob Marley, Jamaica gained cultural respect around the planet, but by the millennium the island was beginning to lose that global appeal. Ragga made for 'the yoots' in the middle of urban cities didn't expand into other cultures as much as straight-up reggae had because it was too self-obsessed. Black Americans picked up on aspects of reggae and ragga, as can clearly be heard in R&B and hip-hop, but they've gone one better. Blind emulation of the American blueprint and the wrong drugs has knocked Jamaican music off track.

But there's always hope; you should never underestimate Jamaica's ability to come up with a fresh take on matters. All that's needed is more self-interpretation, because that's what helped such a tiny island grow from being a pit of colonised misery to culturally colonise the planet with such positive vibes. Jamaica remains very much a paradox, though, with its Rastafari roots spirituality consciousness facing off the rude bwoy ragamuffin element in the dancehall. Although, that's what makes the place so interesting. It's a paradise for some and a pair of dice for others.

My relationship with the land of my parents has been as complicated and contradictory as anyone else's, I guess. I've always regarded it as a place of work and play, but it's never been a home, and Jamaica still has as much trouble identifying me now as it did back in 1978. When Rick and I flew into Kingston with the (mostly white) crew to make *One Love*, as usual I went through passport control first. The officer on duty told me to take my sunglasses off, which I dutifully did. I stood there for ages as he looked at me, then at the crew behind me. He asked me the usual questions and I responded in my best English ('cos I'm on my best behaviour), but he's faced with a dread in scruffy clothes and all these white guys behind asking 'What's wrong, boss?' It just doesn't make sense to him, somehow.

Finally, he says, 'You t'ink you're smart, eh?' and starts ranting at me. Two senior officers had to physically remove him from his post so that we could get into the country. He couldn't understand what was going on and was convinced that whatever it was, it couldn't be legal. I simply didn't compute to him and looking at his confusion I was reminded of something from the past. His look of bewilderment was not too dissimilar to that on my grandmother's face when I knocked on her door.

Fast forward seventeen years or so and things are still not simple with me and Jamaica.

I was there with my family on a holiday – me, my (white) wife and two teenage daughters. Because of the way I look, local guys who'd usually be hitting on the women didn't, because they thought I was a local and had my hustle on, which they respected – and I worked it! It gave me some peace of mind; I could be accepted among Kingstonians – but only for so long and not in every situation. One evening on the

Letts family holiday in JA, 2019.

same visit we rolled up to Rick's Place in Negril, with me driving our rental and the doorman approached the car, leant over and said, 'Right m'man, drop the tourists, park over there and bring me back the keys.' To which I replied, 'No, bredrin, this is my car and my family, so you park it over there. Thank you.'

More than forty years after my first visit, I was still constantly reminded of the vast cultural difference between my existence and that of Jamaicans of my generation. Whenever I work there, I have to walk a line between being the boss and also a brother, to look out for them and instruct them on what to do. Which isn't easy and partly why to this day making *Dancehall Queen* is the thing I'm most proud of.

We held the UK premiere of the movie in Brixton, at the cinema where I'd first seen *The Harder They Come*. I was happy to see that the Ritzy, as it was now called, was a lot smarter than when I was a kid and it was called the Classic. Back then it was a fleapit and the back row was permanently occupied by dirty old men in long macs. Walking down the red carpet on the night with my parents made me incredibly proud. So was seeing friends from back in the day there. What I wasn't so proud of, though, was that my children – Audrey and I had a daughter, named Amber, in 1992 – were not present. The final break between Audrey and I had happened while we were wrapping up filming in Kingston, and by the time of the UK premiere in October 1997, Audrey, Jet and Amber were no longer talking to me. The only compensation I had was that finally Grace and I could be together.

What's the Move?

Interior. Early morning, bright sunshine pours in through an open window. Reveal a small, cluttered office. The walls are covered with yellow Post-it notes, every surface has recording equipment on it, among the clutter are small cameras, assorted wires and leads, microphones, booms. Underneath the plain wooden self-assembly desks that stand against every wall are a range of black canvas holdalls and plastic carrier bags that spill items of clothing, shoes, reels of masking tape and paper files. On the largest desk against the wall adjacent to the room's only door sit a large screen and a couple of large video and audio players. A handful of people stand and sit about, yawning, stretching and talking inaudibly. A tall, elegant blonde woman stands, leaning against a desk by the playback and editing equipment. She's smiling and chatting with the man seated in front of her. The atmosphere is calm, until the door is thrown open and a bustling female carrying a clipboard and stern expression enters. She points at the tall blonde and speaks to the man in the seat.

'Her! She's gotta go.'

I lean back, puzzled. 'What?'

Suzette repeats, 'She's gotta go.'

'But why, and no, we're not finished,' I try not to shout, 'we've got to do pick-ups.'

Grace is looking annoyed and confused. I put a hand on her arm in what I hope is a calming gesture.

Suzette shakes her head briefly. 'I don't care, word from London. Grace has to go. She can't be here any longer, Don.'

'Why not, what's happened?'

A sigh from Suzette and then she explodes the H-bomb that has been heading toward me and Grace for years. 'Audrey knows about Grace, and she's kicking up hell with Chris, who doesn't want the movie to be disrupted. We have to meet the schedule, you know that.'

'Hang on,' I stand up ready to argue, but Grace stops me.

'It's OK, Don, you're almost done anyway.'

Suzette nods at Grace. 'We've booked you on a flight to JFK this afternoon, so get your things together. A car'll take you.'

Grace gives me half a smile, a kiss, and leaves. All I can do is watch her walk away. I can't argue with Suzette, I can't demand Grace stays or I go with her. I want to leave with Grace, but I have obligations to *Dancehall Queen* and everyone working on it, which means I have to get it finished. I fall back into the chair and try not to think about what happens when we wrap.

A week later I was back in London and Grace was in hospital in New York with a bad case of tonsillitis. While she dealt with doctors and illness, I tried to keep calm and reason everything out with Audrey. The irony of my situation was that Grace made me want to be worthy of her love, to be a better person than I felt I was at the time, to be the kind of person that she'd want to be with. It must have sounded like a bare-assed insult to Audrey, and maybe it is, but I didn't want to leave her and our kids because it wasn't the kind of thing that a man – went my thinking – who Grace could love would do. If we hadn't had Jet, I probably would have slipped out of the relationship with Audrey in 1986, but now he and Amber were there, and I love my kids. Audrey and I went to therapy to try to make sense of what was happening during the months after she'd been told about Grace, but in the sessions all I could think and say was, 'I really fucked up.' No amount of justification could make things better, the whole affair bounced around my brain for weeks. I tried to explain how I met and fell in love with Grace at a time when, as a member of B.A.D., I could have taken advantage of groupies, one-night stands, and had lots of meaningless sex, but I didn't want to. I didn't want to have to explain to Audrey how I'd given her an STD, and that wasn't an excuse it was simply my truth. It didn't help things with Audrey when I added that Grace and I hadn't slept together until a year after we'd met and that we'd first become friends. Audrey didn't appreciate the fact that Grace and I had an old-fashioned courtship, and formed a close friendship before it became a love affair. There's never a good way to tell your partner and the mother of your children that you have been in love with another woman for ten years. Or, if there is, I sure as fuck didn't know about it.

Naturally, Audrey threw me out – of both 'my' place and hers because I gave her and the kids ownership of the Bassett Road flat, which never excised my feelings of guilt.

The therapist we saw suggested that I try to get my thoughts and feelings in order by writing about what had happened and how I felt. I started a kind of diary and what follows are those bits of it worth reading (I hope). They include notes from trips to New York and random observations of a man in the grip of an emotional and existential crisis. This is how I was, back then:

It's 1996 and I'm forty years old. I'm also in the process of leaving my wife and two kids for another woman. Well, we're not actually married, but when you got kids, you're way past married anyhow; any fool can say 'I do'. Grace is her name and until we got caught, we'd been having an affair for about ten years, which is only two years shy of my time with Audrey. Jet, my son, is eleven, Amber my daughter is four. I love them dearly, I love their mother too, but not as much as I love Grace...

It's 4.30 a.m. the desperate hours in which only the desperate dwell – unless you're on a dancefloor, and I'm years from that.

I'm sitting here in a small room that Trish has so kindly let me use in my hours of need. I got one of those Sony wide-screen TVs but that's still at Bassett Road, right now I'm watching a cheap six-inch screen version. Went to a party but left after an hour, don't feel like talking, not ready to socialise. Being out when you're performing below par is damaging to your health!

Tonight's movie is *Waiting to Exhale* [1995] which opens with one of the four female protagonists proclaiming, 'I've given you eleven years, raised two kids, and you're leaving me for a white woman!' She proceeds to burn all fifty of her man's fine suits and his B.M.W. Love – what can you say? I hope my future ex-wife doesn't see this. Ain't it funny how whatever crisis is going on in your life, when you turn on the T.V. there it is being shown back at you. Someone once said the movies are reality and reality's a nightmare. No shit.

End of August, Carnival Time... can you believe I been coming for 25 years? Jungle carries the swing this year – and the last, come to think of it.

Now it's 5.30 in the morning, and I'm in the S/FX zone but seriously and it is in this state that I will try to put into words the root of my current confusion. For now, I'll keep the run-up brief although it's very much part of the story that got me to this place. I think either way I'd be here. Basically, in true movie cliché I got busted for playing away from home. Seems common enough, except that this is with a woman I've been seeing at every opportunity for some 10 years: Grace.

*   *   *

Can you imagine being so bored or miserable or both that you walk down to Avenue D. N.Y.C. to try something new – score $100 worth of crack from the projects and then smoke till dawn, only stopping for a brisk walk to Max Fish for a quick double J.D. and coke? Little was his name, as he was in size and in his outlook on life. He said that his mum died at 30 a junkie and his dad at 35 an alcoholic, and it would cost $20 dollars for him to procure. Oh yeah, he also said he was fucking himself up and that he didn't know why.

I gave him $20 to help him on his way.

I love this town, it brings the devil out in me. Walking around at three a.m. and the streets pulsate like it's six in the evening. This place oozes sex, drugs and rock 'n' roll – no, make that rap 'n' ragga. The Fugees' 'The Score' is currently destroying the place. There's a new-found confidence here, the place is no longer fascinated by all the 'tea bags' with their Eurotrash.

Fuck writing it, that ain't the problem. It's the THINKING. Yet it would make for an interesting approach, I guess. This in a nutshell has been an eternal problem for me, the choice between the right thing, the wrong thing and the cool thing. Put another way it's what I describe as my daily battle between God and the Devil. Why does Jesus whisper, why does the Devil shout?

So, I power down and start to watch a video *The Brothers McMullen* (1995) and guess what? One McMullen is having an affair dilemma.

The next morning I'm reading Irvine Welsh's *Ecstasy* and poor old Rebecca Navarro has just discovered her beloved Percy has been fucking her over for years.

That evening Cathy threatens to kill Cindy if she finds out she's up to her old tricks on *Eastenders*. Cindy, you see, is no stranger to extra-marital affairs. My fascination with this subject matter is not without foundation, of course.

Went to the 'marriage guidance' session this morning, the fifth.

*   *   *

I'm on my way to New York to see the woman I love. The strain of the past two months has driven me to desperate measures. What with the utter collapse of my personal life, caused by me, by the way, coupled with the strain of bullshit politics on the movie I'm trying to complete has really got on top of me. If you knew me, you'd understand how serious this is, the very fact that I've put it in print is a cry for help. But who can help me? Where is the manual? I've never been one to pick up and run but I need something. I need to...

Picked up at the airport by Limo, check into a suite at Morgans.

Does all this information really give any insight into where I'm coming from? Maybe I should just skip to the juicy stuff: the two-timing—forever-lying-self-gratifying-hedonistic way I've lived my life. But this is the smoke screen, delaying tactics that will serve quite nicely until I'm ready to face my demons.

*   *   *

MEMORIES WERE MEANT TO FADE, THEY WERE DESIGNED THAT WAY...
T.V.s HAVE FEELINGS TOO... FOOD IS FOREVER...

*   *   *

Back in London, last night Jet informed me that he wants to change his last name so it's the same as Audrey's. His reasoning being that when I eventually have another child his or her name will be Letts and he would not like that. When I ask what makes him think I'll have another child, he reluctantly tells me that Audrey says so...

*   *   *

I'm in Brighton watching Dreadzone, my head distressed by a two-hour phone argument with Grace the night before. I guess it's the stress of the situation i.e. in two months' time she will arrive to start a new life with me and in the meantime, we are physically separated. Which would be difficult enough without being complicated by the fact that I've left Audrey, Jet and Amber for this new life, but Audrey is about as mad as that woman in *Waiting to Exhale* (the one who torched her husband's entire wardrobe and B.M.W.). Anyhow, these arguments with Grace leave me totally fucked. They hang over me like a cloud, possibly because I guess I'm mostly responsible, and if I don't get this right, I'll blow everything. It's not that I'm always right, it's just that I'm never wrong, and that's the problem.

As I'm watching the show, I get that uncomfortable 'spectator' feeling accompanied by a subtle ache to be on-stage. Just as I'm about to wallow in my sorrow a girl runs up, kisses me on the cheek and says, 'You're one of my all-time heroes!' For a mere millisecond my spirit lifts. It's funny how a moment of recognition can make your day. Is this what one would call a sign of insecurity? The next day I'm reading the new *Q* magazine and I see a namecheck regarding the 'Heads. What does two times a millisecond make?

*   *   *

7.00 a.m., this is the first attempt to add to my ongoing saga in about two months. Between confusion and a trip to Jamaica to finish the movie, I've not had motivation. I was summoned to New York to meet Chris Blackwell for a meeting regarding the movie and we flew to Miami on

Friday in his private jet, and checked into the Marlin, one of his hotels. Spent the early hours of the morning bullshitting with Bono. The next morning we flew to Jamaica. We're whisked through customs like royalty, then driven to Strawberry Hill to watch the Mandela film with the prime minister of Jamaica. I should be impressed, but I got other shit on my mind.

Sometimes, just for a moment, everything comes together and I'm happy. Usually when I'm driving in my car, the light's just right and it all clicks. But it only lasts as long as whatever track is playing on the stereo, the catalyst for this chemical reaction.

Did I mention that in one of the visits to the therapist, I confessed to being a media-created monster, armed with a remote control? Forever seeking the next fix, be it visual/aural/mental/sexual or oral. Amazingly superficial about anything of depth, and at the same time deep about the superficial. Jeremy told me there were two of him (personalities). He asked how many me's there were? I replied, 'as many as I need'. Problem is, I thrive/survive like this. You've heard the expression 'channel surfing'? Well I guess I'm 'life-surfing', always looking for the next big one. If I haven't seen the movie then it doesn't exist, if I don't like the program then I'll change the channel.

*   *   *

Grace arrives in three days' time, will the phoenix rise from the ashes? I've been a total asshole the past few days. I'm used to being in control and for the first time my remote ain't working.

Chrissie Hynde once told me that we're all ultimately on our own in this world, I must remember to ask her if she still believes that.

What is existentialism? How do you even spell it?

Presently Jet is not speaking to me since he found out there's another woman in my life. I'm finding this difficult, and I realise he's expressing his hurt in the only way he knows. It's just like me trying to deal with another me, which if I've managed to convey anything about myself and my family will illustrate what a potentially dangerous route that is. In my heart I know I have to make the effort to remedy this situation. What's scary is my potential to say fuck it and walk away.

It was recently reported that the Artist Formerly Known As Prince lost his first child due to birth complications. For some reason this really depressed me. I was also really upset that Tyson lost against Holyfield.

*   *   *

January 10, 1997. 7.30 a.m. Grace is here, she's upstairs, asleep. I'm 41 today. I could be depressed about that but the whole event was swamped by two days spent arguing. Love will tear us apart, if we let it. Why does she put up with an arsehole like me? I hope I don't drive her away. My time with her has erased all that's gone before. I love this woman. She makes beautiful shapes from negative space. I've never wanted to really show myself to anyone, but I want to reveal myself to her; I need to, desperately. We fell in love – and I think this is the only time I would use that expression 'fall in love'. It was her personality that got me first. I didn't even realise it was happening. All previous relationships were premeditated orchestrated acts of lust or ego. I saw, I conquered, I came.

Not this time.

*   *   *

Today I married the girl of my dreams.

Grace arrived in London just in time for New Year's Eve 1996, and we moved into a room of our own in Leo's flat on the Harrow Road. We lived there for a while, but it wasn't a big place, so we began house hunting early in the new year. We couldn't afford anywhere of a decent size in Notting Hill but found the place we've lived in ever since. It took me a while to really love living here, because as far as I was concerned it was the wrong side of the Harrow Road, but when we found it I looked in the garden and thought, 'At least it's got outdoor space, which I haven't had since I was a kid.' No idea why, but it still amazes me that I now 'own' a tree. It was a two-bed ground-floor apartment carved out of a large Edwardian redbrick house just north of Ladbroke Grove. I say 'was' because since we've been here we've added a basement to accommodate the two daughters we had in 2001 and 2005. I guess that the basement work was a sign that we weren't going anywhere, that we'd finally dug in. We were married in November 1997, quietly at a registry office (Jeannette was a witness) with no party or any fuss. We didn't want to upset Audrey, who'd never officially been my wife. Then we found the apartment and it's turned out to have everything I need, even if I didn't know it then. I understand it now. We did the place up, got married and then made a family. All of which had to be paid for, of course, and, fortunately, I could earn doing things I enjoyed.

Signing the register with Grace, 1997.

Westway to the World

Interior. Day. A high-ceilinged warehouse space with a curved, brick roof, lit by strip lights hung on chains. A steel staircase at the left of the space leads to a mezzanine. The ground floor is filled with bulky shapes covered by dark sheets of heavy fabric, tables with various pieces of camera and film equipment and crates with lids loosely set on top. The only daylight comes through a steel-framed window taking up the top quarter of the entrance, which is closed by corrugated metal gates, into which is cut a door. Once a car repair garage, the space is now a movie equipment store and hire shop. Enter through the door a white male, mid-thirties, hair receding, ears and nose protruding, looking uncertain as to where to go. On the mezzanine two men look up from the desks where they're seated opposite one another. The bulkier of the men shouts down to the intruder.

'Wha' ya want?'

'Looking for Don?'

I get up and move toward the steps. 'Yeah. Mal?'

'Yeah. Hi, Don.'

We meet at the bottom of the stairs and shake hands. I perch on a bar stool off to the side and he sits in an old chair and gets a notebook and pen from his bag.

'You found the place OK then.'

'Yeah, though I thought it'd be in West London, not King's Cross, but it's a lot easier bike ride from Camden which is good.'

'You're a brave man cycling in London.'

'Not really. What is this place, if you don't mind me asking?'
Mal points to the various cameras and film equipment lying about.

'It's our warehouse and office, me and Rick rent equipment out. Anyway, what's up?'

'Trish said we should meet, and I need to get an idea of what you want to do. I asked her what the band want to talk about, and she said, quote, "You're the journalist, you work it out."'

I laugh. 'Yeah, sounds about right. All I know is that they've decided to tell their story.'

'So,' Mal says, 'I was thinking we'd start them off talking about 1968, 'cos Joe was 16, Mick and Paul 14, and they were coming of age at a time when the world was on fire. There'll be lots of great footage from newsreels of '68 you can use, right? The Grosvenor Square riot, Paris in May, that kind of stuff.'

'Yeah, but are they alright with that? Does Joe want to talk about his school, or Mick about his nan?'

'I don't know,' he shrugs. 'I guess we'll find out when we start filming. I also asked Trish about a title and she said they don't have one, so I was thinking 'No Elvis, Beatles or Rolling Stones', 'cos she says that we'll end the film when Mick is sacked. Which means we cover 1977 to 1984, just like the song says.'

'Yeah, that sounds alright.' I look up to the mezzanine. 'Yo Rick, that sound good to you? Rick!'

He stands up and looks down at us. 'This is Mal. Mal, that's Rick, he's the producer.'

Rick nods down at us. 'A'right.'

Mal waves back and says, 'Cheers, Rick.' Then he looks at me again.

'What do you think about getting some other people interviewed for this?' he asks. 'Trish says the band probably only want them to be on camera, but we have to get Bernie if we can, right? And Kosmo. I can get Tony Parsons to talk about the *NME* tube interview. Baker and Johnny Green should probably also be interviewed, and Terry Chimes. Which reminds me, how's Topper, any idea?'

'I haven't seen Topper for a while,' I answer. 'But he has to be in this. Not sure if Bernie would want to be in it, though.'

'OK, well, I'll speak to Bernie – he came into my office a few weeks back banging on about how he wanted to write a book telling the world how he invented The Clash and punk, that it'd be the only one worth reading. I couldn't get a word in edgeways. And just as suddenly as he'd appeared – without calling – he left.'

'Sounds like Bernie.'

'OK, well I guess we have to see what the band say. See you next week in Bromley By Bow – where the fuck is that anyway?'

'Down the Mile End Road, Mal. You got a car?'

'Yeah, don't worry, I'll find it. See you.'

With that he puts his pad and pen back in the bag, shoulders it and leaves. Rick comes down the stairs and asks, 'Why's he doing this and not you or Salewicz? He doesn't know any of them like you two.'

'We'll get more complete answers.' Rick looks confused, so I explain. 'When you question someone you already know, you don't get the whole story because they assume you know enough to read between the lines. Mal can do this, he knows his shit and the band are OK with it.'

In July 1998 The Clash, who had talked about doing a film for years but only now decided that the time was right, travelled separately and on different days to 3 Mills Studios to sit in front of a camera and talk about their lives. The film producer is Tricia Ronane (Trish), Paul Simonon's wife at the time, mother of their two sons and managing business affairs for The Clash. I always knew that there was a great story waiting to be told on film and that eventually I'd get the call

Filming the 'Rock The Casbah' video in Texas with The Clash, 1982.
(L–r) Joe Strummer, Mick Jones in camouflage mask, Paul Simonon.   DON LETTS

because of our history. I also had a lot of previously unseen footage of The Clash that even they didn't know existed.

Tricia and I had begun to set up the shoot a couple of weeks before this meeting, and we'd discussed what we'd like to see in it. Good music documentaries reflect the time and capture the era in which they were made, and I really wanted that to be the case with *No Elvis, Beatles or Rolling Stones* (it didn't become *Westway to the World* until after we'd wrapped). I didn't want to make the usual MTV rockumentary or *South Bank Show*-style documentary where the director or producer puts their slant on the story. It was clear from the moment that Joe came in for his interview – the first of the bunch – that he was treating this very seriously and had thought about what he wanted to say. I'd not heard a lot of the stuff he told the camera about his life before The Clash – the relationship he had with his father and his brother in particular – and I got the distinct feeling that, although he knew I couldn't use a lot of it, he wanted to get it off his chest (some of it ended up in Julien Temple's film *Joe Strummer: The Future Is Unwritten*, in 2007). I was genuinely surprised at how honest he was throughout the filming, which took about five hours including the lunch break. After a few false starts, with Joe having to be reminded to put his questions into the answers because there wasn't going to be a voice-over – most bands have problems stringing a couple of sentences together, but The Clash never did – he talked and talked. At times he was really happy, but he was clearly troubled by things that he'd done and now regretted. Joe's direct apology on camera to Mick was really powerful and the tears in his eyes were genuine. I wasn't expecting anything like that from him or the others, especially Paul, but they all ended their interviews in tears, or close to it. There is real regret and love for each other shown in that film.

I know people have questioned why the narrative ends when Mick gets sacked, but *Westway* is the story of The Clash, not the Clash Mk II. Mick was into every single damn detail of the film. He was interviewed for about three hours and we all thought it went pretty well, but when Mal said that was the final question, Mick looked up at me and said, 'Can we do that again?' I asked, 'What, the last question?' to which he replied, 'No, the whole thing.' Mick had come to the interview a little anxious, on the defensive, and on camera he came off as being reserved. So, we shot the interview again the following morning, before the scheduled session with Topper. Although none of the band were planning to be at the studio at the same time, Mick said he wanted to hang around to see Topper. Because he was still troubled by addiction at the time, Topper hardly appears in the original cut of *Westway to the World*, but for the few moments he does appear, he is scarily honest. 'I'd like to apologise to them for letting the side down, for going off the rails, but if it happened again, I'd probably do the same thing,' he says, and I admire him for that. I always thought of him as being like Frankie Machine in Nelson Algren's *The Man with the Golden Arm*.

The film also includes interviews with Terry Chimes, Johnny Green, photographer Pennie Smith and Tony Parsons. I tried to get Bernie involved and he said no. Mal also called him and was told: 'Only I can make a Clash documentary.' Although originally released in 2000 in the UK, it won a Grammy Award for Best Long Form Music Video in 2003 (it came out in 2002 in the States). Not expecting to win, no-one from the band or record company went to the show, only me and Grace. The organisers hadn't been informed that I was there, so when they announced the award they said something like, 'Sadly director Don Letts can't be here tonight.' They were interrupted by me shouting from the back of the hall, where I'd sat not expecting to be in the running, 'Hold tight, I'm coming for my Grammy!' I ran to the stage and got there out of breath, and with mixed emotions. Joe had died unexpectedly just eight weeks earlier, and the shock hadn't worn off by the time I was onstage holding the tiny statue in my hands.

When someone close to you dies suddenly it's impossible to grieve at first, because you simply can't believe that they're gone. Joe wasn't showing any signs of illness; he'd been recording with his new band The Mescaleros, planning a tour and along with his second wife Lucinda had moved to Somerset where he walked a lot, chilled and was writing songs. It was a total shock that he was killed by an undiagnosed heart problem, which had probably been there since birth and could have taken him at any time. But he died just before Christmas 2002 when he and his family were gathering for the holiday. None of those who knew and loved Joe felt there was much to celebrate that year. In the weeks between his passing and the Grammys I'd find myself picking up the phone to call him about something and then remembering that he wasn't there. The thing was, I hadn't said goodbye and that's not the way death should work. Joe was never far from my thoughts and in that moment onstage in New York as I accepted the Grammy, I couldn't help but think that it had been given because of his death. If it was, I thought, he wouldn't like it because the film was about The Clash, not him, and besides he'd never have been happy with winning on a sympathy vote. I also felt a little uneasy because I could see there was a danger people would create a legend out of Joe, which would separate him from the band. Joe would agree that winning awards is not why any of us got into doing what we do, but when they're handed out it's important that recognition goes to everyone involved, equally.

As it turned out, winning wasn't exactly a blessing for me, because although my brethren thought it was cool, I didn't get any work offers for six months. Apparently, the logic in the world of movies is that once you've won a Grammy you'll be more expensive to work with. Fortunately, later in the year Sony asked me to edit *The Essential Clash*, a compilation DVD featuring all the videos I'd directed for the band, plus a few I hadn't. It also included the trailer for the *Clash on Broadway* movie and interviews with the band done for the *London Weekend Show* in '76. But more importantly, Joe Strummer's *Hell W10* film was included. Joe directed it in West London during January and February 1983 as a side project between touring and recording. I have to hand it to him, he was a natural director, and if he said, 'Go and jump off a cliff,' people would (and I'd film it).

Strummer had a knack of making everyone feel that they were special and had a role to play in the big picture, even though in many cases it was obvious to me that they didn't. He could rally anyone with his enthusiasm and *Hell W10* is a perfect example of that. Nobody got paid for being in the film, which involved filming throughout many long nights. It was a silent black-and-white movie in which Paul Simonon played Earl and Mick Jones an underworld gangster called Socrates who were at war over a consignment of heroin. After Joe finished the film, he forgot about it and it disappeared until *The Essential Clash* DVD. We only had it because years earlier I'd been given a VHS copy by a guy who'd picked it up at a car boot sale. It was a cutting copy of the original and as far as we know the only one that exists. So, I put a soundtrack to it using some obscure unreleased Clash instrumentals and, because I wanted to keep its original vibe, didn't clean it up too much. It's rough and ready but without doubt the vibe cuts through. Mick Jones is particularly funny hamming it up as a villain.

The Clash may have ceased to exist as a creative unit in 1984, but they are accepted as 'the only band who matter' by a new generation of music fans who've discovered their enduring musical and cultural genius through streaming and social media. I continue to be involved in recreating their audio-visual catalogue, too. For the 25th anniversary of the release of *London Calling*, I made *The Last Testament* (which had been the original title for the album) in which Clash consigliere Kosmo Vinyl tells the story of the making of the double LP that *Rolling Stone* had voted the album of the 1980s (even though it was released in December 1979 in the UK). *Last Testament* includes some amazing footage of the band working on songs in Wessex Studios with legendary producer Guy Stevens, whose inspirational technique included pouring wine in pianos and smashing chairs in the studio while they try to lay down tracks. Sony put it together with a remastered edition of the album and it sold to fans old and new, earning reviews that consistently put it in the Top 10 of legendary rock albums of all time.

One thing the Grammy did do for me was put me in the frame with the BBC to make documentaries about the kind of left-field artists who I loved, and who'd had a similar impact on music and culture as The Clash. Not that they were always easy to work with, as Gil Scott-Heron proved at the end of 2003 when I was commissioned to make *The Revolution Will Not Be Televised: The Story of Gil Scott-Heron*.

The film was named after Gil's landmark track 'The Revolution Will Not Be Televised', a merging of highly charged political poetry with a laidback soul/funk groove, because it's rightly credited as being at the very the root of hip-hop. The influence of his lyrics can be found in Black culture across the world, and in the 1970s his albums sold in equal numbers to white and Black fans. In the 1980s he collaborated with Stevie Wonder on getting Martin Luther King's birthday made a national holiday in the USA. Sadly, though, by the 1990s his career was in decline and he'd developed a drug problem. In 2001 he was arrested and sentenced to three years for possession of cocaine – he was on parole when we made the documentary – which was ironic given how vehemently he'd been against drugs in his songs. In the film Gil is very honest about his problems. When one of the contributors suggested he was 'suffering for his art', Gil counters, 'Look, I'm not suffering for my art, I'm suffering for some shit that I took.' As clear-eyed and honest as he was on camera about his problems, our relationship was strained, although I knew it wasn't personal. As Public Enemy's Chuck D puts it in the film, 'He's trying to keep it together while the whole time having this fucking gorilla on his back.' He was arrested and bailed while we were in New York, for possession of a crack pipe. But I couldn't let what he was going through cloud my view of what he'd done in the past. He'd put out an album and two books by the time he was 19, at a time and in a place where there was almost no Black cultural support at all. Gil turned up for his long interview with us two-and-a-half days late. As I said before, I like to make my problems my assets, but he pushed things to the nth degree. He seemed to be amazingly resilient, though, even if now he did look like he'd been in a car crash. Gil Scott-Heron once described his records as 'survival kits on wax; instructional pieces on how to move things forward and make things better'. I told him that I'd like this film – which featured contributions from Mos Def and Richie Havens, The Last Poets, Linton Kwesi Johnson and Clive Davis – to be a survival kit on celluloid. Sadly, his survival was short-lived, and Gil died in 2011, aged 62. He was only seven years older than me.

The BBC liked my Gil film enough to offer me the chance of making one on Sun Ra, which I titled *The Brother from Another Planet* (2005). The only track I really knew by him was 'Space Is The Place' but I knew that he was to jazz what Lee Perry is to reggae, and I thought, 'He's a Black man who broke new ground – I'm there.' I naturally gravitate toward anybody Black who breaks out of the confines of prejudice and expectations of how they're supposed to act. People who are trying to push the envelope, like Sun Ra, George Clinton, Prince, Jimi Hendrix, Sly Stone and Arthur Lee, who are not defined by their colour. Sun Ra broke with the presiding orthodoxy of jazz by bringing in electric keyboards, synthesisers and embracing the Moog, and when everyone asked, 'What the fuck are you doing, that ain't jazz?' he replied, 'Jazz is what I say it is.' Sun Ra predated the punk DIY ethic by starting his own record label in 1956, creating hand-drawn sleeves and selling records at gigs in the sixties. He'd died in 1993, so I interviewed Marshall Allen, his saxophonist for more than thirty years, along with people like Thurston Moore from Sonic Youth, White Panther leader John Sinclair, and Wayne Kramer from the MC5 who had all been inspired by him – and who were also featured in another project I'd begun as this one was in production, *Punk:Attitude*. MC5 and Sun Ra often played gigs together during the early sixties – which on the face of it seems incongruous – pushing spaced-out free-form jazz from another planet alongside hard-edged Detroit garage rock. But John Sinclair saw some kind of idealistic connection between the two bands. I saw it as exactly the same as when I played hardcore dub reggae to the white punks at the Roxy. I included footage from a previous documentary called *Sun Ra: A Joyful Noise* in *Brother from Another Planet*, along with *Space Is the Place*, a 1972 film written by and starring Ra and his Arkestra. In the 1972 movie they land on a distant planet and set about bringing Black people to it from Earth. Ra had to put up with segregation in Alabama when he was growing up and was naturally inclined to think that Black people should leave this planet and go somewhere else for a better life. Ra's views brought Afrofuturism into sharper focus, but after listening to all the Sun Ra albums that I could get hold of (there are fucking hundreds of them), I realised that most of his music was going over my head. Sun cosmology; numerology; and whatever 'ology' he could lay his hands on were worked into Ra's music, and even Marshall Allen admitted that he 'didn't quite get it'. But to Ra everything was meaningful, and he mixed electronic sounds with jazz long before Miles Davis did.

Like Ra, George Clinton was an outrageous, loud and hard-to-miss brother who made some genre-busting albums with a collection of musicians who he moulded into a musical collective to bend to his will. When the BBC asked me to make a similar hour-long documentary about Dr Funkenstein (we titled it *Tales of Dr Funkenstein*, 2006), I had to say yes. I'd grown up listening to Funkadelic and busting moves on the dancefloor to the Parliament catalogue, both of which were products of the Clinton musical imagination. The film featured contributions from Macy Gray and Outkast's André 3000 as well as from Clinton. Before getting down for the funk of it, though, I had to properly explore the relationship between American and British punk.

In 2005, some thirty years after the first stirrings of the UK punk movement, I was approached to make *Punk:Attitude*. I originally had reservations about it, but then thought, why do we keep returning to punk and why does it still capture people's imaginations? Punk rock spawned photographers, graphic artists, writers, and people like me. Not many other movements have 'anniversary' celebrations and exploration every five or ten years – totally missing the point, of course – and that speaks volumes about the impact of punk.

I decided to approach the film with the idea of showing punk in context: i.e. that it didn't begin and end in the 1970s. Plus, if it happened before, it can happen again, and looking around today, it sure needs to.

If I'd have gone to people like David Johansen, Siouxsie Sioux or Tommy Ramone and said I want to make a nostalgic documentary on punk rock, they would probably have told me to take a running jump. Instead I presented my story of punk as an ongoing dynamic that started way back and had been here for hundreds of years. It is about an attitude that doesn't only exist in music, and most of the music produced today is probably the last place you'll find it. It's there in the writing of Albert Camus, the art and films of the surrealist movement, the films of Buñuel and comedy of Lenny Bruce, for instance. I wanted to include Marcel Duchamp in the original edit, but one of the producers asked me what band he was in... I obviously had to spotlight the Ramones, the Sex Pistols and The Clash, but what I also tried to do was give airtime to people who hadn't been afforded much before, especially when considering what punk was.

Punk:Attitude was quite a difficult project to work on for many reasons, but the main one being that it was a co-production between a UK- and a US-based company. I had to ignore each of their versions of what punk 'was' and worked toward 'a truth', instead of 'my truth' about the matter. There were a few people I would have liked to have featured but couldn't – Iggy Pop in particular, but he was working on another documentary at the same time. Patti Smith was on tour so we couldn't get her either. Lou Reed would have been great, but as everyone knows, Lou's Lou... But the idea behind *Punk:Attitude* was bigger than any single contributor and it was never intended to be an A to Z of the movement. Still, the original cut was three hours long, and I had to edit it down to ninety minutes for the release. That was partly because of the cost of acquiring archive footage – which in one case was £10,000 for twenty seconds. I also had to deal with some rights managers' prejudice against punk as well as that of a number of people we were interviewing. It really pissed me off when I was refused the use of any Nirvana music or footage, for instance, because I really wanted to place them at the peak of one of the narrative arcs. I think that Kurt would have been the first to admit that Nirvana wouldn't have existed without punk.

When I was making the film, I never worried about how it would be received. I never do that. I worry about how I receive these things and the rest is a bonus. *Punk:Attitude* seemed to strike a chord, though, and I spent nearly a year promoting it at various film festivals around the world. It was weird going out and pontificating about something that really is instinctive and intuitive. You end up talking about something that you should be doing.

It almost drove me mad after a while, especially when that idiot stands up (there's always one) during the Q&A and asks, 'Why wasn't this group or that group in it?' Still, while making it I got to spend time with some old friends and made some new ones too, like the awesome

Henry Rollins and John Sinclair. Strummer was a huge inspiration throughout its making, and at times it felt like he was sitting on my shoulder whispering, 'Shut up and get on with it.'

I dedicated *Punk:Attitude* to Joe, who continued to be a part of my working life.

In 2008 I put together *The Clash: Revolution Rock*, a history of the band using only live footage, and a couple of years later got to work with solo film of Joe and the people behind Strummerville for a documentary with that title (for Sky Arts), which also included Damien Hirst and Billy Bragg talking about his Jail Guitar Doors charity, which helps rehabilitate young offenders through playing music. It premiered at the SXSW Festival in Austin, Texas in 2010, which was cool. Making *Strummerville* and interviewing people who weren't even born when The Clash were playing, it was great to see how Joe's spirit, energy and attitude were inspiring and helping a whole new generation.

My connection with The Clash didn't end there. Twenty-one years after making *Westway*, Sony asked me to create a director's cut of the film, but I said that would short-change the fans and instead suggested using unheard stories from the original interviews with the band, to make a new film. I cut out the talking heads footage completely and used The Clash's testimony as voice-over for more visually powerful imagery. In the 2021 version of *Westway to the World* the viewers – many of whom I imagine were born long after the band had split – will hear the voices of Joe, Paul, Mick and Topper while watching them at their physical and musical peak, doing what they did best: performing in front of live audiences and for the camera, or walking the streets of London and New York, soaking up atmosphere and devouring cultural influences in order to send them out to a wider audience. It's a different film, but the message remains the same and it's edited to be more appealing to a generation who've grown up with Facebook (launched 2004), YouTube (2005), Twitter (2006), Bandcamp (2008) and Spotify (2008). They need visual stimulation to catch their attention, and The Clash were always a great spectacle.

Everybody Needs a Holiday

Interior. Night. The Royal Festival Hall, London. Several people mill around in a windowless, brick-lined corridor with doors off either side. Pan along the hall and we see the inside of one of the rooms, which is a functional, shiny-floored dressing room. Clothes are hung on pegs or folded neatly on benches. A table at one end of the room is loaded with mineral water, fruit, packets of food, beer and a couple of bottles of wine. A skinny middle-aged man in a brown three-piece suit with a yellow handkerchief in his top pocket that matches his tie is fitting a strap to his black-and-pearl Fender Telecaster Custom. Seated on a bench staring at a mobile phone sits a man in a light, loose-fitting linen suit, white linen shirt and light woollen hat, which is filled with dreadlocks. A dread wearing a long, light duster coat, deep blue trousers, bright red shirt and solid black wide-brimmed hat leans into the doorway.

'We gotta go on, guys,' Leo says.

'Alright, let's go,' agrees Mick.

I don't move.

'Don, y'comin'?' asks Leo.

'Fuck man.' I don't know what else to add.

'What's up, Don, you can't be that nervous,' Mick says.

'I just got a message that Amy's died.'

'Huh? What, Winehouse?' Leo looks shocked.

'Yeah, fucking overdose or something, at home.'

'Shit,' Mick looks shocked. 'When?'

'A few hours ago apparently, dead when the ambulance got there.'

I throw my phone down, feeling devastated, rub my eyes and get up.

'Fuck it, man. Let's go and play "Everybody Needs A Holiday" for Amy, yeah?'

'Sure,' Mick nods and we head out to the stage.

It was July 23, 2011 and Big Audio Dynamite were headlining the Saturday night gig as part of the London Is The Place For Me Festival, which celebrated the contribution that Caribbean culture has had on the capital city. I'd really been looking forward to it, not just because of the event, but also because Grace, Liberty and Honor were in the audience and as a special treat we'd arranged to sing 'Happy Birthday' to Grace who didn't know anything about it (the crowd sang along, too). It turned out to be a very bittersweet night, though. I'd heard Amy Winehouse long before I met her, and the thing that struck me and everybody else, I guess, was her vocal style. She took every style of Black music and turned it into something that was completely unique to her. I was really impressed when she shouted, 'Shut up, I don't give a fuck!' at Bono during the *Q* music awards ceremony in 2006. I was cheering inwardly, not because I didn't like Bono, but because all pop stars need to be kept in check. The music business needed people like Amy, I thought, because they'd become few and far between. She was a lyrical gangster, somewhere between Salt-N-Pepa and Sarah Vaughan with a completely modern style. I really liked 'Me And Mr Jones', subtitled 'Fuckery', which gives a raw, honest female point of view on sex in a way that The Slits had done. I was lucky enough to get to know Amy quite well and she reminded me a bit of Ari in being totally upfront and confrontational. At Glastonbury in 2008 I was finishing my DJ set when someone told me that Amy was asking for me onstage – apparently she was about to sing her version of the Toots song 'Monkey Man' when she said, 'The only person at Glastonbury who knows about

With Amy Winehouse at the *Q* awards, 2004.

reggae is Don Letts. Where's Don Letts?' I eventually made it backstage to thank her just as Jay-Z was about to make his controversial Glasto debut, when Amy grabbed me and Grace and marched us past Jay-Z's bodyguards on to the stage where we stood next to Beyoncé just as he dropped his take on Oasis's 'Wonderwall'... Absolutely astounding. Amy, that is.

So, when B.A.D. played 'Everybody Needs A Holiday' that night at the Royal Festival Hall it was with deep feeling and genuine affection. The whole gig felt special, and we had some great reviews for the final London gig on our reunion tour — we were off to Japan the following week, then the US before returning to the UK for some festivals.

That Big Audio Dynamite had re-formed for the tour was partly because in 2010 Mick and I had worked on a 'legacy' reissue of the first B.A.D. album, and listening to *This Is Big Audio Dynamite* I thought, 'There's a lot to be proud of in what we did.' At the time Mick was rehearsing and then touring with Damon Albarn's Gorillaz, who included Paul Simonon on bass, which I hadn't seen coming when I'd filmed Paul in another of Damon's side projects, The Good The Bad & The Queen (in 2006). Mick really enjoyed being back in a group, he said, even if it was someone else's band and Damon was the frontman.

Then, when all the ex-members of B.A.D. met up at the christening of Leo's first son in late 2010, someone mentioned that a B.A.D. fan group had heard a rumour that we were going out on tour. We all thought the idea didn't seem like a bad one and, after a couple of drinks, Mick said, 'Let's do it.' The time was right, and we had plenty of support from friends, family and the business in the shape of Gerry Harrington, a big-time Los Angeles movie agent (for Brad Pitt, Sylvester Stallone and Nic Cage among others) who happened to be more in love with rock 'n' roll than Hollywood. He'd managed Joe for the final couple of years, as well as Tom Waits and David Johansen. He was also friendly with Chrissie Hynde and owned a huge collection of music memorabilia (sadly he died in 2013). Through Gerry we were booked onto some great gigs and festivals.

Have to say that I couldn't turn down the chance to go on tour with the guys again and with Grace in plain view. For us to be on the road and out in the open was a great relief. Plus, what better way for a bunch of geezers to see out a midlife crisis? I ain't the Harley-Davidson type, and the buzz from hearing thousands of people sing along, dance to music that you're making and then shout for more, has to be so much better and safer than riding a hog down a highway (is that the right phrase?).

Once it was all agreed, everything happened so fast we didn't have time to write any new material, so decided to only play songs from the first four albums. Rehearsals went smoothly, and we picked up pretty much where we'd left off in 1990. Everyone had remained friends and there was no 'catching up' to do. We all lived in West London and our lives were intertwined in many ways (Mick's daughter Lauren and Jet were the same age and close friends), which meant that we spent all the time in the studio getting into the songs again. I had to buy some new stickers for the keyboards (albeit larger ones) and get to know the new tech, things having moved on considerably since we last toured. I also had to reacquaint myself with the lyrics, while Mick also used new tech in the shape of a teleprompter set up with song lyrics next to his stage monitor. But it didn't take more than six weeks

B.A.D. reunion tour promo, in the shadow of the Trellick Tower, 2010.
(L–r) Greg Roberts, me, Mick Jones, Leo Williams.

to get into the groove and we hit the road running – well stylishly strolling – at the first gig in Liverpool on March 29. Although we'd never been a major chart band – I always said we were more cred than bread – B.A.D. were a great live act and the love and energy coming from audiences from that first date gave our covered wagon medicine show all the support we could ask for. For the first few gigs things were really rocking, and the first home-town London shows (after Glasgow and Newcastle), two nights at the Shepherd's Bush Empire, were described by one reviewer as 'excellent' and filled with 'classic after classic'. After four more sold-out shows in Nottingham, Leeds, Manchester and Bristol we seemed to be moving effortlessly toward America.

But, as Sun Ra used to say, 'Ain't nothin' all beautiful, you gotta have some ugly in it,' and unfortunately unknown to us, one of our number was heading for his own personal ugly.

I was a bit apprehensive about the reception we'd get and how our stuff, which was more than twenty-five years old, would hold up in America. Turned out I didn't need to worry about that and our first shows in America since 1989, at the LA Roxy, went down a storm. It was great seeing Rick Rubin, Steve Jones and the Red Hot Chili Peppers in our dressing room after the show. Two days later we had Hollywood royalty in our Winnebago at Coachella – Danny DeVito spent the afternoon with us, holding court and making everyone laugh. He was a big fan – who knew? The show was a new experience for us, since that kind of festival didn't exist when we first toured, but the *LA Times* liked it. Their reviewer wrote: 'The world seems to have caught up to the cut-and-paste jumble of rock and dance cultures that was the Big Audio Dynamite mission... Though B.A.D. isn't credited with shaping the future of music in the way The Clash is, one can hear B.A.D.'s genre-carelessness in Gorillaz, LCD Soundsystem and even Sunday night headliner Kanye West, among dozens of other Coachella acts.'

We were in New York three days later and the NYC crew were out in full force in the shape of old pals Jim Jarmusch and Matt Dillon, along with photographers Josh Cheuse and Bob Gruen, plus others. Again, the show was excellently reviewed, but it would be memorable for another reason to us, because that was when it became clear that we needed to make a change in personnel. Luckily we had Davo (Andrew Davitt), Mick's guitar tech, with us, and being a mate and a seriously accomplished musician and artist in his own right – I'd directed the video for his band Johnny Boy's single 'You Are The Generation That Bought More Shoes And You Get What You Deserve' in 2004 – Davo stepped up in fine style and it was a pleasure to have him onstage with us for the rest of the tour, which began two months later, in June 2011, with a warm-up for Glastonbury in Bournemouth.

I've now been DJing at Glasto for more than twenty-five years, but June 29, 2011 is the only time I ever got to appear with a live band onstage, and, of course, it fucking rained. Not only that, but we were getting weird vibes from the crowd who didn't seem to really be into us and didn't look right, either. It felt like they were holding something back, I commented to one of the stagehands as we came off, and he said that was probably because they were mostly all there to see the unnamed 'surprise' act who were coming on in a while. It turned out to be Radiohead.

The sun shone for the next two festivals we played, in Serbia and Spain, which were both great fun, and then came the Royal Festival Hall. Which was memorable not only for Amy's death and Grace's birthday surprise, but also because everything felt musically right and the audience were really up for it. The *Guardian* said in their review of the gig that 'The Bottom Line' 'sounds as relevant as ever', and that 'B.A.D. wrote some terrific songs', which was strangely encouraging – we weren't just our own tribute act, or one-hit wonders mining the nostalgia mother lode, which I'd never wanted to be. We flew out to Japan to play at Fuji Rock Tokyo at the end of July, which has a reputation as Japan's own Glastonbury and I'd always wanted to visit. It was a lot like Glasto, except the rain was even heavier and I had to take refuge in the Strummerville wagon which was on site during the midnight monsoon. We got to follow Lee Scratch Perry onto stage in Japan too, which was cool.

We flew from there to LA for the first of a series of gigs throughout August in America, beginning at LA's House of Blues. Some of the dates included support from Bad Brains, who were immensely powerful live, and you gotta love H.R., the singer – one night I found him still in the dressing room just as the rest of the band started in on their fourth number.

We were booked to appear on the *Late Night with Jimmy Fallon* show in New York on August 3 and for it had worked up an unreleased track that Mick and I had written more than twenty years earlier, titled 'Rob Peter, Pay Paul'. I think it's one of the best things Mick and I wrote, and it seemed to go down well. Jimmy Fallon then joined us to sing on 'E=MC^2', and when we'd finished he came to our dressing room, bringing with him Tony Bennett and Freida Pinto, the star of *Slumdog*

Millionaire (2008), who I greeted in my underpants. We weren't expecting visitors, which is why there's a photo of me in my boxer shorts standing next to an embarrassed-looking Freida somewhere around... We also had a great show that night at the Brooklyn Bowl venue in the city, and after a gig in Philly the following night we made our way to another festival, and another strange reception. Perry Farrell's Lollapalooza festival began in 1991 as a touring circus for alt-rock acts like his own Jane's Addiction, but by the time we appeared it had settled into a three-day event at Chicago's Grant Park. We were on in the early evening when there was still plenty of daylight and I was kind of surprised to see a bunch of dudes – I assumed they were male but it was hard to tell with their hoodies up – out front. Our set was greeted with a mixture of boredom and hostility, but when CeeLo Green who came on after us had exactly the same response from the crowd, it made me feel a bit better. When the headliner appeared in exactly the same black hoodie as worn by most of the crowd I finally understood that this was all they'd been waiting for – Eminem (if it was him under the hood). Still, the after-show party hosted by Perry Farrell made up for nearly everything, and the following night we played a great gig at Prince's club First Avenue in Minneapolis, at which Mick's mum, Renee, turned up.

After one more gig in LA and another festival on August 12 – Outside Lands in San Francisco – we headed back to the UK for the end of the B.A.D. reunion tour at three more festivals (including a French one in the middle). V Festival on August 21 was an interesting contrast to the Beautiful Days festival we'd played two days earlier, because Beautiful Days was run by indie folk-punks The Levellers, who'd come up through the traveller scene of the late 1980s. Their festival prided itself on having no sponsorship whatsoever and the audience looked like they'd been following the band since forever. V, on the other hand, was sponsored and named for Richard Branson's Virgin, and the audience were all fresh-faced, very, very young, probably festival virgins, in fact – and the lights went out at 11pm, sharp!

The final festival – and gig – that Big Audio Dynamite played was Bestival, on the Isle of Wight. The island put on an outdoor rock event in 1968, predating Glasto by two years. That initial Isle of Wight Festival was the first, proper, American-style rock festival in the UK and in 1969 it became world-famous when Bob Dylan & The Band made their first live appearance in three years – just eleven days after Woodstock, which Dylan had refused to play. It was estimated that almost a quarter of a million people invaded the Isle of Wight that weekend. In contrast, there were 45,000 for the weekend we appeared on the isle at Bestival (September 8–11, 2011), and the headliners were The Cure and Brian Wilson. It was great fun, although hardly the orgy of sex, drugs and rock 'n' roll of the original festivals. But that was cool because we were all past that and B.A.D. went out on a natural high.

After it was all over, I thought of how it had been an honour to tread the boards again with Greg and Leo. We've remained close over the years, we still collaborate on Dreadzone, we're long-time friends and always will be. It was a real pleasure to be onstage with Mick Jones. He moves and grooves like no-one else, and when the spirit takes him it's a genuine delight to watch that smile of his widen as the music flows. At times on that tour I looked across the stage and thought I was watching a rock 'n' roll Tony Soprano. I think I'd do it all again if only to see him looking that happy...

Rewind

Interior. A small, darkened room filled with flat TV screens on desks
against each wall. There are no windows. Most of the desks are
unoccupied, chairs pushed in, leads and headphones coiled neatly
on hooks hung under each one. Wiring snakes up the wall to each
screen and various boxes on which the screens sit. In a corner
two men are seated side by side at a digital console, watching a
screen as it flickers with colour and black-and-white images. The
colour images, faded like old Polaroids, are from vintage live news
footage which was shot from an upper-floor window. It shows
scores of people being chased along a road and around a corner by
black-uniform-clad British police officers. Fast cut to five policemen
awkwardly carrying a Black youth between them. Stretched as if
about to be thrown on a bonfire he is angry, his contorted face oddly
in contrast to the clean white shirt and smart khaki trousers he's
wearing. He looks as if he's been forcibly removed from a family
dinner or restaurant meal. Cut to elevated shots of ambulances
and police motorbikes tearing past crowds of police before a green
police bus with a smashed windscreen rolls into shot. Angle shift
skyward to follow a police helicopter flying low overhead. Pan down:
in longshot a police bus stops in the middle of a street strewn with
bricks, dustbin lids and cars lying on their sides, their wheels
sticking out and looking like a dog asking for a tummy tickle.
Officers jump from the bus and half a dozen or more begin attacking
a lone white male, while the others chase youths away from the
camera, picking up temporary 'road closed' signs and bin lids to

use as shields against the occasional milk bottle or brick thrown at them. Cut to a wide shot of a crowd of people – men, women, children – in smart summer clothes running toward the camera, framed on their right by the elevated section of the Westway, and to the left trees and a fence. Smoke rises in the distance. Screams and shouts can be heard.

'There!' I stop the footage. 'Look at that – people all dressed for a party. Normal, working-class families who've dressed for a day out at the end of the summer, looking forward to an evening dancing, maybe a barbecue, laughing with friends and smoking a spliff – and what happens?'

My editor switches the screen to a shot of uniformed police running at the camera en masse, truncheons drawn, a blank look of determination on their faces.

'You get whacked with a truncheon.'

We're watching news footage of the Notting Hill Carnival riot of 1976, the one at which the infamous picture of me was taken that ended up on the front of the *Blackmarket Clash* album. By the way, what the photo doesn't show are the hundreds of brothers behind me about to kick off.

That was 2009, and I was watching archive footage for use in a documentary tracing the fifty-year history of the Notting Hill Carnival. Titled simply *Carnival*, it turned out to be my first self-financed film and that was because – amazingly to me – I couldn't get anyone to commission it. That year was the carnival's 50th anniversary, and I was particularly surprised that the BBC passed on it. They'd filmed every single carnival for news purposes, including the first in 1959, which wasn't held in Notting Hill, but inside St Pancras town hall in King's Cross. I thought it'd be an easy decision for them to say 'yes' because they basically had the programme in their hands, the usual archive footage costs would be nothing. All it required was for some relevant interviews (I got Jazzie B, Norman Jay, Rudolph Walker and Sir Trevor McDonald among others) and the history to put everything into context. Yet I couldn't get anyone at the corporation to see why it was important, and they all passed on the opportunity to make a film about what is without doubt a culturally significant event.

It was important to me that the real story of the carnival be told then, and maybe that was because my parents were old and frail, my mum suffering dementia, my dad not as mobile as he used to be. I felt that their story, of their lives and of their friends in England, needed to be told before they'd gone. This was years before the Windrush scandal, but it seemed to me that the origins of the carnival needed to be shown as truthfully as possible, as much to reclaim it for them as anything else, and to say to the country that here was something which they should treasure, and it had come from immigrants.

The first carnival, organised by Claudia Jones, the Trinidadian founder of *The West Indian Gazette*, was her attempt to show that the people of Notting Hill who'd suffered racist attacks (one of which killed Kelso Cochrane in 1959) were part of a rich and vibrant culture that the rest of London could and should see and experience. It was held in January, which is when they have carnival in Trinidad, but was held inside because that's not the time of year in London to go out in skimpy West Indian outfits. The location of carnival moved around over the next few years and got to Notting Hill in 1966 when a local activist called Rhaune Laslett, who wanted to bring the community together through a street event, helped organise things with the local West Indian, Polish, Moroccan and European communities. Everybody was invited, regardless of colour, culture or class. The event began as a kids' street party and then a steel pan player called Russ Henderson decided to take his instrument for a walkabout while playing, and people followed him as he marched through Notting Hill. It wasn't about sound systems at all in the sixties; it was much more of a traditional West Indian calypso-style Mardi Gras carnival and intended to be a reminder of home and their former lives for my parents' generation. But by the time we came to it in the seventies it was a very different affair and had become more a statement of how we felt about being Black in Britain 'today' and that this was our home. Then carnival was about us and our experience, and it had become a lot more politicised. The struggle it had emerged from was a part of why we went, we couldn't forget the racism our parents, and we, suffered. I wanted to make that clear to the latest wave of immigrants suffering bigotry and racism in England in the film, to show that carnival was for them, too. Perhaps it might inspire them to create something similar within their own culture, or just join in. It's important to put the conscience back into the party that carnival has become, because its politicisation has been pushed into the background over the years. Too many people think that the Notting Hill Carnival is just another – albeit huge – street party and all about

More than six decades after the birth of rock 'n' roll.
Older and... 2014.   BETINA LA PLANTE

getting stoned, dancing and copping off. It is all of that, but that's not what drives carnival; cultural exchange is the reason for its existence as well as persistence in the peaceful interaction of traditions going back generations. Hopefully that comes across in the film.

Carnival was the first of a series of historical documentaries I made in the following years. Maybe that's a natural result of getting older, but I never thought that I'd become a nostalgic old man, and I'm not – at all – and yet in the second decade of the twenty-first century I became the go-to director for historical documentaries about youth culture. I went from being someone who made films about culture as it was happening to become a historian of that culture. Even when I got to make documentaries about something new, it invariably involved an aspect of looking back, or was about someone who'd been a big part of pop culture in the previous decades.

That was partly because of six 'Subculture' films I made for the Fred Perry YouTube channel in 2012, which had hundreds of thousands of views. Although each episode is only ten minutes long (to suit the social media generation), when seen together they make up an hour-long history of British youth culture from Teddy boys in the 1950s through mods, skinheads, soulboys, punks, the two-tone movement of the early 1980s, right up to millennials. Without meaning to, I created films that grabbed the attention of a generation of people who were not born when I started making documentaries (as well as plenty of people who're my generation).

Those Fred Perry subculture films have been amazingly successful, and schools use them to teach kids about modern history. When I was told that I remember thinking, 'Does that make me a teacher?' And I guess the answer to that is yes, it does, even if it was never planned that way. But I'm OK with that, because it means I'm still relevant and able to tell an audience the history of how we got to here, from there, and about how I got there and Black again. The films let me explain how my passage through the dominant white culture of the past fifty years has made me more understanding and supportive of an Afrofuturist worldview.

Making the series I couldn't help but notice how every youth culture from Teddy boys onwards, through mods, skinheads and so on, relied significantly on a Black presence, even if the subculture was anti-

Black, as Teddy boys obviously, and some skinheads, were. *Fred Perry Presents Subculture* is a testament to how essential Black culture has been to British culture. Although Teddy boys, for want of anyone else to fight with, chose West Indians to attack, their younger brothers who became 'mods' borrowed essential elements of fashion and lifestyle from the first-generation youth of the Windrush immigrants. The original skinheads went further than elements of style and also adopted Jamaican music for their soundtrack. Soulboys relied purely on Black American music to make their feet dance, but punks took to the then emerging roots reggae of the mid-1970s as if born to it. Two-tone wouldn't exist without the coming together of Black and white youth. I wasn't entirely sure why, but the most watched of all those short films was the one on skinheads, and that made me want to explore the phenomenon further. Happily, the BBC agreed that there was something in the skinhead movement that needed further investigation, so they hired me to make *Skinhead* in 2016. That was the first time I stepped in front of the camera and 'presented' a documentary that I was also directing. It trended on Twitter when first screened and caught the attention of a lot of people, including pretty much every 50- and 60-something skinhead or former skinhead, if the number who approach me at gigs to talk about it is any kind of indicator. They all tell me how much they loved the film because it's the truth about the movement as I remembered it – from my perspective as a 12-year-old, chubby, four-eyed, Anglicised rude boy, the original inspiration for skinheads – and that it wasn't all about white working-class idiots being racist.

Skinhead touched more white working-class men than punk did, because punk was too freaky for a lot of them. The original skins adopted the look partly because it was anti-hippy – being part mod (American Ivy League-look Oxford shirts by Ben Sherman, Levi Sta-Prest white jeans, loafers by Weejuns, Baracuta 'Harrington' jacket), and part rude boy (pork pie hats, two-tone tonic suits, Crombie overcoats, highly shined brogues). Like most subcults, skinhead evolved out of opposition to a dominant culture, which at the end of the 1960s was middle class dominated – all long hair, loose, flowing, multicoloured clothes and music you couldn't dance to. Skinheads were generally white working-class, blue-collar kids whose fathers had done national service and who had nothing in common with their sons, who wanted a scene of their own. And it was mostly male at the time. There were always girls who dressed to please the boys and had their own fashion, but the prime movers were always men, as it was with nearly all British youth culture. Being a skinhead meant being in an easily recognisable gang, it gave a sense of belonging to socially estranged teenagers, regardless of skin colour. By the end of the sixties the look had changed slightly, with the Ivy League shoes being replaced by British-made Dr Martens AirWair 18-hole boots, all the shirts having to be checked and braces worn regardless of whether they were needed. Unfortunately, though, that new 'uniform' was pretty much the invention of a 50-year-old Canadian-born hack named James Moffat, who wrote a series of books about a skinhead called Joe Hawkins under the pseudonym of Richard Allen. Although the author of more than 290 books, his *Skinhead* series was by far his biggest success, which is a shame because Moffat made Hawkins racist, violent and fatally appealing to teenage boys in search of an anti-hero.

As skinhead started to spread outside its ground zero of the multiracial council estates in London propelled by the *Skinhead* books, the movement became more politicised and the National Front infiltrated the ranks of skinhead football fans, recruiting them to their poisonous cause. Which is when skinhead was soiled with the indelible stain of racism. As the film shows, even two-tone bands like The Selecter, The Specials and The Beat had to deal with Sieg Heil-ing skins who were there for the music (all Jamaican-influenced) but thought they had to act like right-wing thugs. By this time skins had swapped the Harrington for USA Air Force MA-1 flying jackets, the Dr Martens for steel toe-capped work boots, and the Ben Shermans for T-shirts. In the 1980s 'Oi' skinheads were overtly racist, angry and violent, and although I couldn't relate to them, I could relate to the growing sense of discontent across the land, which exploded in the Brixton riots of the early 1980s.

In the summer of 1981, after around 200 skinheads rampaged along Southall High Street smashing windows on their way to an Oi gig, the pub where it was being held was attacked and set on fire. The media called it a race riot started by right-wing skinheads and from then on it became a predominantly racist, white power movement.

That view was rammed home by the media, who, whenever they wrote about 'skinheads' from then on, had to include the words 'Nazi' and 'white power' somewhere in the article. Consequently, that became the commonly held perception of skinheads, which was so far from its multicultural beginnings as to be a travesty. In contrast to the ages-old British media tendency to create urban folk-devils from spontaneous youth movements which arise as part of the natural ongoing dynamic, and then kill the movement, I hoped my film might just persuade people that not all skinheads are or were racist, and that the cross-cultural roots of the scene are worth exploring and celebrating.

The Story of Skinhead gave me the idea to make another film exploring the roots of British subculture for which I could draw on personal experience. What's more, I could include a largely unseen archive of footage I'd shot over the summer of 1976 and 1977. *Two Sevens Clash* (2017) was an attempt to properly position Black culture at the heart of the most disruptive subculture of the 1970s (and arguably ever) and explain the myth and the reality of the 'punky reggae party'. It is the most personal film I've made. Someone once told me that music doesn't affect change, it only reflects it. I made *Two Sevens Clash* to prove them wrong, because music played a huge part in making me the man I am, and a generation of other people like me who they are, too. In the summer of 1976, I carried my Super-8mm camera everywhere and filmed everything, including drives through Brixton, filming through the windscreen of my Plymouth Satellite. Footage of people going about their everyday lives in the bright sunshine looks as if it might have been shot in Kingston but when intercut with racist graffiti and torn National Front posters on the walls around those same streets it presents the reality of life for Black people in England at that time. I used family portraits of my parents under a first-person voice-over, in which I tell parts of what you've already read in this book (if you've read it this far). The film also includes live footage of Big Youth, Prince Far I and loads of punk bands, vérité shots of the carnival that year – different to the stuff in *Carnival* – chosen to show that there were plenty of white youth there, too. As I say in the v/o, the riot wasn't a Black-and-white thing, it was a wrong and right thing. Making *Two Sevens Clash* was an attempt to have something to point people toward if they're really interested in what happened back then. Almost forty-five years after the event lots of the people who were there have given their version of what happened (their point of view, remember, which is not necessarily the truth), and in *Two Sevens Clash* I present mine in film and sound. But that doesn't mean that I've finished with it all, because now I'm at a stage in my life when I'm apparently a living, historical document and constantly consulted on this stuff.

I guess that *Two Sevens Clash* is also a letter to my children, and I hope that they'll watch it and get an idea of what life was like for their old man. Jet and Amber, being older, know something of the punky reggae party, but for Honor and Liberty their old man's life story is 'boring' (even though their mates love *Dancehall Queen* and are genuinely impressed that I made it!). Life for them has been, and continues to be, so different to not only their parents' but also their older half-siblings, too. I saw all my kids born, and although I missed much of Jet and Amber growing up, I have been there pretty much every day of Honor and Liberty's life so far. I guess that they each know something of their roots, and over the years Jet and I got to know each other a lot better, having been estranged for a while when his mother and I split. Having long, detailed conversations with any of them about

My holy trinity: Liberty, Grace and Honor, 2019.   PAOLA PIERONI FOR DINNY HALL

family history isn't always possible (and if truth be told they don't really seem to be that interested). They have more important things to do, as they see it, and I get that. So, I hope that maybe at some point they'll sit still long enough to watch the forty-five minutes of *Two Sevens Clash*. They can even have the director with them for a personal Q&A if they like.

When I'm Sixty-Four

Interior. Day. Tight shot on an area filled with keyboards, lit by one single silver-stemmed bedside lamp with a bell-shaped cloth shade, an old-fashioned brass desk lamp on top of an upright piano missing its front casing, and ambient light through a glass door. At the piano, in front of which are suspended microphones on long stands, sits a dark-haired man in a grey shirt with a white collar, sleeves rolled above the elbows. He's wearing a wristwatch on his right arm, his ears are covered by black headphones. We view him side on and his left profile looks familiar, with its small, bird-like nose and slightly sleepy-hooded eyes. He's probably somewhere in late middle age. After playing a few notes he turns to look straight into the camera, smiles, winks and starts to sing,

'Your day breaks...'

Paul McCartney was singing 'For No One' to me, three days after I'd told him that I'd once written out the words of exactly this song and shown them to a girl I fancied, telling her that it was my poem. That's Paul McCartney the ex-Beatle, writer of some of the best pop songs ever written. Sir Paul McCartney, who I'd almost worshipped when an Apple Scruff and used to hang about outside The Beatles' offices in Savile Row on Saturdays with my best mate Froggy, hoping (in vain) to catch a glimpse of the band. The closest we ever got came one day when we managed to blag our way into the ground-floor offices after a sympathetic doorman took pity on us because it was pouring with rain. I'm sorry to say that we repaid his sympathy in the only way we knew how, by stealing Beatles-headed notepaper, pens, an ashtray and some black-and-white photo negatives. I added them to my collection, of course, the one which grew to be the second biggest in England and was swapped for an American car in 1976.

Now there I was, forty-five years later, directing Paul McCartney, having been hired by his production company to make a short film for the 2013 album, *New*. It wasn't the first time we'd worked together, because we'd 'sung' a chorus of Bob Marley's 'One Love' in a video I made in 1984 for the song, as part of the promo video for *Legend*, but that had been a flying visit for Paul. For *Something New* I got to spend weeks at his studio in Sussex filming Macca and his band as they rehearsed for a world tour to promote *New*. Which was a major trip for me. When he played 'For No One', the fact that he'd remembered what I'd said was amazing enough and, later when I was interviewing him, I almost felt like crying. I couldn't help but think back to what his music meant to me, how my whole life had come from music, that in a way I was sitting there with him because of his music in the first place. If asked, I'd have said I was pretty jaded by the time I got to here, because I'd worked with a lot of people and knew a lot of famous artists. But working on that film at Windmill reminded me of what it was to be a fan again and sitting there asking him questions, I couldn't help but recall how I'd felt back in the sixties. At one point when shooting the band going through their set, every single number of which was an enormous hit, I was so taken with the moment I almost dropped my camera. In contrast, the tech dudes and roadies were all preoccupied with their phones or some such. To them this was just another day. But I'm only a few feet away from Paul McCartney and it feels like he's really playing this stuff for me. When sitting opposite him in the garden as he played an acoustic guitar and 'wrote' a new song, I thought about how far this scene was from that scruffy council house in Brixton when, aged 10 years old, I'd listened to his voice as it came out of my Dansette. It also reminded me of the passing of John Lennon, because the day before he was shot in December 1980, Bob Gruen had given him my showreel to view in connection with me directing a video for a single from *Double Fantasy*. Bob asked John to leave it with the doorman at the Dakota building for him when he'd watched it. Despite all the confusion on the

At home with Sir Paul McCartney, 2013.

fateful night, Bob somehow got through to the doorman's office where he found the tape, which John had dropped off on his way out.

That remembrance of things past begins to occur more often as you get older. Or, at least to me it has. As I approached the age of 60, I'd tell people that it was no big thing and I didn't want a party – I was too preoccupied with the making of the skinhead documentary for the BBC at the time to even think about it. But Audrey – we'd made peace by then – baked me a cake and insisted to Grace that they throw me a small party anyway. Everything was fine that night but there were some very old friends in my kitchen and there was a lot of talk about the past. I don't remember my 21st, 30th, 40th or 50th birthdays being a big deal in any way, and definitely not any kind of milestone. But I realised when I turned 60 that, in the previous decades, I'd been working so hard and doing so much that there was always something to be thinking about other than getting old. I always knew pretty much what had to be done in the year to come, and having a birthday in January helps with that, but at 60 there was slightly more time to consider what had already been done, as well as what I was going to do.

Not long after that birthday, and for the first time in my life, I began to wake up in the mornings feeling ill, and not cold-like, but deeply ill, in my gut. I saw a doctor and, because of my age, he immediately sent me to the hospital for scans. There were cysts on my kidneys, they said, but it wasn't too bad; they were age-related and not stones. After a series of more invasive (and painful) tests they told me that the condition had to be monitored, but thankfully not operated on. Before that, though, there were a couple of weeks when it was thought that they might be cancerous cells, during which I wavered between thinking 'I've had a good innings' and listening to Father John Misty's 'Ballad Of The Dying Man', feeling sorry for myself. I still have to get my kidneys checked regularly, but so far, it's all fine. Or as fine as can be expected for a man of my age.

Before reaching the age of 60, I'd suffered hardly any health problems, just a cyst on my eye which had to be lanced when I was in the middle of an acid trip while DJing at the Roxy in 1977 (I had it done at St Thomas's outpatients and caught a taxi straight back to the club). Yet three years after the kidney problem I was hospitalised for the first time ever with a bout of something called diverticulitis. That was scary for a few weeks, until the doctors told me what it was and how to manage it. Have to admit that it made me feel my age in a way that I really hadn't previously. I'd sailed through life's traditional markers and they hadn't meant shit to me. Driven by work, I never had the time or inclination to ponder the meaning of life. It's said that you're as old as you feel (or the woman you feel...), but here's the thing: there comes a time in life when you're as old as you are, no matter how preoccupied you might be with other stuff.

My 'other stuff' includes a weekly radio show on BBC 6Music, which I'm anal about getting the right mix of old and new stuff for.

I usually take a few days out of my week to put it together, working alone, listening to as much new material as I can and then adding the right blend of old songs, hopefully. I'm not saying the show's perfect and that each one is great, but I try to do the best job I can, every week. In my own mind I'm making a mix-tape like the ones I made back in the seventies; they're non-disposable, permanent in a way that online playlists aren't. I can't do things any other way. I don't like to hear umming and erring on the radio, so I semi-script shows and pre-record them, cutting out any hesitation or dull bits. It's not exactly back-breaking work, I know, and it's a hell of a lot better than working as a bus driver or chauffeur or at a job for which I'd have needed those science qualifications that I so spectacularly failed to get. My parents both died before I got to 64, but I think that eventually they appreciated that I'd not done too badly for myself, despite not going along with their plan for me to get the best kind of job on offer to a Black man in the 1970s – one which would not have involved music, film or any kind of art. I thought of both my parents when, on November 17, 2018, I stood in front of a bunch of professors and academics clutching my Honorary Doctor of Letters award for contributions to culture in the UK. I was wearing a gown just like everyone else at the University of West London, although they had to make allowances for the hat (I wore the most appropriate 'crown' in my wardrobe) as I looked around the hall. At that moment I would have given the world to see the look on the faces of Mr and Mrs Letts rather than the somewhat confused reaction I was getting from other graduates and their families.

I'm glad that I grew up in England when I did. I wouldn't be the man I am if I hadn't grown up suffering and learning, living and loving, in London. I sometimes wonder that if I'd grown up in Jamaica, if my parents hadn't made that journey to the wet, grey and windy mother country, and I'd been raised there, would I be the person I am now? I don't know, but I suspect not.

Burnin' and Lootin'

Interior. Day. On a large, mostly blue sound stage in a TV studio sits a soberly attired white female with a pen and notebook, her back to a vast white desk, empty but for a glass of water and laptop. She faces a giant screen that is split vertically down the middle. On the left-hand side, a young Black man wearing a black baseball cap and black hoodie sits in a sparsely furnished room. To the right sits an older Black man with a grey-white beard, wearing a green knitted hat holding a profusion of locks, a camouflage pattern summer shirt and lightly tinted brown sunglasses. Behind the older man are a set of shelves with various small items of family-related memorabilia, to the right of which hangs a black-and-white photograph of a smartly dressed man wearing a pork pie hat, white shirt, tie and a long-drop jacket with a white pocket 'chief, leaning on what looks like a very large speaker cabinet, holding a vinyl record. [It's 'Duke' St Leger Letts with his Superstonic Sound System.]

The woman has prepped the men for the interview on Channel 4 News, to discuss the re-release of Bob Marley's 'Burnin' And Lootin'' and the power of protest music in the wake of the worldwide Black Lives Matter protests. The younger man – David 'Sideman' Whitely, a DJ, actor and musician – makes a point about the lyrics of the Marley song being relevant now, fifty years after they were written, that they speak to the BLM movement.

The camera switches to the interviewer, Jackie Long.

'So, Don, you're shaking your head a lot there, but here we are fifty years later and what has changed?'

'I'm shaking my head in agreement because not a lot has changed, evidently. Sam Cooke sang a long time ago that "A Change Is Gonna Come", in what, '63? That's nearly six decades ago and obviously things haven't changed, and that's led to where we are today. That song ["Burnin' And Lootin'"] is a lament for the thousands of years of crap that Black people have had to put up with, and it's a warning. It's a warning, that if you don't do the right thing... burning and looting.'

Jackie responds to ask, 'But does it speak to a failure of protest music? You mention Sam Cooke, I think of Marvin Gaye singing "What's Going On" – that could be a piece of music that we're still playing today.'

'I don't think it's a failure of music. You say music hasn't changed things, but music has the potential to change people, and people are things. Bob believed in music as a tool for social change. It wasn't about selling you sneakers, it was about changing your mind. And that's what's made me who I am today. I'm a great believer in protest music and as a form of social change. The protests going on now have already changed things – the chokehold has been banned in Minnesota, some states have introduced laws which say that if officers see cops acting up they have to intervene. So things can change – it's just a shame that we've had to get so extreme before things happen.'

The interview carries on, and Sideman says that he thinks the term 'protest music' diminishes what's going on at the moment, that the marginalisation and murder of Black people isn't just a 'protest song', or a TikTok dance. Jackie brings up a recent event when a statue of a seventeenth-century slave trader (Edward Colston, 1636–1721), which had been erected in 1895 and designated as a Grade II listed monument in 1977, was pulled down by people on a BLM march in Bristol. It was then rolled into the harbour, the whole event captured for posterity on a hundred or more smartphones, images from which flew around the world via social media and mainstream news channels.

Turning to me, she says, 'Can I ask you about the statue, because the prime minister has spoken about how we shouldn't be erasing history, that the statues belong to our history. What do you say about that?'

I shake my head, feeling really pissed off. 'We ain't talking about erasing history, we're talking about telling the goddamned truth. They say that Colston's statue shouldn't have been taken down because of all his charitable activities, but you wouldn't put up a statue of Jimmy Savile, would you? What do you think the British Empire was made of, if not criminal activities? We gotta get real here, and people have to understand that this misrepresentation of history gives right-wing boneheads justification. Churchill, that whole "bulldog spirit" thing, I know this is really going to piss people off, but to a lot of people of colour on this planet the British Empire was not that far from the Third Reich if you're really honest.'

The camera swivels to Jackie who smiles uneasily and shifts in her chair. 'That will upset a lot of people,' she says, sounding unsure whether to be happy or scared about that. I carry on, regardless.

'Guns and nuns, that was how the Empire was built and the government should be acknowledging the fact and saying, "Yeah, it ain't cool, putting up statues that make you feel like second-class citizens." But they haven't done that, so we've had to take things into our own hands. Do it for ourselves, because it's taking too long. Those guys taking down the Colston statue in Bristol, *that* rocked my world. Because they opened the door to the truth and reality. In the twenty-first century, truth is the most radical weapon we have at our disposal. To shine a light on the legacy... Plenty of people seem to love our culture, but not so many like *us*, and we really – all of us – need to educate ourselves. Drop the hate and educate. Look at the sum total of Black history, the thousands of years of Black creativity pre-slavery, and the hundreds of years after that in which we've contributed to civilisation. As bad as slavery was, that's the stuff I focus on and that's why I don't feel like a goddamned second-class citizen. Everything you can put up [about the history of white culture and civilisation] I can match you and probably pre-date you.'

When the piece is aired later that day my inbox floods with requests from other news shows to appear, from journalists asking if I'll be interviewed and from radio producers if I'd like to do live on-air pieces about the BLM and statue debate. I say 'No' to everyone. I had my say and that was it.

Or, almost.

Most days during that long, often hot and humid time of lockdown in 2020, I sat in a daze in my garden, feeling glad that I'm no longer young, which is really selfish, I've got kids, after all, but... I finished the

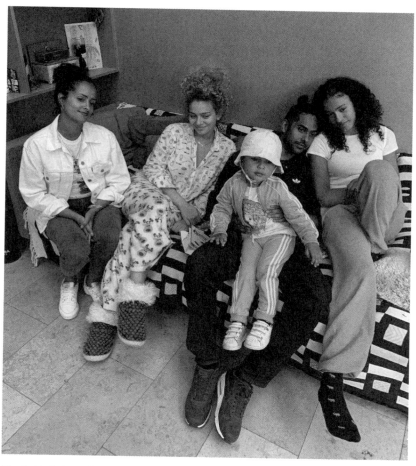

The Letts future. (L–r) Amber, Liberty, grandson Kaio, Jet and Honor, 2020.

interview with Channel 4 News saying that I was optimistic, because my default setting in those instances is to say that. But really, I mean about the distant future, in twenty or thirty years' time, not right now or tomorrow. And to a young person, what does that mean? You might as well say 'never'.

What made things darker and more ominous to me over the first six months of the pandemic was that it seemed like every day I heard stuff which showed how vulnerable Black people are. The number of Black people killed by the police in America in 2020 was reported by CBS News to be 164 people in the first eight months. Most infamous among them being Breonna Taylor, a 26-year-old medical worker who was shot eight times by police in her own home in March, and George Floyd, 46, who was suffocated over almost nine agonising minutes in broad daylight during an 'arrest' in May. Later that month, white vigilantes in South Georgia shot and killed Ahmaud Arbery, 25, while he was jogging through their neighbourhood, and in August Jacob Blake, 27, was shot seven times in the back by a white police officer in Wisconsin in front of his children.

In the UK I read that Black people are four times more likely to be killed by cops, and far more likely to die from coronavirus (so if Covid-19 don't get me then the cops will). Apparently, the number of Black people stopped and searched is stupidly higher than other ethnicities and naturally, as lockdown eased, Black people were fined for not wearing a mask way more often than white people. A July 2019 report on maternal morbidity rates at Oxford University found that Black women are five times more likely to die in childbirth, but it didn't get widespread press coverage until August 2020. It is relentless. I read and heard government-approved stories and statistics, yet the government denied that there was any institutionalised racism in Britain. But what are those numbers saying? It's painfully obvious, and since it was the government's own numbers being quoted, it inevitably means that things are far worse. Every time I heard a politician say 'We're all in this together', I wanted to punch them in the face.

Because of the pandemic, the deadline for this book was extended, even though we'd finished it on time, just as the lockdown came in. When everything stopped and, like everyone else, my life was put on hold – no gigs, no going into the studio for my radio show, no new commissions for film or TV – it took some time to work out when, or if, things might ever get back to normal. Although, the thing is that 'normal' was never *normal* in the first place, and therein lies the problem. Months after we'd delivered the book to the publisher, we began to rewrite the ending, and at the time all I knew was that there was no going back to life as it was before March 2020, and not just because of the coronavirus.

In July I received several requests to join all-Black creative enterprises, which made me think, 'We're back to that again?' It reminded me of the time Channel 4 TV asked me to make something for them in the mid-1980s, and in the first meeting with the commissioning team they said, 'We gotta get an all-Black crew.' I thought then, but didn't say, 'I just want the best crew!' Thirty-five years later, given the way things are with the BLM movement, it's horribly ironic but I'm probably guaranteed work for the next ten years, I reckon, but only because I'm defined by my colour. Which is partly why the invite made me hesitate, why I didn't leap at the idea and reply, 'Yeah, let's do it!'

Then I asked myself, why was that my instinct? Where's my head at? I thought long and hard before it came to me: I'm tired of being Black. I just want to be Don Letts. I don't have a problem with being Black, it's the rest of the world that has the problem. The whole thing did make me question myself and my work, though, and I went through it all to check if I'd 'done the right thing' all the time. And I think I did. It's up to others to pass judgement, but I'm OK with it. At the same time, I know that while you think that the ground you've gained is something to be proud of, reality is always waiting to slap you down; for the rest of the planet it might as well be the 1950s or something.

When Mal came over to discuss how we might end the book, I was filled with contradictory thoughts, questioning motives and reasons for doing anything. I do what I have to, to survive, to care for my family and hope that it can also benefit other people in some way. That's all you can do, I think. Of course, I'd like to be comfortable; I don't believe in suffering for your art, but that's what I wish for everyone. You can benefit from doing righteous things and I've been lucky enough to not have to do anything that I didn't want to or that I'm ashamed of.

The thing is, I'd rather tear myself down before anybody else does. That's what this is all about. I realised early on that I don't want to be a star or a fan, that there's a natural hierarchy to life and I've been trying to find where I fit into it my whole life, while at the same time playing by my own rules. When I saw Marvin Gaye onstage in the early 1970s, I looked around at the audience and realised that some people want to be fans and idolise others, and that I didn't. I recognise that need but I just don't have it. Since then it's been a part of how I am and how I work. I'm not afraid to express an opinion to anyone, I'm not happy to be led by others. I play the game, of course, knowing when to hold back 30% of my opinion and knowledge because white boys get scared or annoyed if they realise that I know more than them.

Sitting in my garden with the sun streaming down, Mal and I watch one of my white cats creeping up on a butterfly. I jump up to shoo the cat away and the cabbage white takes off into the middle of the enormous gunnera which has grown so large that it virtually splits our long London garden in two, so that now you can't see the house from my office.

Stepping back to my chair, Mal asks, 'So, what's our conclusion?'

'Conclusion?' I pause.

'Yeah,' he says, 'a snappy final line, the payoff...?'

'You want a final line? Here's one: human beings – what a bunch of fucking wankers.'

He laughs. I'm half-serious. 'That's our final line. When you get down to it, regardless of colour what a bunch of dicks we are. We're killing the world and don't seem to get it. Wildfires and freak weather are destroying communities around the world, while corona has spread like an ancient plague. Yet instead of everyone coming together to try and fix things, governments and big business are figuring out how to make money from it – we don't deserve to be here.'

There's what feels like a final pause.

'But you can't say stuff like that, can you?'

Mal shrugs, 'Well, there is no end – just a point at which we have to stop.'

I nod in agreement, 'There ain't no conclusion. The only thing I've got is that as long as there's another day, there's always another opportunity.'

Fade to black...

Postscript

Fade up from black, to a street scene. Day. In black and white.

A piano plays a mournful march as a portrait of Mahalia Jackson wearing a hooded shawl comes swaying into focus. The camera pans down from the photo that has been made into a placard nailed to a plain piece of wood, which is being carried by the shaven-headed Irish singer Sinead O'Connor. The camera is filming her impassive face a few steps in front of her as she walks along the middle of a London high street with people passing on both pavements. There are no cars in sight. Sinead looks past and around the camera, and as she moves her head she reveals the tattoo 'All Things Must Pass' on her neck. Suddenly a stark black-and-white photo appears full screen. In it, four young Black men stare full on at the camera from a distance of about ten feet. One of the men, his face half hidden by a mask, has a placard sticking out of his backpack bearing the words BLACK LIVES MATTER. Two more photos of female BLM protesters flash on screen, before cutting back to Sinead, as she begins to sing a traditional spiritual song that Mahalia Jackson recorded in 1956.

'Soon I will be done with the trouble of the world,
trouble of the world,
trouble of the world.
Soon I will be done with the trouble of the world,
going home to live with God.'

The camera reveals she's wearing a large sweatshirt bearing the words
BLACK
LIVES
MATTER
over skinny black jeans and heavy lace-up boots.

Filming 'Trouble Of The World' with Sinead O'Connor (and Mahalia Jackson), Peckham, London, August 2020.　　BEN BEAUVALLET

Later in the video Sinead wears an all-black hijab with only her face and tattooed hands showing – on her right are the words 'The lion of Judah shall break every chain' and on her left 'Lumen Christi' (the light of Christ).

It was the first 'job' I'd been able to do outside my home in six months, filming in Peckham, South London, in early September 2020. Sinead – who'd 'reverted' to the Muslim faith in 2018 – donated proceeds from sales of the single, which would be released in October (Black History Month in the UK), to various Black Lives Matter charities. The photographs displayed throughout the video had been taken by John Behets at different BLM marches and protests around the country during the Covid lockdown.

When the edit was done, I thought that the 'new normal' perhaps wasn't that different after all. I was back behind a camera, capturing a unique moment, filming a cultural and spiritual rebel on the streets of South London. The song is as old as the protest it hoped to benefit and the wrongs it sought to right. I sat back and realised, damn, I'm here and Black again.

FIN

Acknowledgements

...wonderful world: Grace, Liberty, Honor Letts / Amber Letts / Jet & Kaio Letts / Naomi Crowest, Leo n' Honeybee / Desmond Coy / Leo Williams / Norman Letts / Ashley Letts / Jeannette Lee / Raoul Shah / Daddy G / Kamba & Fumie / Pablo D'Ambrosi / Jon Beckley / Tomo, Miki, Mito / Frank Wilson / Chris Blackwell / Audrey De La Peyre / Mick Jones / Jim Jarmusch / Paul Simonon / Michael Koppelman / Shin Okishima / Stussy Tribe / Luc Vergier / James Daley / Fred Perry Massive / Phil Hunt / Mark Vennis / William Badgley / Bob Gruen / Fred Rubio / Gerb / Josh Cheuse / John Lydon / Simon Mattock / Jeff Barrett & the Heavenly Crew / Chris Salewicz / Rick Elgood / Miyako Tanabe / Tricia Ronane / Gary Stonage / Third Man Records / Caroline Baker / Humphrey 'JR' Murray / Tony 'T' Thompson / Sheila Rock / Sam Bully / Jane Ashley / Biff / Trojan / Greg Roberts / John Behets / Paul Burgess / Guy Gillam / Linton Kwesi Johnson / Sinead O'Connor / Nigel House & Rough Trade Records.

Mal thanks the very much-missed literary agent Cat Ledger (1958–2020), Jane Phillimore, John Conway, Rocket 88 Books, Peter Silverton, Tricia Ronane, Glen Matlock, Andrew (and John) Krivine, Grace Letts, Noel 'Razor' Smith, Julia Halford, Imogen Gordon Clark, David Barraclough, Sophie Hicks. And the sounds to write to; Culture, Dr Alimantado, I Roy, Studio One, Tappa Zukie, Trojan Records, Motown, Stax, Retro Soul Radio, Nile Rodgers, The Sound of Philadelphia, Teddy Pendergrass, Salsoul, LKJ, The Clash, Big Audio Dynamite, PiL, BBC 6Music, Eric Dolphy, Mark Springer, Kendrick Lamar, Steve Reich, Gavin Bryars, Marvin Gaye.